Exploring Consciousness

Exploring Consciousness

Rita Carter

University of California Press
Berkeley   Los Angeles

For Rose and Norman,
with eternal thanks for this small spark of it.

University of California Press
Berkeley and Los Angeles, California

Published by arrangement with Weidenfeld &
Nicolson, The Orion Publishing Group Ltd.

Text copyright © Rita Carter, 2002
Design and layout copyright © Weidenfeld &
Nicolson, 2002

ISBN 0-520-23737-4
Cataloging-in-Publication data is on file with
the Library of Congress

Printed and bound in Italy by Printer Trento S.r.l.

10 9 8 7 6 5 4 3 2 1

Contents

Introduction

How does the feeling of this book in your hands, the perception of these words, the thoughts they provoke – this whole, private inner world that you are experiencing right now – arise in a universe that is made of molecules? What *is* this thing we call consciousness?

The question is known, famously, as the 'hard problem'. It is so hard, in fact, that when I started to research and write about the brain and its workings I planned to steer well clear of it, just as cognitive scientists had contrived to do for a century. My previous book, *Mapping the Mind*, therefore dealt only with the (relatively) 'easy problems' – the biological underpinnings of emotion, perception and thought.

Consciousness is the frame that embraces all experience. Thus, like the air we breathe, it is remarkably easy to ignore so long as you hurtle forward with your sights set to laser-beam focus. For me, however, writing about the 'easy' problems only brought the more essential mystery into stark relief. Why should the oh-so-physical fizz and buzz of electrically charged brain cells be associated with this other, apparently non-physical thing we call consciousness? And so the hard problem got to me, as it does, eventually, to everyone who is unwise enough to Think Too Much.

Alas, I cannot claim that, Having Thought, I have solved the problem. This book will not let you into the secret of consciousness, because I don't know it. Nor, I think, does anyone else. Nor does it propose a radically new, improved theory. And it certainly doesn't tell you everything there is to know on the subject.

However, assuming such an unlikely paragraph has got past my editor, I will explain what it *will* do ...

Those who have thought long and hard about consciousness have come up with a solid body of work – empirical findings and theoretical proposals – which contains, I think, more than a hint of an answer to the hard problem. What I present in this book is an overview of that hard-won information, in a form which, I hope, anyone can understand.

It reveals the subject of the inquiry – human awareness – as it really is and not how we intuitively think it is. This newly realized view of the phenomenon requires new ways of thinking about it and I show – through the work of those who have struck out on such paths – where they might lead. Most of all I have tried to show how the traditional approaches to the problem, the philosophical, scientific and experiential routes, might be brought together.

As in all fields dotted with ivory towers, the study of consciousness has until recently been carved up between different disciplines with the practitioners of each seemingly convinced that their approach, and theirs only, will eventually lead to enlightenment.

Neuroscience, for example, has revealed a great deal about the biological processes that accompany consciousness, and many books have been written that claim to explain how physical events give rise to subjective experience. On closer examination, however, most of them turn out to be theories about the 'easy' problems – how the brain processes information, not how it turns it into feelings, thoughts and perceptions. The only comprehensive theories which deal directly with the hard problem are those that claim it does not exist – that consciousness simply *is* physical processes and everything else is illusory. That is a neat idea and may turn out to be correct. But few people – myself included – are satisfied by it.

Conventional psychology ignores the hard problem and concentrates on creating models of mind which are essentially practical; while philosophy has traditionally dealt with mind as though it is something entirely unconnected with the brain – as unsatisfying, in its way, as a purely physicalist approach. Most infuriatingly (for those of us who seek both intellectual and emotional satisfaction) many mystical and religious traditions simply claim to 'know' some ineffable truth through being. They offer no 'solutions' because they do not acknowledge a problem.

This rigid demarcation is finally collapsing because it is becoming clear that the puzzle of consciousness will not yield to an explanation on any one level. Suddenly, there is a search for synthesis. Today, the study of consciousness is like a huge neighbourhood feast to which everyone is contributing their favourite concoction. What follows is – if you like – an aerial view of those offerings, with suggestions as to how they might be combined. Even if (as is quite likely) you end the book with more questions than answers, I think you will find it has not been a waste of your time. Consciousness is the means by which our view of the world, including ourselves, is derived. But, as you will discover, it creates a curiously distorted view because it is not the transparent 'window' it seems to be but a filter – allowing through only that which we are disposed to take account of. Exploring consciousness itself – identifying its limitations and illusions – may therefore help us not just to know ourselves better, but to see everything else more clearly too. And so, please – enjoy.

Some (Possibly) Boring but Important Notes on Language

Consciousness is the frame through which we see the world, and language has evolved to describe things as seen through it. This book, however, goes *outside* the frame – and normal language does not always stretch to accommodate the expanded view.

For example, seen through the frame it appears to me that 'I' am separate from my brain. But one of the strongest schools of thought in modern neuroscience is that brain function and self are one and the same. If this is correct, every sentence that contains a statement like 'you move', or even 'your brain tells you to move', perpetuates a myth. It is more accurate to say 'the brain (that is you) moves the body'. But even that is not quite right. The brain and body are not separate either – the brain extends its tentacles to the tip of your toes and the body owns the brain as much as the brain owns the body. If every reference to 'brain', 'me', 'you' or 'I' in this book was written to accord with this view it would read like mumbo-jumbo. I therefore use normal sentence construction throughout, unless I am making a particular point. Please bear its limitations in mind.

The other language problem is lack of vocabulary. There are no ordinary words for many of the concepts surrounding consciousness. Consciousness itself is a relatively new word – it seems to have arrived only in the seventeenth century. Until then the word 'conscience' was used both for what we now think it to mean (a sort of inner moral dictator) and for what we today call consciousness. Shakespeare, for example, was probably referring to consciousness when he wrote 'conscience doth make cowards of us all'. And in some languages the two notions are still served by a single word.[1]

Nor are there commonly accepted single words to distinguish various states or levels of consciousness. The flickering smidgeon of awareness we might imagine to exist in a mayfly shares the same label as intense human emotion. Some writers make up their own terms for various states: 'core' consciousness; 'creature' consciousness; 'phenomenal' consciousness; 'access' consciousness; and so on. As yet, though, none of them are universally agreed, and different writers sometimes use the same term to refer to different states. For this reason I have not adopted any of these terms, but use instead everyday words. However, I sometimes use them in an uncommon way.

'Information', for example, means any sort of signal that is capable of affecting a living organism, including things like light waves or vibration. And by 'knowledge' I mean the effect of that information (the firing of brain cells, for example) whether it is conscious or not.

'Concept' is another word that has an odd meaning here. I use it both in the normal sense – to mean an idea – and to refer to the physical mechanisms that lead or force us to see the world in a certain way. An example is the interpretation of certain wave lengths as 'red'. The idea 'wavelength x = red' is not conscious, but it is an 'idea' nevertheless, because 'red' is not 'in' the wavelength but 'in' our brains and minds.

I use the word 'unconscious' not to mean some Freudian pit of suppressed desires but simply to mean a state in which there is (almost certainly) no subjective sensation – no 'what it is like to be'. An example would be dreamless sleep.

'Subconscious' means a state that (like unconscious knowing) is not reportable – but which might be conscious and unreportable only because the person does not lay it down in memory. (I try not to use this word too much.)

As for the word 'consciousness', I hope its meaning is made clear in each case by the context. Generally I mean by it the 'lights-on' state in which we are aware of our surroundings and aware that we are aware of them. I use experience in a similar way.

Another word problem is this: there are two very broad views of consciousness. One (mainly associated with the Western materialist tradition) is that experience is generated, or simply *is*, neural activity. The other is that it can be separated from brain function, and that neural activity is merely the means (or even just one means) of tuning in to it. I lean, personally, towards the first view, but I think the other is interesting and could possibly be correct. To reflect this open-minded (though not gaping) stance consistently through the book I would frequently have to resort to painfully elaborate sentence constructions, e.g. 'neural activity which generates, or is, or is (usually) associated with, or gives access to, consciousness.' To spare myself (and you) this I generally refer to neural activity as generating, producing or being associated with consciousness.

One final point: there are lots of 'isms' in this book. There is no way around this, as far as I can see. Every 'ism' is a shorthand term for an idea, theory or concept which, if described in full each time, would lead to dullness and repetition. Please bear with them.

[1] Antonio R. Damasio, *The Feeling of What Happens* (London, William Heinemann, 1999), 232.

A Stream of Illusion

'When you are a bear of Very Little Brain, and Think of Things, you sometimes find that a Thing which seemed very Thingish inside you is quite different when it gets out into the open and has other people looking at it.'

Pooh Bear from *Winnie the Pooh*, A. A. Milne

Please do not think about your nose. Just forget that you have that fleshy protuberance altogether.

Successful? I doubt it. Your consciousness, like mine, constantly roves in time and space – switching from a passing face, to the origin of the universe, to tonight's dinner or the tickle in your toe – seemingly at the behest of your will. It is like an all-enveloping movie, behind which the self lurks like some shadowy director calling the shots.

The intuition that this 'I' is in control is, however, almost certainly illusory. Your brain is subjected to a continuous barrage of cues – light waves that activate your retinal cells; vibrations that ruffle the hairs in your cochlea, molecules that latch on to the receptors on your tongue and in your olfactory bulb; molecular assaults on the nerve endings in your skin and changes in body cells that send urgent messages up your spinal cord. It is these stimuli that dictate where the action goes next, even if you are not consciously aware of them. The most compelling cues are immediate, personal and odd. They snag your attention, and where attention goes, so does consciousness. So if you are asked not to think about your nose – an immediate, personal and decidedly odd request – it is almost impossible not to do so.

By now, however, your brain will have checked out the status of your nose and (I hope) found it to be okay. The show has moved on.

So, what are you conscious of at this very instant? Start with the obvious: certainly you will say that you are conscious of these words; their meaning; the look of them on this page; perhaps the book itself and maybe even the place in which you are reading it. You might say you are also conscious of the state of your stomach (if you are hungry); the temperature (if it is too hot or cold); or maybe you are conscious of a slight headache; the drone of traffic; or some lingering feeling of irritation or elation from a recent social encounter. Sensations, thoughts, emotions; all jostling for attention ... a rich and full mix.

Question two: Are you clear about the contents of your consciousness? Can you say, precisely, which things are conscious and which are not? Of course (given a cue like this) your mind may rove around and yank up memories and ideas which were not conscious an instant ago. But at any precise moment would you say there were things that were in consciousness (this question, for example) and things that – though known to you, like your middle name or the rain outside – are definitely not? In other words, do there seem to be two distinct levels of mind – conscious and unconscious – with a clear division between them?

Question three: How does it feel from moment to moment? Does your consciousness flow smoothly, continuously, and in real time? Or does it lurch along, punctuated by jump-cuts and freeze-frames, flashbacks and fade-outs?

Final question: Whose is it, this consciousness? If that seems a daft thing to ask it is because, if there is one thing about consciousness that seems incontrovertible it is that it is yours – your own, single, private, unshareable world.

Now, impertinent though it is to throw doubt on your private introspection, the assessment you have just made of your own consciousness is almost certainly incorrect. The contents of one's own mind seem to be the single thing we can talk about with absolute confidence, but in fact we are very unreliable witnesses and nothing about consciousness – not even the assumption that it is yours and yours alone – is as clear-cut as it might at first appear.

Take that seemingly fulsome contents list. Sight plays a huge part in human consciousness, and visual perception is probably better understood than any other sort, so it is a good place to start. Glance up, momentarily, at your surroundings. What were you conscious of in that first split second? Not everything, certainly – you are limited, after all, by your field of vision. But within that field you probably thought you took in more or less the whole scene, albeit not in detail. If you are inside a building, for example, you would probably report seeing the walls, the carpet, the door, a table, the window and the view beyond. Certainly you would say you were aware of the main objects, at least to the extent that if you looked up again you would notice if one of them disappeared.

So try this. At the end of this paragraph, without looking up again, close your eyes and try to bring the scene around you to mind. Recall the table – what sort of legs does it have? What does it have on its surface – was there a cup? A magazine? If you are in your own home you may be able to visualize the table clearly, and you may know there is a magazine and a cup on it because you just put them there. But exactly where on the table is the cup? Which way does its handle point? What does the magazine cover look like? Do this for each element of the scene and note exactly what appears in your mind's eye. Unless you are one of the few people with eidetic (photographic) memory, when you concentrate on these images you will find they become hazy. If you are in unfamiliar surroundings the image you conjure in your mind will be even hazier. In fact, the chances are that in that first glance you were fully conscious – that is, conscious enough to give a report – of no more than four or five objects or aspects of the scene. This seems to be the limit of our capacity at any one moment.[1]

The lines show the eye movements and the circles the resting-points of a person looking at a painting as detected by eye-tracking apparatus, Only the regions within the circles are consciously registered. Such experiments show that an observer typically focuses on four or five small parts of a scene, and continues to scrutinize only these details even when they go on looking at the same thing for some time. Yet their subjective impression is that they have observed the whole image. The fact that they have not studied the whole scene usually only becomes apparent when they try to recall it and find they can't.

A gorilla (actually someone in a gorilla suit) walks through the middle of a basketball game. An observer, intent on the game, will often fail to notice such an extraordinary event – a phenomenon known as inattentional blindness.[4]

Our startling lack of consciousness of what is in front of our eyes was demonstrated in an experiment, carried out at Harvard University, in which students were invited to sign on for an (unspecified) experiment by filling in a consent form. The form was handed to them, from behind a counter, by a young man with blond hair, wearing a yellow shirt. When the form was completed, the man took it and moved behind a bookcase, ostensibly to file it away. In fact, while he was out of view, another man – dark-haired, and wearing a blue shirt – stepped into his place. The second experimenter then emerged from behind the bookcase, handed the student an information pack and directed them to the 'experiment room' – where 75 per cent of the students were found to be totally unaware that they had just dealt with two entirely different people.[2]

In another experiment, subjects watched a competitive ball game being played in a room. They were told to watch the moves carefully. Halfway through the game a woman carrying an umbrella walked slowly across the foreground of their vision, from one side of the room to the other. Barely anyone noticed.

Our tendency to miss things we are not primed to look for is called, in neurospeak, 'inattentional blindness'. Scientists have been studying it for just a few years, but magicians have used it since the year dot.

'Change blindness' is a similar phenomenon, and demonstrates that, even when you are invited to concentrate on a scene, huge changes can take place in it without you noticing. If you look at the two pictures on page 15 you will probably spot almost immediately that they are different. The change is not small or marginal – it is quite big, and right there in the centre of the picture. If these pictures were presented to you one after the other, in quick succession, you would expect that the difference in them would leap out at you, much as it does when you see them next to each other. And, indeed, if you alternate between the two pictures without leaving a time-gap between them, the change does show clearly. But if you alternate the pictures with a tiny period – just one fifth of a second – of blackout between them, most people fail to see any change at all.

In one series of change blindness experiments, none of the subjects noticed when a large building, smack in the centre of the picture, shrunk by a quarter between glimpses. None of them saw that two men exchanged hats of different colours and styles. And 92 per cent failed to spot the sudden disappearance of a group of 30 puffins on an otherwise uninhabited ice floe.[3]

Recent research into change blindness shows you don't even have to leave a gap. If you alternate two different pictures rapidly and, at the moment of each change 'splatter' unaltered areas of the image with a few small blots, the

It is quite easy to spot the difference between these two pictures when they are side-by-side (the plane's engine is missing in the bottom picture). But if the images are shown in succession, with a brief blackout in between, very few people notice the change, even though the engine is in the centre of the picture.

difference in the pictures can go unnoticed for more than half a minute.[5] The only changes that are not masked by the splashes are those which capture our attention instantly – typically the central or 'action' part of the image, or something that has particular emotional salience, for example a facial expression or a scene of social interaction like a kiss.

Within-the-moment visual consciousness is not, then, the rich and detailed panorama we think it is. It is limited to a handful of clear perceptions, and the apparent detail is an illusion. Our minds are fooled because consciousness

Professor J. Kevin O'Regan
Laboratoire de Psychologie Expérimentale
CNRS and Université René Descartes, France

Vision – The Grand Illusion

When we look around we get the impression that we see everything that is out there. The conventional way to explain this is that the scene is represented inside our brains and what we are aware of is that internal 'picture'. But change blindness demonstrates that this isn't so. We are only aware of a tiny bit of a scene at any moment – even though it doesn't feel that way.

The way I explain this is that the knowledge which gives us sensory awareness is not of objects but of an ability – an ability to act in a particular way. For example, we 'see' something when we know we can do certain things with our eyes and bodies and expect very particular changes in our sensory input.

Take the sensation of redness. Most people would say that you see red when there's activation of a brain mechanism that represents redness. But that just won't do, because it doesn't explain why that mechanism should give us a feel of red. This problem evaporates, however, if you think of seeing red as knowing that certain things will happen if we do certain things. If I shift my eyes off a red object, for example, the differences in the way the retina samples colours in peripheral vision changes incoming stimulation in a way that is typical of red. Knowing this law – and knowing that it is currently applicable, constitutes the feeling of red. It is a practical kind of knowledge – know-how, like the feeling of driving a car. You can't describe the 'what it's likeness' of driving in every detail, but all the things you can do, like press on the accelerator and know the car will whoosh forward, are what it's like. Similarly, all the red-related things you can do constitute the feeling of red.

So qualia (the elements of conscious experience) are not what we tend to think they are. In particular, although we talk about particular qualia as though they are going on continuously, if you really think about it you realize this ongoing quality is actually just a consequence of the fact that every time you check to see whether you are having that particular quale – well, you have it! It's like looking in the fridge to see if the light is on. Every time you do it, it is – so you think it is always on.

One of the interesting consequences of this view of sensation is that it suggests that if you could 'beam into' a person's brain a stimulus that produces the changes we expect from, say, a red-related action, the person would 'see' red

Our patchy awareness of what is in front of our eyes can be dangerous. NASA researchers put commercial airline pilots in a flight simulator and asked them to 'land'. On some approaches they superimposed the image of a stationary aircraft right in the middle of the runway. One in four pilots blithely landed on top of the obstruction.

even if the stimulus was not itself red. There is even some evidence to show this happens: in one experiment, blind people were equipped with video cameras which turned images into vibrations, and these were then transmitted to their skin. When they manipulated the camera, so the vibrations altered in response to what the camera registered, they learned very quickly to sense the presence of objects in front of them – to the extent that they behaved as though they could see them. If something loomed up in front of them they jumped back.[1] Another related finding is what's called the 'face sense' of the blind: they sometimes feel the presence of nearby objects as a light touch on their faces. Although this is felt as a tactile experience, it is actually derived from auditory stimulation – if you block their ears with putty they no longer get it. So it might be possible to create devices which allow blind people to 'see' and deaf people to 'hear' – or even to create entirely new sensory experiences by combining sensory experiences – a sort of acquired synaesthesia.

[1] Paul Bach-y-Rita, *Brain Mechanisms in Sensory Substitution* (New York and London, Academic Press, 1972).

unfolds in time, and the construction of our experience depends on merging the consciousness of one moment with that of the next. Our impoverished visual perceptions are fleshed out by our memories of the perceptions that went before, and our expectations of what will come next. So great is the illusory nature of vision that it is possible to construct the entire experience of seeing without any sensory input at all. In a rare condition known as Anton's delusion people who become blind (usually due to a severe stroke) continue to believe that they can see.[6] Such a state seems hard to credit, but it is may be just a very extreme example of something all of us do the whole time.

Kevin O'Regan, an experimental psychologist at the Université René Descartes, France, believes that almost everything we see is, in effect, a 'grand illusion'. The few items which catch our attention in a scene are directly sensed while everything else consists of nothing but the knowledge that it is there, and that if we turned our attention to it we would bring about certain neurological changes which would provide us with direct knowledge of them. We get an impression of rich, all-round cinemascope not because we have a picture in our brain but because whenever we think about whether we can see something, our attention is drawn to it and information about it therefore immediately becomes available. The sensation of seeing something comes, not from a replica of the thing being created somewhere in the brain, but from the knowledge that information about it is at this moment available.

It is, says O'Regan, rather like being rich. A person with a billion pounds in the bank feels rich because she knows it is there, not because she spends her entire time taking wads of notes out of a hole-in-the-wall. If the money was not there she would not know until she next needed some and found she could not get it.[7] Of course, says O'Regan, seeing has much more of a 'real feel' than feeling rich. To account for this difference, O'Regan notes that, among other things, seeing is intimately linked to body motion: the slightest eye or head shift brings new information flooding in, so we don't have to think about how we are going to get it. To feel similarly 'really' rich, a person would need to be able to access their money just by reaching for it.

If O'Regan is correct, a person with Anton's delusion would be rather like a person who had spent their fortune but – due to an administration error – kept receiving bank statements that showed it to be intact. They would not realize the truth until they wrote a cheque and found it bounced. Similarly, a person with Anton's delusion can operate very happily as a fully sighted person until they physically collide with objects that happened not to be in their imaginary picture of the world.

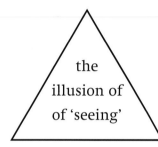

the
illusion of
of 'seeing'

The difference, then, between the person with Anton's delusion and one with normal vision shows only in their interaction with the world. The former will trip over things rather more often than the latter on account of their sight being wholly illusory rather than mainly so. But their visual *experience* will be similar.

If normal sight is a matter of 'knowing' you can see, blindsight is the opposite: seeing without knowing it. During the First World War stories emerged from the trenches about soldiers who – though apparently blinded by head injuries – still dodged bullets. They seemed to be guided by some sixth sense. In 1917, a possible explanation for the phenomenon emerged, when the English neurologist George Riddoch described what is now known as blindsight.[8]

Blindsight is observed most easily in people who have patches of dead tissue in the primary visual cortex (V1). V1 is, in one way, like a mirror: if an object is at the edge of the visual field, it is processed by neurons at the edge of V1, and if the object is in the centre of the field central V1 neurons respond to it. Dead tissue in V1 therefore create spatially corresponding blind spots (scotomas) in the visual field. Although people with scotomas claim to have no visual awareness in their blind spot, when a moving object crosses it some of them are able to report with 100 per cent accuracy the direction in which it is moving. Because they are unaware of it, however, they only report it when they are prompted to 'guess'. The subjects themselves are usually, at first, staggered to discover that their guesses are correct.

Recent research on blindsight subjects has revealed that it is not just movement that can be reported on – one 'star' blindsighter can tell the shape and colour of a target as well as its motion, and even the expression on an 'invisible' face.[9] Blindsight – or something very like it – has also been demonstrated, in cleverly devised laboratory experiments, in people with normal vision.[10] So has 'blindtouch' and even 'blindsmell'. In one experiment, for example, people were asked to smell two phials of liquid, each of which had a very weak odour – one pleasant (amyl acetate, similar to bananas) and the other nasty (butyric acid, a bit like rancid butter). The smells were so weak the volunteers claimed they could not detect them at all. However, when prompted to 'guess' which one smelt nice and which was nasty, they were very successful.[11]

Studies such as this suggest that sensory information which does not make it to consciousness may nevertheless influence our behaviour. Places that somehow don't 'feel right'; people who seem curiously attractive for reasons we can't work out – perhaps the effect they have on us is due to our unconscious processing of their aversive or attractive odour.

The Elusive Quale

Subjective experience is something that it is 'like' to have. This description was introduced by philosopher Thomas Nagle in a famous paper: 'What is it like to be a Bat?'[1], and although clumsy, so far no-one has come up with anything better.

A single element of experience is known as a quale (plural qualia). The most obvious examples of qualia are sensations – individual sights, tastes, smells, and so on. But qualia may also be thoughts, emotions and memories. Thoughts might not seem as obviously 'like' something as, say, a smell. But if you examine it you will find that the experience of, for example, thinking about an elephant is quite distinct from that induced by a thought about your tax bill. They share a certain type of cognition (just as seeing red shares colour perception with seeing blue) but they are not exactly like one another.

It is easy to reel off examples of qualia, but they are maddeningly difficult to define. Are they – as they seem – some ineffable 'mind-stuff' that can never be pinned down in the material world? Or some special, condensed kind of 'knowing'? Or are they more like know-how – the ability to transform a wave of light into vision, for example?

One of the most famous thought experiments, devised originally by philosopher Frank Jackson, illustrates these three competing views of qualia.

Mary is a colour scientist who has spent her entire life locked up in a room which is entirely black and white. Her skin has been treated to disguise its pigment, there are no mirrors in which she could see the colour of her eyes, and there is no window through which she can see the outside world. (In practice, anyone brought up in this environment would soon lose the ability to see colours even if they were presented, because the colour-processing parts of their brain would atrophy or be hijacked by another sense. But anything can happen in thought experiments, and in this one Mary's colour faculties are somehow preserved despite her weird situation.)

Mary is not just any old colour scientist – she is the best in the world. In fact, she knows everything there is to know about colour. That means *every*thing – not just what we know today, but everything that can ever, ever, be known about it. She knows about the properties of various wave lengths, the way they are processed by the human eye and the brain, and the way that processing affects the body. She knows which colours are usually attached to which objects, and how they alter in different light conditions. She knows the lot.

One day her captives decide it is time to test Mary's knowledge, so they

present her, for the first time in her life, with a coloured object to look at and ask her if she knows what colour it is. To make it a proper test they take a banana, which they know Mary will expect to be yellow, and colour it blue. Now, the question is: when Mary sees the banana, will she have a new experience – a colour 'quale'? Or not?

There are three putative answers to this. The intuitive one is that Mary's first sight of blue will give her a new quale. She will gasp and say: 'So that's what blue is!' (Or, more likely, 'So that's what yellow is like!') Another is that she will react in the same way – but only because at the moment of seeing the colour she gets a new ability – the ability to process information she already has but in a different way. A third possibility is that she won't gasp at all, but will say something like: 'So who had the bright idea of colouring the banana blue?'

The first option (favoured by dualists) reflects the view that qualia are 'real' things that Mary is experiencing for the first time. The second (the functionalist argument) maintains Mary is just using her existing knowledge in a new way. The third view supposes that qualia is what Mary has already – incredibly complete, but essentially ordinary knowledge.

[1] Thomas Nagle, 'What is it like to be a Bat?', *Philosophical Review*, 83 (1974), 435–451.

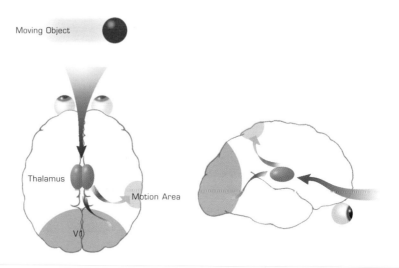

Moving Object

Thalamus

Motion Area

V1

Blindsight probably occurs because some of the light-borne information about a moving object is sent directly to the motion-processing area of the cortex, bypassing the primary vision area V1. This short-cut prevents the information from contributing to consciousness, but it does allow it to be used to direct movement – hence a blindsighter, when prompted, can point to a moving object

Blindsight is used extensively in consciousness research because it seems to offer a testable way of distinguishing between mere knowledge and qualia. At first it seems obvious to say that a blindsighter has the first, but not the second, and this, by extension, seems to support the idea that qualia are 'real extras' to simple information processing. This assumption doesn't necessarily stand up to closer scrutiny however, as philosopher Daniel Dennett, in his book *Consciousness Explained* demonstrates.

Suppose, says Dennett, that we have a 'superblindsighter' – someone, say, that has half his visual field obliterated, yet has the ability not just to know about motion within that blind area, but to know *all* incoming visual information, colour, movement, shape, form ... in other words, all the information we usually associate with normal vision. The superblindsighter will not, at first, be able to report any of it unless they are prompted to guess. But suppose he teaches himself to make spontaneous guesses, instead of waiting to be prompted from outside. And suppose he prompts himself repeatedly, second by second. Suppose further, that he comes to have complete confidence in his guesses – stops being surprised that they are right and accepts that the guesses are necessarily what is 'out there'. To an outside observer he would now be behaving precisely like a normally sighted person. Not only would he be able to move around the area in which he is 'blind' without bumping into things, he would be able to use objects within it, respond to gestures, read books; he would also report on it – could read aloud, for example, or select a red tie from a blue one. Internally, too, the two halves of his visual field would be in many ways similar in that they provided identical information, even though the brain activity which produced it was different. But would what he got from these two brain states be exactly the same? Or would the blindsight half lack that crucial element – qualia?

Dennett argues that it would not. Qualia, he claims, is just this state of knowing, and knowing you know. Like a person with Anton's delusion the superblindsighter would believe he could see normally – and he would not be deluded, because (unlike the person with Anton's delusion) his perceptions would be accurate in that they would be triggered by external stimuli. 'Superblindsight' and normal vision are therefore one and the same.

In theory it should be possible to tell if this is true just by finding a blindsighter, training him, and then asking what it is like (if it is 'like' anything). One blindsighter, Graham Young, does seem to have got better at his peculiar skill since taking part in countless studies, and has sometimes said that the visual stimuli give an 'impression' of motion. But the nearest thing there is, to date, to a superblindsighter is a monkey who behaves perfectly normally despite having had her whole primary visual cortex surgically lesioned.[12] Her astonishing ability to know what is there – to reach for food, move around obstacles, manipulate objects and respond to others – proves that it is possible to function normally without the 'normal' brain states that produce sight. Unfortunately, though, she cannot tell us what it is like.

Just as we enjoy an illusion of spatial completeness of visual consciousness, so we also feel as though experience is continuous in time. This is reflected in the words 'flow' and 'stream' that we commonly use to describe it. Yet even this smooth progression turns out to be illusory.

Take the words on this page. You probably think you are conscious of most, if not all of them, even though you are only actually reading this particular line of print. And that consciousness seems seamless, does it not? It doesn't flicker or jump – so long as you continue to look at the page the words stay stolidly within your consciousness.

In fact your consciousness of the words is punctuated by gaps – it is only in retrospect that these gaps are edited out. This has been demonstrated by an ingenious experiment. Your eye is travelling along this line in a

series of   ballistic jumps   called saccades,   each of which traverses the space of three or four words. A computer-controlled tracking device, locked onto your eye movements can calculate at the start of each saccade precisely where your eye will alight. It can be linked to a computer with a VDU displaying a page of text in such a way that, while your eyes are in the middle of a jump from one group of words to another, the text which your eye is about to land on is changed. If you are not linked to the eye tracker, the lines of print on the VDU are seen to be in continual, squirming motion. But if your eyes are linked to the tracking device you see a solid chunk of text, just like the words on this page. Providing the word changes which are made while your eyes are jumping make sense, you will not notice that anything odd is happening. Anyone not locked into the eye tracker will see the changes because their saccades are out of synch, so their eyes will be landing on the words as they change. But for you, with your eyes in mid-air, the changes go unnoticed and your consciousness of the text appears to be unbroken.

Similarly you could watch the text change from an upper/lower case arrangement

LiKe ThIs

to one

llkE tHiS

without spotting it. When David Zola, the psychologist who devised the experiment, first tried this on himself he thought his equipment had broken down because he could not see that anything was happening.[13]

These unnoticed gaps are present in our perception of everything. If you look, consciously, at one particular thing, it effectively blinds you to anything else for up to half a second. This period is called the 'attentional blink' and can be demonstrated by flashing a visual stimulus to a person, then flashing a second stimulus up in its place for a fraction of a second. The more complex the second stimulus, the longer it can be left in view before the subject becomes conscious of it.[14] Asked about it afterwards, however, subjects never report a 'blank' between the two stimuli – their brains retrospectively 'fill in' the missing moment. This filling in is similar to the spatial infilling that occurs in the visual field where each of us has a blind spot created by a gap in retinal nerve cells which react to each part of the field. You can experience it by holding the image opposite about 40 centimetres (fifteen inches) from your face, closing your right eye, fixating on the small yellow circle, and moving the page slowly towards you. At some point the square in the centre of the circle will fall into your blind spot – the area of the retina where the optic nerve leaves the eye and there are no light receptors. The area covered by the

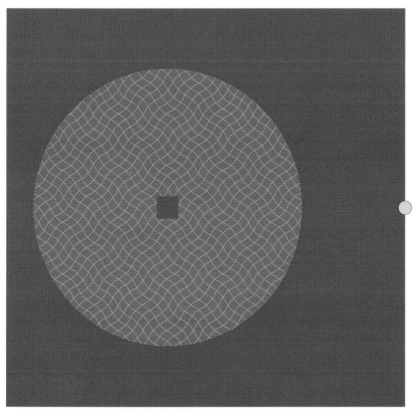

Do you really 'see' the centre, or do you just think you see it? Visual awareness of a particular area in space is generally thought to be created by the activity of the visual cortical neurons that are concerned with that spot. And that activity, in turn, is generally thought to be the result of light information travelling from the eyes and triggering the neurons. In this case, though, there is no light-borne information coming from the centre of the circle. The wavy lines in that patch are illusory. What seems to happen is that the brain (unconsciously) assumes that the centre of the circle is the same as the rest and this idea is subjectively indistinguishable from sensation produced directly by external stimuli. Some researchers think that the (literally) sensational effect of such an idea is brought about by the 'higher' brain areas that create it stimulating appropriate activity in the 'lower' areas of cortex which normally respond directly to outside stimuli. The experience of seeing the centre of the circle is therefore created by the same type of neural activity that produces awareness of the rest of it – it is just that the activity is triggered by the brain itself rather than by information coming in from outside. Others argue that the neural activity which encodes the idea is sufficient to produce the conscious experience.

So far experiments have not resolved the debate. It may be that visual, and other types of awareness, can be created by neuronal activity either at a 'higher' or 'lower' level. Or it may be that both levels of the brain must be active.

square will not suddenly go black, however – rather you will have the impression that it is filled by wavy lines, like the rest of the circle. You do not see a gap – what happens instead is that your brain fills in the blind area with what surrounds it, in this case white.

We also feel that our subjective flow of time is synchronous with outside events – something happens 'out there' and we know about it 'in here' immediately.

Wrong. Consciousness is not immediate – it takes time to be fleshed out. There is a full fifth of a second delay, on average, between the time a visual stimulus arrives at the brain and the time it becomes conscious. And the gap between receiving information about a complicated stimulus and becoming conscious of what it means – that you are in the presence of a person wearing a blue coat, for example, rather than just being in the presence of a large blue form – is about half a second. During this split second, the brain does a phenomenal amount of preconscious work in order to turn a stream of electrical pulses into a conscious sight, sound, emotion, thought or perception. The signals that come into the brain from the sight of the person in blue, for example, are shunted to various parts of the brain where each element is separately dealt with before being put together to form the conscious recognition of the person. The visual areas distinguish colour, distance, size and movement; the face recognition area detects that it is a person; the limbic system (a clutch of organs, mainly beneath the cortex, which generate emotion) attach familiarity to it; and memory regions contribute information such as the person's name, their personal attributes, what they are doing standing in front of you and so on. All these activities finally combine in a conscious perception: 'It's John!', complete, perhaps, with something like: 'Early, for once!'

The more complicated an incoming stimulus, the longer it takes the brain to process, so different inputs take slightly different periods to emerge into consciousness. We don't usually notice the time lag, or experience things in a different order to that in which they occurred, because our brains either backdate, or rearrange our experiences (rather like an editor cutting a film) so they seem to happen in logical order and in real time. We are not generally aware of any of this back-room processing – all we get, consciously, is the perception, and not any inkling of how it is produced. It is as though the gateway to consciousness is too narrow to allow this deluge of information-processing to pass.

Such an arrangement makes perfect sense if you assume that consciousness is an evolved method of dealing with the external world, because to be aware of all the part-formed perceptions that are being processed in the brain at any time would be hopelessly confusing. Consciousness, it seems, arises on a need-to-know basis and it doesn't need to know about anything until that something has been constructed by the brain into an object or an event that can be acted upon. It needs to know about the presence of a person in a blue coat – not the presence of blue lightwaves, movement and form in a particular part of the visual field, and so on. Similarly, if we want to know what day of the week it is, we just want to know it is Thursday – not that yesterday was Wednesday, the day before Tuesday and so on (which may, or may not, be how a normal brain works out what day it is – we don't know if it is precisely because we are not conscious of it. Indeed, every brain may do it differently). Damage to certain parts of the brain, however, can sometimes provide conscious access to these backroom machinations, resulting in bizarre sensory experiences, like a colour in a different place from the object it is attached to.

There is a problem, though, with this idea of evolved consciousness. If it is like it is because being that way is more useful than it being another way, it implies that consciousness itself – rather than the brain mechanisms associated with it – has an effect on behaviour. And, as we shall see, it is very difficult to see how that could be the case because consciousness itself is not (apparently) a physical force, and only a physical force can affect a physical system and thus change its behaviour. This is just one of the ways that consciousness, on close examination, slithers out of the explanatory systems that can so neatly account for almost everything else.

It gets weirder still. Not only does consciousness not progress continuously in time – it is not even locked into the present moment. The immediacy of consciousness is yet another illusion. In fact it is constantly backdating itself in time, and under certain circumstances it can even appear to reverse time.

Imagine living in a state in which the physical things you encountered exerted their effects half a second before you were conscious of them. Time and again you would find yourself constantly 'not knowing what had hit you' – sometimes very literally – until after the event.

In fact that *is* the world in which we live. Although it takes on average half a second for the unconscious mind to process incoming sensory stimuli into conscious perceptions, we are not aware of this timelag: you think you see things move *as* they move, and when you stub your toe you get the impression of knowing about it immediately – even if the pain (for different reasons), takes a little longer to get through.

This illusion of immediacy seems to be created by an ingenious brain mechanism that backdates conscious perceptions to the time when the stimulus first entered the brain. If you stimulate certain parts of the brain directly, however, the backdating mechanism does not kick in. In a series of extraordinary experiments (of which more later) neuroscientist Benjamin Libet, now of the University of California at San Francisco, discovered that direct brain stimulation could be used to produce an effect that seems for all the world like precognition.

Libet worked with patients whose brains were exposed during surgery for epilepsy. This type of surgery is often carried out with the patients awake, in order that they can report to the surgeon what happens when a particular area is touched and thus help identify the spot(s) which need to be operated on. Brain tissue does not have pain receptors, so the patients do not suffer – and several researchers (with the patients' consent) have taken advantage of such operations to find out what happens when an electrode stimulates the exposed brain directly.

Libet's experiments involved stimulating an area of the brain known as the somatosensory cortex. This is a strip of tissue which curves around the surface of the brain like an Alice band, and is divided into sections, each of which responds to information from a different part of the body. Touching a spot on the somatosensory cortex produces the same subjective feeling as touching the corresponding part of the body. So a stimulus applied to the 'hand' area on one side produces the sensation of a touch to the hand on the opposite side of the body (human sensory wiring crosses over in the brain so each hemisphere controls the opposite side of the body). He also stimulated the patients' hands in the normal way. Libet's first finding was that it took about half a second for the patient to report conscious awareness of the stimulation. There was barely any difference in this delay whether the stimulus was given to the hand, or directly to the brain, because the nerve pathway from hand to brain is so fast that the brain registers the stimulation almost immediately. The half second, then, seemed to be due to the brain going through the process of 'spreading the word' about the event to wider-flung brain regions which turn it into a conscious perception. This demonstration of the processing time required for consciousness is not surprising now, although when Libet's experiments were carried out, in the 1970s, it was a revelation. But what Libet went on to discover was something that is astonishing still.

Although the processing-to-consciousness time had been established as being similar in both hand and direct brain stimulation, Libet found that when two stimuli – each of them lasting a quarter of a second or longer – were applied to the hand and brain respectively, the one given to the hand was reported as occurring first. Further, if the direct brain stimulus was given and *then* the hand stimulus was applied 150 milliseconds or so later, the hand stimulus was still reported as coming first. Somehow, the order of outside events had been turned around in the patient's brain, so the latter one was experienced as happening before the earlier one.

On the face of it, this seems impossible because, as Libet established, cortical signals take the same 'real' time to process to consciousness whether they were originally sent from the hand or created by a direct touch from an electrode. So consciousness of them should have been reported as occurring in the order that they were applied. That this did not happen in Libet's experiment raised the possibility that consciousness can trick itself into sensing that it occurred before it actually did.

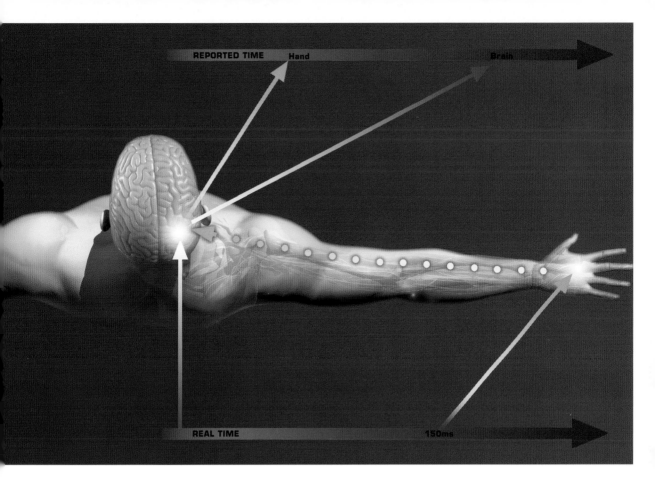

When a stimulus applied directly to the somatosensory cortex is followed very quickly by a touch stimulus to the hand, the subject reports experiencing the hand stimulus first.

And that, indeed, is what seems to happen. Not just in experiments, but all the time, in our day-to-day life – consciousness of events are 'backdated', so that consciousness seems to arise at the same time as the events actually take place. We actually live our lives half a second out of synchrony with the external world – but when we report on the external world we do so in the belief that we are keeping pace with it.

This trick seems to be contrived by a part of the brain which lies beneath the cortex, and by nerves in the body. Sensory signals coming from the sense organs and the peripheral areas of the body travel to the cortex along very fast pathways that pass (with the exception of olfactory signals) through the thalamus. This centrally located brain nucleus acts in part as a sort of relay station, directing sensory information to the appropriate part of the cortex. Although signals arriving at the cortex seem thereafter to be processed to consciousness in the same way as those given by direct cortical stimulation, it seems that their means of arrival affects the way we 'report' them – even to ourselves. We 'know' about the sensation half a second after the arrival of the information at the cortex, but in that moment of 'knowing' we slide the event back in time by almost precisely that same half second it took for it to become known. So our conclusive consciousness of it – the one that we know we know and can thus report on – is that it occurred at the time when our brains first registered it, not the time when our brains first made us *aware* of it.[15] If you cannot be sure about the what, the where and the when of your consciousness, can you be sure that at any given moment you were conscious at all?

Think of a stomach rumble that alerts you to the fact that you are hungry. Your body must have been wanting food for a while (stomachs only rumble when they are empty). But were you hungry for that time, or did your hunger only arise when you heard your stomach complain? Compare it to something else: your body sends signals from its periphery to the brain the whole time, not just on demand. If you think, now, about the bottom of your feet you will become conscious of the feeling of the ground, or your shoes, on the soles of your feet. The signals carrying this information from your feet to your brain have been flowing all the time, but was the feeling they now convey there before you thought of it? And what about your mood? Are you a bit down, today? Or slightly anxious? In love, or in mourning? Whatever your current disposition, is it something you were consciously aware of before you read those words? Or did reading the words act as a cue that turned a mere brain state into a feeling that you supposed had been there all along?

Whatever your answer, there is no way you can be sure you are right. The question is a bit like asking whether your refrigerator light is permanently on. It may seem to be because every time you open the door, there it is, shining. If you didn't know about fridges, it would be logical to assume the light is there the whole time. And so long as opening the door is the only way to look into the fridge, the question must remain unanswered.

It is possible that a huge amount of our lives is lived in a state of mind which is, in a similar way, unreportable. Most people, for example, know what it is like to get lost in a daydream while driving, and to travel miles without any memory of doing so. Only when something happens to alert us to our situation – a child runs into the road, say – do we snap back into full awareness of the present moment. Our inability to remember anything before our attention was engaged suggests that we were not conscious until that moment – that we lapsed into a robotic state in which our bodies went on acting even though no-one was 'at home'. It is a reasonable assumption, but it is not necessarily true, any more than it is necessarily true that the light goes off when we close the fridge door. Maybe consciousness is permanently on, even when we subside into what seems like unconsciousness. It may be that we are conscious, at the time, of those seemingly blank miles, but we simply fail to lay down any memory of it.

Similarly, it is conceivable that we are conscious when we are in dreamless sleep, or under anaesthetic. The reason we do not remember anything about an operation could be because we fail to remember the pain, rather than that we fail to experience it at the time. This possibility is implicitly acknowledged by anaesthetists – along with the drugs which put their patients to 'sleep', they also routinely use drugs which prevent the laying-down of memories, 'just in case'.

Unlike the fridge-light conundrum, the uncertainty surrounding the presence of consciousness is profound. If you really wanted to find out about the light you could rig up a camera inside the fridge, with a timing device which would set it off after you've closed the door. Assuming the camera did not have a flash, if the resulting photograph showed a panorama of chilled foods you could deduce with some confidence that the light stayed on, and if the photograph was black you could be pretty sure it went off. But there is no comparable way of deducing when consciousness is 'turned on' – even in your own head. Behaviour is no guide: the distracted driver, for example, reacts appropriately to things like red lights, lines on the road, other vehicles, as well as steering, braking, and accelerating. But there is no way of knowing if she is conscious. There is no way, even, for *her* to know, because the moment she poses the question she ceases to be distracted. It is perfectly possible that things like braking, steering and so on, are merely the effects of unconscious brain processes. But it is also possible that they were conscious acts, which were instantly forgotten.

In order ever to know which is correct, what is needed is some overt marker of consciousness – the equivalent of taking a photograph inside the fridge. The ability to observe and detect brain processes directly through brain imaging machines and EEG has given hope that such a marker can be identified, and the pursuit of 'neural correlates of consciousness' (NCC) is currently top of the consciousness research agenda. The ultimate ideal would be to devise a sort of 'consciousness meter' – a helmet-type device, perhaps, which could be popped on a subject's head to indicate if the lights were on inside. But, of course, the search for NCC is itself snagged by the reportability problem: the only way to correlate brain activity with subjective states is to get your subject to report on their state. Which brings us full circle... So, even if neural correlates of

Higher and Lower Orders

The idea of a conscious state being one in which there is a 'doubling-up' of knowledge is a 'higher-order representational' theory of consciousness.

'Representational' means that the contents of consciousness are 'representations' of things rather than the things themselves. The feeling of 'redness', for example, is brought about by neural events in the brain (a representation) – it is not redness itself.

Representational theories are of two kinds: first-order and higher-order. First-order theories state that the initial representation of red is directly experienced. For example, the neurological changes brought about by the impact of 'red' light is the first-order representation of red and it is also the experience of red.

'Higher-order' theories state that the first representation (the neural event(s) correlating with the impact of red light on the retina) requires a second representation in order to endow the representation with the subjective 'feel' of redness which is experience. The second representation is an additional neural event (or events) which reflects the first and brings about awareness of it. (For a more detailed description of one such theory see David Rosenthal on *The Higher-Order Thought Model of Consciousness*, page 45.)

At first sight, first-order representational theories seem to have the advantage over higher-order theories. Intuitively it seems that the effect of, say, red light, automatically brings awareness of redness – to add another layer seems unnecessary. But the evidence shows that this is not the case. Apart from blindsight – a clear demonstration of visual knowledge which is not conscious – there are cases of people who, after brain injury, find they can no longer consciously see the form, position or spatial orientation of objects, yet can grasp them accurately. One woman, for example, can only see colour and texture – so if you place a banana in front of her she is aware only of something yellow and smooth – somewhere. Yet if asked to grasp the 'yellowness' she will reach out and pick up the banana as competently as anyone else – her hand goes to precisely the right spot in space, and her fingers are poised to curl around the fruit – there isn't the hesitant feeling about and clumsiness typical of a truly blind person. Clearly the knowledge of the banana's position, shape and size is represented in her brain and is able to guide her actions.[1] The only thing that is missing is her awareness of that knowledge. Higher-order theory accounts for this strange phenomenon – what is missing is the second-order representation that would ordinarily make her aware of the first.

One obvious objection to higher-order theories is that they invite what philosophers term an 'infinite regress'. If a representation requires a second one to make the first one conscious, that higher representation further requires a third order one to make that conscious – and so on. However, higher-order theory does not demand that a second-level representation is conscious – indeed, most higher-order representations are thought to be unconscious. They are rather like the unconscious processing that underlies language – all we know about is the end result (a flow of meaningful words) not the brain mechanisms that produce it.

However, higher-order representations *can* be conscious. This is what happens when we introspect – the second-order representation of, say, red, becomes the conscious 'I am aware of red' by virtue of the unconscious third-order representation 'I am aware that I am aware of seeing red'. And if a fourth-order representation makes the third-order representation conscious the contents of consciousness becomes 'I am aware of being aware that I am aware of seeing red'.

Another objection to higher-order theories is that if every conscious perception (or thought or feeling) has to have a concomitant second-order representation attached to it, our brains would simply become overcrowded. But this is not such a problem if you accept that the apparent richness of consciousness is largely illusory. If the 'stream' of experience is as gappy and impoverished as close scrutiny suggests, at any one moment we only have a maximum of four or five things which are mirrored by higher-order representations. So the cognitive load is not impossibly burdensome at all.

Higher-order theories come in two main types:

Higher-Order Experience (HOE) theories posit a second-order representation which is more or less a perfect reflection of the first order. Like the initial representation that underlies it, this higher experience is 'fine-grained' – that is, dense, indescribable and concrete – not an abstraction but, if you like, a 'sense'. It is created by a sort of 'inner scanner' mechanism, which monitors brain states such as those produced by the impact of red light, and produces another state which is the feeling of redness.

Higher-Order Thought (HOT) theories, by contrast, say that the second-order representation is an abstraction rather than a direct reflection of the base experience. It is not a 'sense' of redness, but a *belief* of redness, and the neural events associated with it are correspondingly different in type from those which produce the first-order representation. HOT theory – in recasting concrete knowledge (direct sensory information, for example) as an abstraction, allows for that knowledge to be interpreted flexibly, so the conscious experience of it is more like a drawing than a photograph. For example, the conscious experience of redness could be 'it seems red' rather than 'it is red'. It seems unlikely, however, that many animals, apart from humans, are capable of this sort of abstraction – so HOT theory, if accepted as the only means by which experience can occur, rules out the possibility of awareness in non-human animals.

This flies in the face of one of our deepest intuitions – when our dog (for instance) greets us with wagging tail it is almost impossible to believe that he is just an automaton, responding to our return with no more awareness than a security light which flicks on as we walk into the porch. Although intuition is not a good guide to scientific accuracy, in this case the consequences of denying the intuition that animals are sentient – *and being wrong* – are potentially awful. So to act in accordance with HOT theory would be reckless.

Accepting the HOE idea (and rescuing animals from zombiehood) does not necessarily require that the HOT theory be abandoned. HOEs and HOTs are usually considered to be different kinds of representations, and as such they would be expected to arise through entirely different neural mechanisms. However, it is possible that they are simply different levels of higher representation, both of which arise through similar mechanisms but at different stages of the cognitive construction process which gives rise to awareness.

The line between higher- and lower-level representation is a grey one because, strictly speaking, every representation bar the very first brain responses to a stimuli is a higher-level representation in that it reflects the representation that preceded it. In this sense a higher-level representation is not sufficient to bring knowledge to awareness – it has to be a higher-level representation of a certain complexity.

The lowest higher-level representation that we seem normally to be aware of is one in which all the sensory elements are bound into a whole. In the visual modality for example, we see colour, form, location and so on all in one – not as separate elements. However, the sensory content is all we are aware of. You may look out of the window and see something small and black flashing across the sky. If asked what you had just seen you might say 'a bird' – but at the time you were probably not aware that is was a bird at all. It was just a sensory blip. You didn't name it, wonder where it was going, reflect on its ability to fly.

Indeed, you had no thought about it all. This type of higher-order representation might be regarded as a higher-order experience.

Some perceptions are more complex than this, however. If your attention had been caught by the bird you might have followed it with your eyes, and been aware that it was, indeed, a bird. You might have actually thought 'bird'. You may have noticed that it was heading towards some landmark that you know to be south, and then gone on to wonder if it was migrating for the winter, which may have led you on to a fantasy about heading south for winter yourself. All these thoughts would have been pulled out of various parts of your brain – the name from the area that deals with words; the thought about migration from your semantic memory system; the landmark from your spatial memory and so on. And the representation of this 'meta-percept' would therefore be a correspondingly larger amount of neural activity than the simple sensory blip. But the activity would still be of the same kind, and created in much the same way. The only 'type change' it will undergo is in terms of our own categorization – the added levels of abstractions lead us to call it a thought rather than an experience.

Normal consciousness may contain both HOEs and HOTs simultaneously. When I look out of the window, for example, I might have a HOE about the tree, but a HOT about the car that has just driven into the driveway. Thus some things are not so much 'in the forefront of our minds' as 'at the top of our minds' – more detailed and complex by being the result of higher cognitive processing.

[1] David Milner and M. Goodale, *The Visual Brain in Action* (OUP Press, 1995).

consciousness become recognized there will always be some degree of uncertainty attached to them.

The only sort of consciousness that one can be sure of (and perhaps the only sort we will ever be *able* to be sure about) is that which is reported, either overtly, by talking about it, or internally, by thinking about it – the equivalent of opening the fridge door. The driver passing a traffic light without incident or comment may or may not be aware of its colour – there is just no way that she, or anyone else, will ever know. Her brain will have the knowledge of the light's colour, but this is merely the response of the visual cortex to the light stimulus and the knock-on brain activity that causes her body to respond to it appropriately. It may not be enough to produce a quale.

However, if the colour of the light makes the difference between her being on time, or late, for an important meeting, she will turn her attention to it as she approaches, and in doing so become aware of its colour. It is the attention she pays to it, and her noting of it – the knowledge of knowledge – that makes it certain.

Reportable consciousness (which I shall just call consciousness from now on) can therefore only arise in a system which is capable of monitoring its own state. You could shove gigabytes of information into a brain-like arrangement and it could use that information to produce any degree of sophisticated responses – but its behaviour would not be conscious unless it was equipped with some 'loop' that allowed it to know about its own cognitive machinations. Thus intelligence and consciousness are not necessarily related at all. Indeed, some aspects of intelligence – expertise, for example – is almost wholly the result of unconscious brain activity. Think, for example, of how much better you dance when you cease to be conscious of what your feet are doing.

In people, self-monitoring often seems to be mediated by language. When you think about what is in your mind it tends to be crystallized, automatically, into words (try it). Some theorists argue that words are essential for self-monitoring, but that leads to the assumption that the only species that can be conscious are those with language capabilities, which, with the possible exception of some primates, means only humans. This is deeply counter-intuitive – anyone who has a pet dog, or even a hamster, finds it almost impossible to believe that their complex and idiosyncratic behaviour could be wholly unconscious.

Intuition, of course, is not a reliable guide, but in this case recent research into the nature of self-monitoring in people supports the instinctive assumption that it can be done without words. When people are asked to give

One way of looking at different types of conscious states is to see them as 'levels', with the most complex and reflective as the highest. Some traditions turn this upside-down and think that 'higher' consciousness results from stripping away reflection and allowing the mind to become empty of thought.

INTROSPECTION

Attention on one's own consciousness – the contents of which are your own thoughts.

E.g. a driver thinking 'I am thinking that I am looking at a red traffic light.'

NORMAL CONSCIOUSNESS

Attention on object of consciousness. Qualia are 'fleshed out' and fully reportable.

E.g. 'red traffic light'.

KNOWLEDGE

Possible moment-by-moment experience but inability to report on it.

E.g. a distracted driver; blindsight.

UNCONSCIOUSNESS

No reported qualia – e.g. dreamless sleep. A living human brain may never actually be unconscious – qualia may be experienced 'in the moment' but instantly forgotten.

EXPERIENCE

REPORTED EXPERIENCE

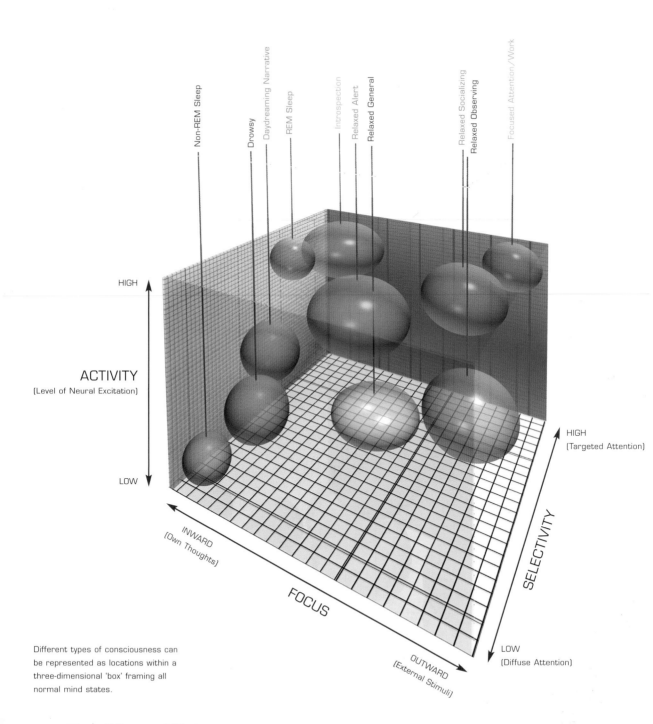

Non-REM Sleep

Drowsy

Daydreaming Narrative

REM Sleep

Introspection

Relaxed Alert

Relaxed General

Relaxed Socializing

Relaxed Observing

Focused Attention/Work

HIGH

ACTIVITY
(Level of Neural Excitation)

LOW

HIGH
(Targeted Attention)

INWARD
(Own Thoughts)

SELECTIVITY

LOW
(Diffuse Attention)

FOCUS

OUTWARD
(External Stimuli)

Different types of consciousness can
be represented as locations within a
three-dimensional 'box' framing all
normal mind states.

an immediate report of what is in their minds at any precise moment, 25 per cent of descriptions include 'non-symbolic thoughts' – that is, thoughts without visual imagery or words attached. A student describing one such thought put it like this: 'I was watching a couple of people lifting something and I sort of knew they were going to drop it. I didn't actually say to myself "Oops – they're going to drop that." – I just sort of saw they were going to drop it because they were carrying it the wrong way. Except that I didn't see it in the way of – like – actually seeing it. It was just – I dunno – in my mind, I guess.' If self-monitoring can be of this kind – an experience of knowing rather than a clearly articulated recognition – it figures that animals without language can do it too.

Even if it is done without words, self-monitoring nevertheless requires an ability to form a concept of a lower-level experience. A concept, in this sense, can be an idea, thought, memory – even the wordless '?' that arises each time something catches our attention. Anything, in fact, that is a mental construction rather than the immediate effect of sensory stimulation from something in the 'real' world beyond our brain. If an organism can't do this it cannot create the dual-layered knowledge that is consciousness.

The proposal that you need to have a concept of a thing before you can be conscious of it seems counter-intuitive – after all, we don't bump into every unfamiliar object we come across. It is less puzzling when you recognize that the brain has certain concepts built in to it: those of space, time and the body it belongs to, for example. It is a bit like being born with a knowledge of the alphabet. You wouldn't automatically read and write because of it, but it would give you the building blocks with which you would learn to form words. By the time we are old enough to consider the matter we have accumulated a near-complete conceptual representation of all the types of things – living creatures, buildings, landscape features – we encounter. These 'close-to' or 'class' concepts are flexible enough to be applied to more or less everything we come across. Nothing is ordinarily so novel that we have to construct a new concept from scratch. Indeed, adapting 'close-to' concepts can bring people very close to being conscious of things, even when the raw information about them is unavailable. A blind person, for example, may hazard that a red quale is 'like the sound of a bassoon', and be right. Certainly their concept contains many of the features of red (rich, warm, deep) and these may even be enough that were they ever to actually see the colour they would identify it correctly.

The need for a conceptual template within which to place a new sensation in order for it to be conscious is demonstrated by cases of people who have been

Knowing Fear

'Doubling-up' of knowledge is required even to make you conscious of being frightened. The emotion is generated in the limbic system, by the amygdala, the organ that reacts to threatening stimuli. Activity here sends signals to the body, preparing it for action (fight or flight), but it is only when a second 'wave' of signals reach the frontal cortex that you actually feel fear.

The amygdala is genetically primed to respond to certain things – almost as though it holds representations of them in its very architecture. Primates, seem to be genetically predisposed to be scared of certain things like crawly insects, heights and certain types of animals – the concept 'snake + danger', for example, seems to be encoded before birth. However, for the concept to become 'active' the creature holding it has to be exposed to a second stimulus, most usually the sight of someone else showing fear of the object. A baby monkey, for example, will show no fear of a snake the first time it sees one. But if it subsequently sees the snake and simultaneously sees its mother reacting with fear, the infant will thereafter itself be scared of snakes. That the fear is not simply the result of picking up its mother's signals was shown in an ingenious experiment in which a mother monkey was conditioned to be scared of flowers, so when a flower was put into a cage containing the mother and her baby, the mother leapt with fright. Unlike when the object was a snake, the baby was puzzled by this rather than scared, and it did not go on to develop a fear of flowers.[1]

Human phobias are very varied, but the most common – birds, insects, snakes, heights – are those that are linked to natural perils which everyone may be primed to avoid. Most people do not become phobic of them, however, because they do not 'realize' their instinctive knowledge and turn it into conscious fear.

[1] S. Mineka et al, 'Observational conditioning of snake fear in rhesus monkeys', *Journal of Abnormal Psychology*, 93 (1984), 355–72.

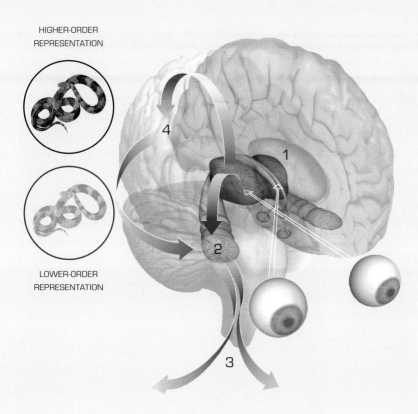

HIGHER-ORDER
REPRESENTATION

LOWER-ORDER
REPRESENTATION

4

1

2

3

(1) The thalamus receives stimulus
and shunts it to the amygdala and
visual cortex.

(2) The amygdala registers danger
(a lower-order representation).

(3) The amygdala triggers a fast,
physical reaction.

(4) Cortical brain processes produce
a conscious image of the snake and
amygdala activity fed to the frontal
cortex produces conscious fear.

Moment to Moment

Psychologists have often tried to discover what goes on in people's minds from moment to moment, but their success has been limited because – short of following individuals around with a notebook – the only way to find out was to gather their reports in retrospect and memories of past moments of consciousness are notoriously unreliable. Russ Hurlburt, of the University of Nevada, has overcome this problem by fitting a large sample of students with electronic bleepers that bleep at random intervals. When it goes off, the student has to observe the contents of his or her mind at that precise moment and make detailed notes. Analysis of the reports has shown that the characteristics of consciousness can be categorized and quantified as follows:

Type of consciousness	Percentage of reports
Inner speech (talking to yourself)	32
Images	25
Unsymbolized thought (a thought without words or feelings)	25
Emotional feelings	27
Sensations (pain etc)	25

(Some reports contain two more categories – hence the percentages add up to more than 100.)

The fact that unsymbolized thought figures in 25 per cent of reports is particularly interesting because one common view of consciousness is that internal verbalization is required for thinking. This suggests that it is not.

Hurlburt's method, called Descriptive Experience Sampling (DES), shows how unreliable previous memory-based experiments have been – and thus what a poor idea we have had until now of what actually goes on, most of the time, in our minds. One volunteer, for example, had no idea that he frequently had angry thoughts about his children until it was revealed by DES sampling because he had forgotten them almost as soon as they occurred.[1] Another student came to Hurlburt after a week with the bleeper and said he did not think it was going off randomly. When asked why, the student replied; 'Because I know I think about sex at least half the time – but it never caught me at it.'

[1] Russell Hurlburt, 'Telling what we know: describing inner experience', *Trends in Cognitive Sciences*, 5:9 (September 2001), 400–403.

blind from birth and then regained the use of their eyes in later life. Even though their brains register visual information they are not immediately conscious of images. They have to learn to see objects by adapting the non-visual representations they already hold of them, such as the concept of how they feel. More subtly, a person who is unfamiliar with wine is likely to be unconscious of many of the tastes in a complex vintage – but may come to taste them once they have been invited to adapt an existing concept (tree bark, full-bodied, sharp etc.) to match it.

The human mind, however, is capable of more than a mere doubling-up of information. It can lift itself by its bootstraps to higher and higher levels of self-reflection in the process known as introspection. To introspect means, literally, to look inside one's mind, and it occurs when the contents of one's consciousness itself becomes the subject of attention. The conscious experience of a red traffic light, for example, is the 'knowing of knowledge' but the thought 'I am thinking about seeing a red traffic light' has an extra 'layer' of awareness on top: the self is monitoring its own self-monitoring. You can build yet another layer on top of that: 'I am thinking about thinking about seeing a red traffic light', and so on. But this sort of thought edifice quickly becomes precarious and tends to topple into confusion at the fourth or fifth level. The thought: 'I am aware that I am thinking about the fact that I am aware that I am thinking that the traffic light is red' is all too much for most people. Just as our consciousness seems able to hold a maximum of four or five objects at any time, so it also seems able to entertain only four or five levels of thought. Most of the time, in fact, we live at the first or second level with brief excursions, perhaps, to the third.

Clever as this layer-building is, the 'higher' levels of consciousness attained through introspection are not necessarily 'better' levels. One way of looking at the accretion of layered awareness is that it builds an ever more complex and meaningful illusion from a reality that is at base mindless. But another way is to regard it as a screen that occludes a richer reality – and that every extra layer makes our view more obscure. Eastern traditions teach that consciousness is enhanced by stripping away the layers until the screen disappears. When the final layer of self-monitoring is dispensed with all divisions – between self and other; object and subject; even between one moment and another – vanish. What remains is a holistic, mindful, fundament – pure consciousness.

This idea – that mind is the basis of reality – is essentially the same as the religious belief that places God as the source of All. Most Westerners, even today, still pay lip service to this idea but a large number of them (probably a

People who are blind from birth and then regain their sight have to learn to see because they have no visual concepts to make their new visual information conscious. These three pictures show the attempts by a newly-sighted man to draw a bus (1) a few days after regaining his sight; (2) six months after; and (3) a year after. In the first image the only detail is the spokes on the wheels, which he knew by touch. This gave him the 'near-to' concept he needed in order to see them. His final drawing, though now quite good, omitted the front of the bus – perhaps because it is the only part he had never touched.

1

2

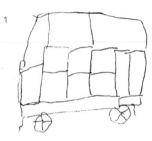

3

majority) also believe (somehow) that matter is the fundamental building block of the universe and that mind arises from it. These two ideas are incompatible and no amount of sophistry can disguise it. Either mind/consciousness/God – call it what you will – is at the root of all things OR matter goes right down to the bottom and mind is just some special physical state or process. Anyone who accepts the classic materialist model as a complete and accurate description of reality is forced, if they think about it, to take the second view.

However, the model has changed. Classical physics is now recognized as, at best, applying only to a part of the universe. When you go down and down to atomic level and below, or up and up to cosmic proportions, its laws no longer apply. Some of the phenomena that seem to exist at these extremes of scale (the 'observer effect' for example) seem to suggest that mind (or information, if you prefer) might indeed be the basis of reality. So at the leading edge of science there is a new convergence between Eastern and Western thinking.

At the time of writing however, it is probably true to say that most scientists engaged in consciousness studies are bunched towards one end of the spectrum – the end where consciousness is just a bit (if a peculiar bit) of the material world. Most scientific research is therefore geared towards answering questions such as how consciousness arises from matter; why it feels as it does; who's got it?; why have they got it?; how did they come by it?; how can we know they've got it? And so on. A decade of research – though failing as yet to come up with incontrovertible answers to these questions – has nevertheless produced many plausible theories and countless fascinating insights. It is these that this book is mainly concerned with.

First, though, let us take a closer look at the spectrum of beliefs about the essential question: 'What on earth (if it is on earth) *is* consciousness?'

Professor David Rosenthal
Philosophy Program and Cognitive Science Concentration
Graduate Center, City University of New York

The Higher-Order Thought Model of Consciousness

All mental states, including thoughts, feelings, perceptions and sensations, often occur consciously. But they all occur also without being conscious. So the first thing a theory of consciousness must do is explain the difference between thoughts, feelings, perceptions and sensations that are conscious and those which are not.

At bottom, the difference stems from the fact that, when a mental state is conscious, we are conscious of being in that state. This is clear from considering that, when one isn't in any way conscious of having a thought, sensation, feeling or perception, that state does not count as a conscious state. And it is arguable that the best explanation of how we are conscious of being in those states is that we have thoughts that we are in those states. Because these thoughts are about other mental states, I call them higher-order thoughts (HOTs).

When a mental state is conscious, we are conscious of it in a way that seems, subjectively, direct and unmediated. We can account for this by providing that the HOTs we have about our mental states do not rely on any conscious inference. Suppose I want something to eat. If I come to have a thought about that desire because I infer from something about my behaviour that I want to eat, my desire won't be conscious. My HOT must arise independently of any such inference.

HOTs need not themselves be conscious. My HOT about my desire to eat won't itself be conscious unless I have a second HOT about it. This explains why we usually aren't conscious of having any HOTs.

Sometimes, however, we are conscious of our HOTs. Though mental states are usually conscious in a relatively unreflective, unfocused way, we sometimes deliberately attend to some particular thought or feeling. We thereby become introspectively conscious of that state. In such cases, we introspectively focus on the state; we are conscious not only of the state, but of our being aware of the state. These are cases in which our HOTs are themselves conscious thoughts. Not only is my desire to eat conscious; my thought that I want something to eat is conscious as well.

It is sometimes urged by critics that the HOT model explains only introspective consciousness. This idea stems from the unfounded assumption that HOTs must themselves be conscious.

But since HOTs typically aren't conscious, we can invoke them to also explain ordinary, non-introspective consciousness as well as introspective consciousness.

Because HOTs are thoughts to the effect that one is in some particular state, it must make reference to oneself. So it might seem that nonhuman animals lack the conceptual resources needed to have HOTs. But thoughts that refer to oneself needn't make use of a sophisticated concept of the self. All that's required is a concept of the self strong enough to distinguish oneself from everything else. And it's clear that many nonhuman creatures must be able to frame such thoughts.

Still, some nonmental creatures presumably do lack the ability to have HOTs. But this isn't on the face of it a difficulty for the model. Many nonhuman species do of course function in ways that establish pretty firmly that they sense things and even have some simple thoughts. But such functioning does not by itself also establish that those perceptions and thoughts are themselves conscious. We can't just rely on subjective impressions to establish which nonhuman species do have conscious thoughts and sensations. When we do figure out which nonhuman species do have sensations and feelings that are conscious, it could easily turn out that all such species also have the mental resources needed for HOTs.

There is a difference between a mental state's being conscious and a creature's being conscious. A creature is conscious if it is awake and can receive sensory information. But that can readily happen even if the creature were never in any way aware of its mental states. So we can't infer from an animal's being conscious that its mental states are ever conscious. In the human situation, of course, being awake always goes with being in some mental states that are conscious, but that need not hold generally.

Because HOTs usually aren't conscious and people are normally unaware of them, we cannot establish their occurrence by being conscious of them. HOTs are, rather, theoretical posits whose occurrence is established by theoretical considerations.

Indeed, the model meshes fruitfully with many scientific findings. It helps, for example, in explaining phenomena such as change blindness and blindsight. The HOT model readily accommodates the nonconscious sensing that occurs in blindsight. And the model can explain change blindness as due to the failure of sensations that result from changes in a scene to become conscious. The model also helps explain cases in which subjects confabulate having various thoughts and desires. These subjects have HOTs that they have such thoughts and desires, and these HOTs make it seem subjectively that they have those states even though they don't.

The HOT model is especially useful in explaining Libet's finding that the neural readiness potentials identified with subjects' decisions occur measurably after their awareness of those decisions. This is to be expected, since the HOTs in virtue of which subjects become aware of their decisions presumably occur measurably later than those decisions.

Some recent brain-imaging work indicates that, when subjects are asked to report their mental states, neural activation occurs in a single brain area, namely the medial frontal cortex.

This is so even when the states monitored are themselves very different in kind, for example, pain, tickles, emotions aroused by pictures, and spontaneous thoughts.[1] The location of activation due to monitoring is also distinct from the locations of the various types of monitored state. This suggests that a single, independent brain mechanism subserves the monitoring that enables us to report our mental states. Since reports of one's mental states express one's thoughts about those states, it is inviting to construe this neural activation as indicating the occurrence of HOTs.

[1] For a summary, see Christopher Frith and Uta Frith, 'Interacting Minds – A Biological Basis', *Science*, 286, i5445 (November 26, 1999), 1692ff.

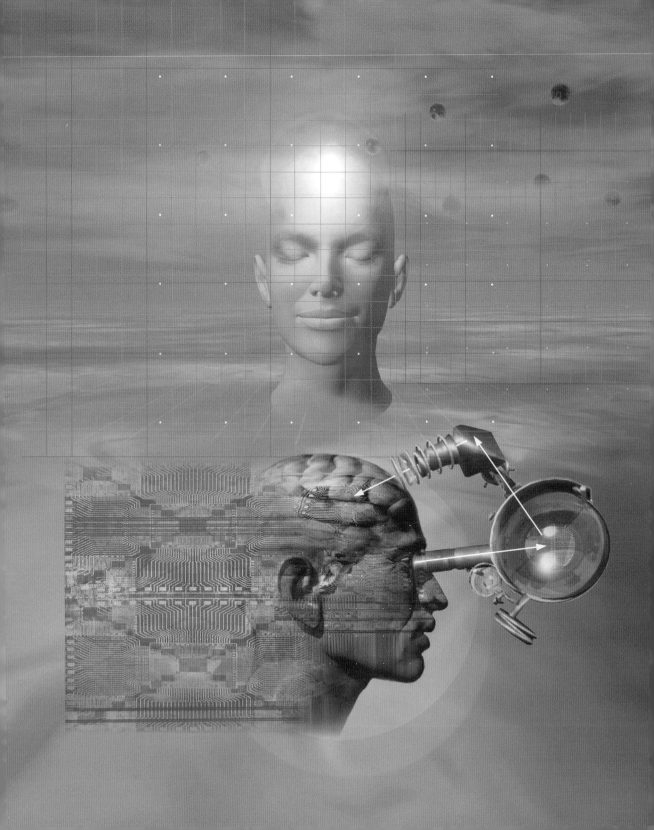

The Hard Problem

'No philosopher and hardly any novelist has ever managed to explain what that weird stuff, human consciousness, is really made of ...'

Iris Murdoch from *The Black Prince*, Chatto and Windus

To be conscious usually means to be conscious *of something*. But the contents of consciousness are distinguishable, in theory at least, from consciousness itself. That is, the cow you are conscious of in the field is a cow, not this ephemeral thing that can be comprised of a grazing ruminant one minute, a feeling of amusement the next, and then a toothache. The contents of consciousness can – up to a point – be quantified, described and examined. But what of the thing itself? What *is* consciousness, and how does it fit into the scheme of things?

Dictionary compilers are more or less defeated by the question. Their definitions are either circular: e.g. 'state of being conscious' (Oxford); or negative: 'not sleeping or comatose' (Collins). And scientific books on the subject generally slither round the question, saying lots about neural correlates (as does this book) but little about the thing the neuronal mechanisms are correlated with. Over the last ten years some 30,000 papers have been published on the subject of consciousness, but for every one that addresses this central issue – popularly known as 'the hard problem' – 99 per cent talk only about the 'easy' peripheral issues: how consciousness is generated; what it contains; who or what has it ...[1]

There is, of course, nothing 'easy', in the usual sense, about the problems discussed in the majority of papers – they are among the toughest that science has ever tackled. But at least they raise questions which appear answerable and which conventional reductive science can reasonably expect to crack in the foreseeable future. The hard problem, by contrast, is qualitatively different because consciousness, uniquely, does not seem to fit into the framework of the universe as most of us understand it. Everything else can be explained (or seems potentially explicable) in terms of physical forces. Even complex cultural

David Chalmers
Department of Philosophy
University of Arizona

Facing up to Consciousness

Consciousness poses the most baffling problems in the science of the mind. There is nothing that we know more intimately than conscious experience, but there is nothing that is harder to explain. All sorts of mental phenomena have yielded to scientific investigation in recent years, but consciousness has stubbornly resisted.

At the start, it is useful to divide the associated problems of consciousness into 'hard' and 'easy' problems. The easy problems of consciousness involve phenomena such as discriminating environmental stimuli, integrating information in the brain, producing verbal reports, and so on. These phenomena seem directly susceptible to the standard methods of cognitive science, whereby a phenomenon is explained in terms of computational or neural mechanisms.

The hard problem of consciousness is the problem of experience. There is something it is like to see and feel and think: in our inner life, we experience the felt quality of red sensations, of anger, of nostalgic thought. It is undeniable that some organisms are subjects of experience. But why should physical processing give rise to a rich inner life at all? It seems objectively unreasonable that it should, and yet it does.

The easy problems are easy because they concern the explanation of cognitive 'abilities' and 'functions' in the production of behaviour. To explain a cognitive function, we need only specify a mechanism that can perform the function. The hard problem is hard because it is not a problem about the performance of functions. Even when we have explained all the functions in the vicinity – discrimination, integration, report, and so on – there may still remain a further question: why are these functions accompanied by experience? The standard methods of neuroscience and cognitive science involve explaining functions of this sort: this is perfect for the easy problems, but it leaves the hard problem untouched.

In most areas of science, functions are all that need to be explained. To explain life, for example, we need to explain the functions of adaptation, reproduction, and so on. Vitalists doubted that physical mechanisms could perform these functions, but when appropriate mechanisms were discovered, the vitalist doubts melted away. The problem of consciousness is puzzling in an

Daniel C. Dennett
Professor of Philosophy
Center for Cognitive Studies Tufts University

Facing Backwards on the Problem of Consciousness

Chalmers' attempt to sort the 'easy' problems of consciousness from the 'really hard' problem is not, I think, a useful contribution to research, but a major misdirector of attention, an illusion-generator.

Francis Crick, in *The Astonishing Hypothesis*, gives us an example of what happens when you adopt Chalmers' distinction, when he says at the close of the book: 'I have said almost nothing about qualia – the redness of red – except to brush it to one side and hope for the best.'[1] But consider what would be wrong with the following claim made by an imaginary neuroscientist (Crock) substituting 'perception' for 'qualia' in the quotation from Crick: 'I have said almost nothing about perception – the actual analysis and comprehension of the visual input – except to brush it to one side and hope for the best.'

Today we can all recognize that whatever came before Crock's declaration would be forlorn, because not so many years ago this was a mistake that brain scientists actually made: they succumbed all too often to the temptation to treat vision as if it were television – as if it were simply a matter of getting 'the picture' from the eyes to the screen somewhere in the middle where it could be handsomely reproduced so that the phenomena of appreciation and analysis could then get underway. Today we realize that the analysis – the whatever you want to call it that composes, in the end, all the visual understanding – begins right away, on the retina; if you postpone consideration of it, you misdescribe how vision works. Crock has made a mistake: he has created an artifactual 'hard' problem of perception, not noticing that it evaporates when the piecemeal work on the easy problems is completed.

Is it similarly a mistake for Crick, following Chalmers, to think that he can make progress on the easy questions of consciousness without in the process answering the hard question? I think so. I make the parallel claim about the purported 'subjective qualities' or 'qualia' of experience: if you don't begin breaking them down into their (functional) components from the outset, and distributing them throughout your model, you create a monster – an imaginary dazzle in the eye of a Cartesian homunculus.

Chalmers has not yet fallen into either of these traps – not quite. He understands that he must show how his strategic proposal differs from these, entirely different way. Because it goes beyond objective functions to the subjective, it is not the sort of thing that a standard account in terms of mechanisms can explain.

Might we expand the underlying mechanisms? Some suggest an injection of chaos and nonlinear dynamics. Some think that the key lies in nonalgorithmic processing. Some appeal to future discoveries in neurophysiology. Some suppose that the key to the mystery lies with quantum mechanics. Unfortunately, while all of these proposals offer new and interesting explanations of objective functions, none explain why these processes should give rise to experience. The same problem arises for any explanation in purely physical terms.

At this point some are tempted to give up, holding that we will never have a theory of conscious experience. I think this pessimism is premature. This is not the place to give up; it is the place where things get interesting.

An alternative approach is to stop trying to reduce consciousness to something else, and accept instead that it is irreducible. This happens often in physics, with features such as mass, space and time: these features are not explained in terms of other things, but are taken as fundamental. One can still construct theories involving these entities, explaining how they interrelate in terms of fundamental laws. In the same way, once we admit consciousness as a fundamental feature, we can then investigate the fundamental laws that govern it. In this way we can go about the business of constructing a theory of experience.

There need be nothing particularly spiritual or mystical about such a theory. Its overall shape is entirely naturalistic: like that of a physical theory, it explains everything in terms of a few fundamental entities connected by fundamental laws. It expands the underlying entities, to be sure, but that happens from time to time. The principles of simplicity, elegance and even beauty that drive physicists' search for a fundamental theory will still apply to a theory of consciousness.

A nonreductive theory of consciousness will consist in a number of psychophysical principles, principles connecting the properties of physical which he recognizes as doomed. He attempts this by claiming that consciousness is strikingly unlike life, and unlike the features of perception misconstrued by Crock: when it comes to consciousness, the hard problem goes beyond problems about the performance of functions ... there remains a further unanswered question: Why is the performance of these functions accompanied by experience? A vitalist can surely ask the same dreary question: Why is the performance of certain functions accompanied by life? Chalmers says that this would be a conceptual mistake on the part of the vitalist, and I agree, but he needs to defend his claim that his counterpart is not a conceptual mistake as well.

When he confronts the vitalist parallel head-on, he simply declares that whereas vitalist scepticism was driven by doubts about whether physical mechanisms could 'do the job', his own scepticism is based on something else: the conceptual point that the explanation of functions does not suffice for the explanation of experience. I submit that he is flatly mistaken in this claim. Whether people realize it or not, it is precisely the 'remarkable functions associated with' consciousness that drive them to wonder about how consciousness could possibly reside in a brain. In fact, if you carefully dissociate all these remarkable functions from consciousness – in your own, first-person case – there is nothing left for you to wonder about.

What impresses me about my own consciousness, as I know it so intimately, is my delight in some features and dismay over others, my distraction and concentration, my unnameable sinking feelings of foreboding and my blithe disregard of some perceptual details, my obsessions and oversights, my ability to conjure up fantasies, my inability to hold more than a few items in consciousness at a time, my ability to be moved to tears by a vivid recollection of the death of a loved one, my inability to catch myself in the act of framing the words I sometimes say to myself, and so forth. These are all 'merely' the performance of functions' or the manifestation of various complex dispositions to perform functions. In the course of making an introspective catalogue of evidence, I wouldn't know what I was thinking about if I couldn't identify them for myself by these functional differentia. Take them away and processes to the properties of experience. We can think of these principles as encapsulating the way in which experience arises from the physical. This is a tall order, but there is no reason why we should not get started.

One possible candidate for a fundamental psychophysical principle is that information (or at least some information) has two basic aspects, a physical aspect and a phenomenal aspect. Experience arises by virtue of its status as one aspect of information, when the other aspect is found embodied in physical processing. In a slogan: physics is information from the outside, while consciousness is information from the inside.

Right now this is more of an idea than a theory. Still, reflection on just what is plausible and implausible about it, on where it works and where it fails, can only lead to a better theory. Most existing theories of consciousness either deny the phenomenon, explain something else, or elevate the problem to an eternal mystery. I believe it is possible to make progress on the problem even while taking it seriously. To make further progress, we will need further investigation, more refined theories, and more careful analysis. The hard problem is a hard problem, but there is no reason to believe that it will remain permanently unsolved.

David Chalmers is the author of *The Conscious Mind* (Oxford University Press, 1996).

nothing is left beyond a weird conviction (in some people) that there is some ineffable residue of 'qualitative content' bereft of all powers to move us, delight us, annoy us, remind us of anything.

Chalmers recommends a parallel with physics, but it backfires. He suggests that a theory of consciousness should take experience itself as a fundamental feature of the world, alongside mass, charge and space-time. As he correctly notes, 'No attempt is made [by physicists] to explain these features in terms of anything simpler', but they do cite the independent evidence that has driven them to introduce these fundamental categories. Chalmers needs a similar argument in support of his proposal, but when we ask what data are driving him to introduce this concept, the answer is disappointing: It is a belief in a fundamental phenomenon of 'experience'. The introduction of the concept does not do any explanatory work. We can see this by comparing Chalmers' proposal with yet one more imaginary non-starter: cutism. The proposal that since some things are just plain cute, and other things aren't cute at all – you can just see it, however hard it is to describe or explain – we had better postulate cuteness as a fundamental property of physics alongside mass, charge and space-time. (Cuteness is not a functional property, of course; I can imagine somebody who wasn't actually cute at all but who nevertheless functioned exactly as if cute – trust me.) Cutism is in even worse shape than vitalism. Nobody would have taken vitalism seriously for a minute if the vitalists hadn't had a set of independently describable phenomena – of reproduction, metabolism, self-repair and the like – that their postulated fundamental life-element was hoped to account for. Once these phenomena were otherwise accounted for, vitalism fell flat, but at least it had a project. Until Chalmers gives us an independent ground for contemplating the drastic move of adding 'experience' to mass, charge and space-time, his proposal is one that can be put on the back burner, way back.

Daniel Dennett is the author of *Consciousness Explained*, (UK, Penguin, 1991).

' Francis Crick, *The Astonishing Hypothesis* (New York, Scribners, 1994), 256.

phenomena, like democracy or a nation's economy, can be broken down, in theory, to the actions and interactions of individual people and, beyond that, to the actions of cells in those people's brains. Behaviour is not the hard problem, because it is easy (in this relative sense) to see how neural activity can produce it. We do so many complicated things unconsciously (including making decisions and judgements) that there is no obvious reason why we should not do everything that way. Yet we don't. Some of our behaviour is accompanied by this weird, seemingly non-physical thing, and there is no clear way to see how, if at all, it fits into the material world.

Science neglected the hard problem until recently, mainly because it was just too difficult to get a grip on. The behaviourists, who dominated psychology until the 1960s, regarded the human brain as a straightforward input-output device. In went a stimulus, out came a bit of behaviour, and anything that might have been going on in between was ignored. This was not born of stupidity – psychologists at the turn of the century made a game effort to explore consciousness through introspection, but foundered on the unreliable witness problem. Attempts to categorize and quantify the 'elements' of consciousness, for example, produced widely varying results. One laboratory came up with 12,000 distinct sensations; another found more than 44,000.[2] So behaviourism came about largely because psychologists found that consciousness was too slippery a customer to be pinned down by the exploratory techniques then available to them.

The behaviourists' approach was spectacularly successful in revealing how, and to some extent why, people act as they do, but in retrospect it is obvious that it left out the most important thing of all: how it all feels.

Scientists are now getting excited about consciousness again, for two reasons. The first is that the discovery of quantum mechanics holds out a possibility of placing consciousness within a scientific paradigm, so it has again become 'respectable' to study it scientifically. The second (more influential) is that it has, for the first time, become possible to study it in a way that does not depend solely on first-person reports. Sophisticated technology – especially functional brain imagers like fMRI, PET and MEG scanners and EEG – allows neuroscientists to look inside a living, working, conscious brain and see exactly what is going on. No need to deduce, any more, what is happening in the black box by watching its output or simply asking people to report on their inner world – you can look at the mechanics directly. This second breakthrough has made consciousness studies appealing even to those who believe that there is no 'hard question' to be answered, and that consciousness is simply a part of the material universe that has hitherto seemed mysterious because it was so difficult to investigate. Such 'hard' materialists are confident that a satisfactory explanation of subjective experience will eventually pop out of their computer-generated brain images and neural firing charts, and a few think it already has.

Philosophers, on the other hand, have been grappling with the problem for centuries. Many of them are now enthusiastically incorporating neuroscientific discoveries in their deliberations, though some think the answer is more likely to be found through abstract reasoning than by playing with expensive machinery. So far the philosophical approach has generated a vast amount of dense conjecture, but precious little consensus. However, most of the multitudinous theories of consciousness – old and new – can be fitted into two broad divisions: monism, which regards consciousness and the observed universe as one; and dualism – the idea that consciousness and the physical world are two different things.

While scientists test their ideas with laboratory experiments, philosophers use thought experiments. These have the advantage of requiring minimal equipment: a brain and (ideally) a comfortable armchair. So anyone can do them.

A thought experiment that investigates the strengths and weaknesses of the one thing or two things argument is the philosophers' Zombie. This not the flesh-eating, dead-eyed monster of the B-movie. It looks, and behaves, exactly – and I mean exactly – like you or me. It is made of the same flesh and blood as a human being, with the same brain wired up in an identical way. And it goes through its life in the same way: its eyes sparkle when nice things happen to it, it cries when nasty things happen, it cuddles and snaps at its children and may even write books about consciousness. The single difference is that the Zombie does all this without any consciousness of what it is doing. There is no 'inner life' for a Zombie. It may go 'aaah' at a beautiful sunset but – unlike you or me – it isn't aware of the red sky at all. The lights are all on but there's no-one at home.

Having established this odd piece of thought laboratory equipment, the experiment now proceeds as follows: everyone furrows their brows and ponders the following question: 'Is it logically possible that such a thing could exist?' Not, 'Is it likely?', or even 'Is it plausible?' Not even 'Do the laws of Nature permit it?' (We don't know enough about the laws of nature to say but, even if we did, this is not the point.) No, the question is – is there anything about a Zombie that makes it impossible, as for example, a triangular square is impossible, or a female cock-pheasant?

What do People Believe?

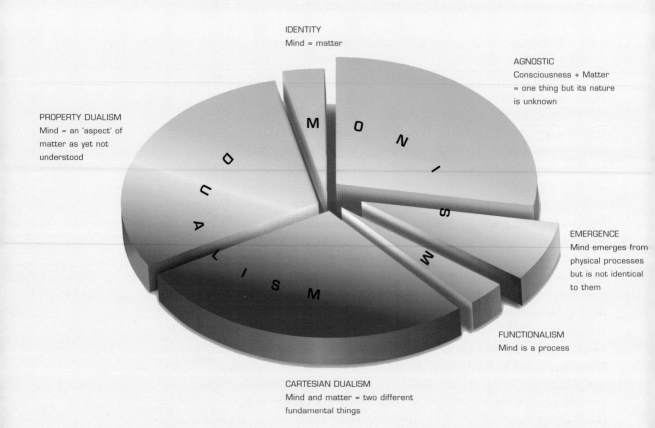

IDENTITY
Mind = matter

AGNOSTIC
Consciousness + Matter
= one thing but its nature
is unknown

PROPERTY DUALISM
Mind = an 'aspect' of
matter as yet not
understood

EMERGENCE
Mind emerges from
physical processes
but is not identical
to them

FUNCTIONALISM
Mind is a process

CARTESIAN DUALISM
Mind and matter = two different
fundamental things

MONISM

DUALISM

Most formal public discussion and writing about consciousness is done by philosophers and neuroscientists, and very few surveys have been done to find out what the non-specialist thinks about it. The few surveys that have canvassed lay opinion suggest the divisions shown above. Very few hold to the 'hard' materialist view that mind and physical processes are identical, nor that it emerges from matter or is a physical process. A survey of scientists and philosophers would look very different.

The crucial point of the Zombie experiment is this: if you conclude that Zombies are logically possible, then consciousness must be 'something extra', over and above the material world. After all, there is no material difference between them and us, yet we have this thing called consciousness and they don't. In other words, our Zombie is the living (-dead) proof of dualism. If, on the other hand, you conclude that Zombies are impossible, it follows that a particular physical construction is necessarily conscious – so the two are of a single material stuff.

Today the most commonly-held type of monism is that consciousness is one and the same as the material world. But there is a far older type of monism implicit in the writings of philosophers as far back as Aristotle. Aristotle did not deal directly with the 'hard problem' as we see it today. In his earliest writings he argues that the 'psyche' was independent of physical matter – a clear case of dualism. But his later works associated mental phenomena with the workings of the body. The student of the psyche, he says, should investigate the behavioural and physiological aspects of his subject – he must know, for example, that anger is the boiling of the blood around the heart.[3]

It is tempting to equate this with modern materialistic monism, but if that is what Aristotle had in mind it is very odd that, in all his writings, he never bothered with the problem of understanding how body and mind are bound. You don't have to think very hard or long about the nature of mind to be struck by the difficulty of seeing how consciousness fits into the physical world, and Aristotle certainly thought long and hard. So why wasn't he concerned with this central issue? The most likely reason is that Aristotle wrote from an essentially different viewpoint to ours. Instead of seeing matter and mind as two, separable concepts, he and his contemporaries may have assumed that everything – each little scrap of matter – had at its centre a spark of life, and thus a shadow of consciousness.[4]

This idea – referred to as panpsychism – has always been, and still is, widely held. It is often thought of as primitive or ignorant, but it has a deep intuitive appeal and most of us have the inkling of it still – when the car breaks down at the worst possible moment, or a piece of windswept paper keeps flipping out of reach it is almost impossible not to feel that the thing 'has a life of its own' and is frustrating us for its own malign purpose.

The appeal of panpsychism only really started to die in the Renaissance, when scientific discoveries began to present the natural world as a mechanical system moved by external cause and effect rather than by the internal forces of intention and purpose. It was this division between mental (or spiritual) phenomena, and the deterministic, reducible natural world, which gave rise, effectively, to the hard problem, and the great minds of the time set to work to solve it.

Modern, material monism was probably not conceivable three hundred years ago – certainly, not enough was known about the workings of the brain for anyone to imagine how it could be. And such a view would have been unacceptable, anyway, for religious reasons. The solution had to leave God, and the human spirit, free of material constraints while allowing science to explore the natural world unhindered. The French philosopher René Descartes (1596–1650) finally found an ingenious solution. He proposed that the human body, along with its more mundane cognitive capacities, was a mere physical mechanism, while the human spirit was made of different stuff altogether, and inhabited a different dimension. The two interacted, however, in the brain. Specifically, he thought that the spirit entered the brain via the pineal gland – a tiny piece of tissue in the middle of the organ – where it influenced the workings of a hydraulic-like system which then produced behaviour.

Cartesian dualism had the same intuitive appeal to those living with the new scientific view of the natural world as panpsychism did to those who knew nature only by their personal dealings with it. The material world was clearly made of one type of thing, and consciousness, equally clearly, was another. The very word 'consciousness' (which appears only to have come into existence around this time) implies this split: 'con' roughly translating from Latin as 'bringing together', and 'scious' meaning knowledge. Most people found the division easy to live with, and still do; the idea – minus the hydraulics – persists among many (probably the majority) of people to this day. Those who thought it through, however, realized that, despite the pineal gland connection, it did not actually explain how mind/body interaction could work. Other explanations were sought, and the one that found most favour – at least among philosophers – was idealism.

There are several versions of idealism, but the best known is that put forward by Bishop George Berkeley (1685–1753). Berkeley loathed the growing scientific world view of his age – that everything is mere matter and is subject only to mechanical forces. He argued that the real situation was its complete reverse: all things are essentially mind (spirit and soul) and perceptions of the material world are merely ideas put into the mind by God. The material world, he claimed, is a vast illusion created by our senses, which themselves are non-material.[5]

Berkeley's idea seems fairly batty at first sight – as it did to some of his contemporaries. Samuel Johnson, for example, declared 'I refute him – thus!', the 'thus' being a toe-stubbing kick at a large and very solid stone. This no-nonsense response to idealism was, of course, vacuous. The stone, the stubbed toe and the attendant pain could be seen as testimony only to the remarkable degree of solidity that an idea might achieve. But it no doubt delighted the 17th-century equivalent of the Man on the Clapham Omnibus, as it still delights those who are comforted by the ridicule of ideas they find difficult to grasp; indeed, most seem to assume the stone-kicking was a triumph of common sense rather than the intellectual stone-walling it actually was. Philosophers, however, took up Berkeley's idealism with enthusiasm, perhaps because it is one of the few theories which it is impossible to disprove. After all, we perceive the world only through our senses – there is no other way to see it. Even a scientist taking measurements from an instrument is dependent on finding out what the measuring instruments show. You can feed the measurements from one device into another, and another – and get them processed by a computer – but in the end someone, somewhere, has to read off and interpret the results. So there is never any way that we can be certain of anything in the outside world – including that there is a world out there at all.

Idealism is a form of monism, though the complete converse of modern materialist monism. It gives primacy to the subjective world of mind and dispenses with the problem of how to reconcile it with the physical universe by denying the latter's reality. Today's materialist monists do just the opposite – they regard the physical world as essential reality and claim that mental phenomena are either non-existent (eliminativism) or one and the same (identity theory).

Eliminativism is the most extreme of the 'hard' materialist views. It is also, perhaps, the hardest to swallow because it challenges our own experience in the most fundamental way – by claiming it does not exist. It looks at the brain from an exclusively objective point of view, and in doing so finds only 'data structures' in the brain. Mental phenomena – pain, say – cannot exist because they are not to be found in the material universe and the material universe is all there is. Thus, pain does not exist – only the neural activation brought about by stimulation of certain nerve fibres.

A moment's reflection seems to defeat the idea of eliminativism, by definition. For what is reflection if it is not consciousness? Real hardliners are not impressed by this, though. The philosopher George Rey, for example, likens it to belief in God. 'Why should one believe in such a God? Why should one believe in such a consciousness? In both cases, of course, people have been tempted to say: "Because I have direct access to it." But such first-person breast-beating begs the question ... the challenge ... is to come up with some non question-begging reason to believe consciousness exists. I doubt there is any to be had.'[6]

Do eliminativists think we are all zombies then? In a sense, yes. Both zombiehood and normal human experience are states involving elaborate information-processing – but neither have this magic thing called qualia. They merely think they do.

The best-known champion of this view is the American philosopher Daniel Dennett, who (though he does not adopt the label 'eliminativist') claims that experience is 'a myth, an artifact of misguided theorising.'[7] He maintains that sensory input produces high-level dispositional states – beliefs, thoughts and judgements – that cause us to act in a certain way. So a certain type of light input, say, produces the judgement of 'red', and that in turn might dispose a person to say something like 'That light is red!' or to stamp on the brake of their car. Over and above these dispositions there is nothing – no internal, ineffable, private experience of red. What we think is a red experience is actually just the operation of the belief that we have it. One argument Dennett employs to support this idea is that the addition of experience to the dispositional states produced by sensory input would not make a difference to behaviour. Qualia are surplus to requirements – and therefore, he argues, there is no evidence to think they exist.

Identity theory, like eliminativism, holds that brain states are all there is. It acknowledges that consciousness exists, but not as something separate from the firing of brain cells. The reason we can't understand it from the outside is that we can't *get* outside it – we are our experience, so there is no way of standing aside from it and examining it from the outside and the inside simultaneously. An example might be temperature. This is the same thing as kinetic energy – a physical phenomenon with no mysterious spiritual properties. It seems to produce this other thing – temperature; but in fact temperature is just another word for the same thing – they are identical and you can't take them apart. Identity theorist Paul Churchland puts it succinctly: 'the human species and all of its features are the wholly physical outcome of a purely physical process ... We are notable only in that our nervous system is more complex and powerful than that of our fellow creatures ... We are creatures of matter. And we should learn to live with that fact.'[8]

Naturally, identity theorists, like eliminativists, do not believe in Zombies. Or rather, they don't believe Zombies are different from people. Given that the physical brain and the mind are the same, they argue that it would be impossible for a creature that had an identical physical constitution to a human being to be in anything but the same state exactly – consciousness (or not) included. Daniel Dennett, for example, points out that a creature which is really physically identical to a human would have neuronal pathways that monitor its own mental processes. This would allow it to reflect on its own (unconscious) thoughts, and these higher-order thoughts would include (unconscious) thoughts about its own (unconscious) thoughts. If you keep cranking up this process of self-reflection you inevitably get to a point where the Zombie thinks the unconscious thought: 'I am conscious!'[9] This illusion, according to Dennett, is precisely what we call consciousness.

It is tempting, when you see the close correlations between conscious states and brain states, to be drawn into thinking that these two things must be the same. And it is attractive because, like eliminativism, it does away with the hard problem. If the tickle (I think) I am feeling in my foot is just this particular state that all the molecules in my body happen to be in right now, there is no 'gap' between feeling and physical state that needs to be bridged. You can stop worrying about arcane philosophical puzzles and start building a complete description of the world, confident that when you have finished, it will encompass everything there is. Easy.

However, if you stand back and think about it, material monism is an extraordinarily radical and counter-intuitive idea. How can a state of matter be a feeling? They seem so clearly to be two quite different types of thing. Intellectually beguiling though it might be, this 'hard' materialism – like behaviourism – feels as though it is leaving out the most obvious and important part.

It is also hard not to feel (as Bishop Berkeley did) that this view of existence undermines the things we hold most precious – our status as autonomous, moral and meaningful beings. If you accept unqualified materialism you are forced to question the existence of free will, deny any notion of spiritual truth and abandon hope of transcendence. God is an illusion, while love is a particular pattern of chemically-mediated neural activity, and morality is best understood as an adaptive survival mechanism. We are robots, controlled by meaningless forces of physical causation. In most of us, even if we can get our heads around the idea, our hearts rebel.

Intuition is powerful because it seems to convey a certainty that intellectual knowledge lacks: 'I know it's wrong,' opposed to 'I think it's wrong.' But intuition is not as reliable as it seems, and furthermore, it changes in the light of experience. The idea that the earth went round the sun, instead of the other way around, once seemed impossible. Even the notion of gravity probably seemed crazy when it was first mooted: An invisible force? That works over a distance? That can make the *oceans* move? You can imagine them falling about down at the Dog and Duck. Yet we have no problem with the idea today. Relativity is still perplexing and counter-intuitive to most of us, but few would dispute its reality. In fifty years it will probably seem as unremarkable as gravity. Quantum physics is totally baffling to most of us: particles that can be in two places at once? That can affect each other without means of communication? That only become one thing or another when we observe them? Yet these things have been shown – as far as things can be – to be true. So gut objections to hard materialism are no measure of its validity.

Materialism has another problem, though – one which has nothing to do with intuition. Although specific brain states can be shown to correlate with specific subjective feelings, it has also been shown that similar feelings can correlate with quite different brain states. Understanding speech, for example, is usually associated with activity in the left hemisphere of the brain, but if the left hemisphere is damaged (by a stroke, for example) it may shift to the right hemisphere, where it will correlate with the activity of entirely different networks of neurons (a different brain state). Thus a particular mental state (understanding words) cannot be said to be identical to a particular brain state – at best it can merely be associated with a particular *type* of brain state.

The distinction may seem a fine one, but once it is made, identity theory becomes vulnerable to the argument of 'multiple realization' – the idea that consciousness could occur in association with all sorts of states. If a particular mental state does not need a particular physical state to occur, it cannot be identical to that particular physical state. This brings it perilously close to being seen (again) as a separate thing which merely attaches to physical states.

There is no need yet, though, to leap back to dualism. There are softer forms of materialism which acknowledge consciousness as a real, distinguishable thing without positing a non-material universe in which it exists, and which do not lock subjective events to one particular physical state. Functionalism, for example, sees conscious mental states as having a similar relationship to physical brain states as software does to computer hardware. According to this theory, it is the processes involved in the brain states, not the states themselves, which are conscious. Thus when a network of neurons fire in a particular pattern and sequence it is the activity, rather than the neurons, that produces the associated conscious state.

Some functionalists believe that only processes within certain types of complex systems, such as an embodied brain, can create consciousness. Others argue that, whatever form the physical hardware takes, if the processes it undergoes are the same as those in the brain, the result is the same subjective state. Given this, it follows that it doesn't have to be neurons doing the firing – if silicon chips, or even chocolate chip cookies, could be induced to carry out precisely the same activity, the system they formed would be conscious.

Like hard materialism, this raises both intuitive and intellectual problems. It is very difficult to imagine biscuits – however many of them and however they are linked up – suddenly feeling heartbroken or starting to worry about being eaten. But that – taken to the point of absurdity – is what functionalism demands. It is even difficult to believe that a silicon brain, wired up to mimic precisely the actions of a human one, would automatically be possessed of human feelings.

Another thought experiment might help, however. Imagine a robot, identical to you except that its brain cells are made of silicon. These cells do just what normal neurons do – they send precisely the same signals to the same places, triggering the same ebb and flow of electric currents, hormones and neurotransmitters throughout the body. Do you think it possible that such a machine could feel differently to you in any way?

Let's say you grant it consciousness (we'll avoid the Zombie) but still think that perhaps it could, say, experience blue when you experience red. It sounds plausible, but now imagine this.

Some brilliant scientist has found a way of shrinking this silicon system so it can be fitted into a human skull as a back-up brain. Imagine such a system is installed in your own head, with a switch that, when flipped, connects the back-up brain to your body. So here you are, with this second brain in your head, and the ability to switch between them. Assume that before you switch to the back-up, you are having a red experience – looking at a red apple on your desk. Then the switch is thrown. Presumably, if the silicon brain was seeing blue when you saw red, the apple on your desk would suddenly switch colours.

Fair enough – it's imaginable. But what happens next? Remember, the back-up brain is sending precisely the same signals to your body as your own brain was before you switched. So your body carries on making precisely the same actions, the same facial expressions, uttering the same words. And the brain itself is functioning in just the same way as your own so it carries on producing the same thoughts. The apple in front of you now appears blue, but you seem totally unconcerned. You don't mention its sudden blueness; in fact, if asked, you would say it was red. Flip the switch again and the apple is red again, but once more you continue without apparently noticing. Flip the switch to the beat of a calypso and you have qualia dancing before your eyes, but you don't know it![10] Is this likely? I leave you to decide.

It is still a big leap from silicon brains to linked-up cookies, and many people find they cannot go all the way with functionalism. The problem with the idea that processes can produce consciousness in things other than the brain is articulated most clearly by the Chinese Room argument put forward by American philosopher John Searle. The Chinese Room is a vast cubicle which contains all the rules for speaking Chinese, along with a man who speaks only English. The rules are written, in English, on millions of cards which are stored in filing cabinets. The cards are also inscribed with Chinese characters which the man can recognize only by shape. The cubicle is connected to the outside world by a letterbox, through which, from time to time, people post questions in Chinese. The man takes these and matches the symbols on them to the symbols on his cards. He then follows the instructions on the cards, which direct him to more symbols, which he copies down onto a blank sheet of paper, and, eventually, posts back through the letterbox. (Luckily, he can do all this at the speed of light.) Those outside find the paper contains the answer to their question, written in impeccable Chinese. From where they are standing, it seems that the person inside the room has understood their message perfectly. But in fact all the man has done is match the symbols – he has no idea what the cards said, no understanding of the question, and no inkling of the meaning of his own reply. Thus, argues Searle, non-neural processes can produce external effects which look for all the world as though they were produced by a conscious, understanding mind when in fact all they are doing is computing.

The counter-argument to the Chinese Room debate is that it is not the man inside who is conscious but the room itself. Or at least, it might be if, in addition to holding information about language it also held all the other information – social, historical, contextual – that a human brain holds. No single component – including the man who goes through the filing cabinets, is itself conscious, but the system as a whole is. Its consciousness is something that emerges from the interaction of the sum of its parts, rather as the movement of a car arises only when all its parts are put together in a certain way and have a certain cause and effect on each other.

The idea that a complex system can produce something that is more than the sum of its parts is known as emergence, and it is common to many theories of consciousness. It creates a new type of dualism in which the 'stuff' of

consciousness is seen as an effect of certain physical processes. It does not necessarily call for any new laws, but as in the Chinese Room, neither can it necessarily be reduced to its individual constituents, because the emergent 'stuff' has different effects, or properties, from any of its parts. Hydrogen and oxygen, for example, cannot dissolve salt. But put the two together as water and they can. Furthermore, they have a new property, wetness, as well as a new effect.

Emergence differs from Cartesian dualism in that matter comes first, and without it consciousness cannot exist. It does not give rise to the intuitive objection of hard materialism, that 'something is missing', but it poses another: if consciousness, though emerging from matter, is not itself material, there is no way within modern scientific understanding that it can have any effect on the physical processes that give rise to it. The physical universe is causally 'closed' in that every movement of every material particle is demonstrably due to one of the known forces of nature. There is no gap in our knowledge of cause and effect which allows for consciousness to influence what happens in the brain. This forces the conclusion that consciousness is epiphenomenal – a mere by-product of brain activity which has no effect on behaviour.

Epiphenomenalism is almost as counter-intuitive as eliminativism, because if there is one thing consciousness seems to do it is to influence our actions. Simple reflex behaviour – whipping our hand away from a flame – is easy enough to understand in mere mechanical terms. But when we ponder a complex situation, weigh the pros and cons of responding this way or that, then make a decision, consciousness seems to be the moving force. So the search continues to find a theory of consciousness which puts freewill back into the picture without embracing epiphenomenalism or the brute materialism of identity.

One way to do this is to suppose that consciousness is an emergent macro-state that not only has different properties from the micro-states that gives rise to it (as water has a different property, wetness, from its constituents) but that it also has different causal effects which 'play back down' to the micro level. So unconscious brain state (or process) X produces conscious state A which has the power to change brain state X into brain state X1 which then produces conscious state A1 – and so on. In other words, once it has emerged consciousness becomes its own creator – no longer dependent on the senseless mechanisms that gave rise to it.

One theory of this kind is that put forward by John Searle, which he calls 'biological naturalism'. Searle's ideas cut across the dualism/monism divide by stating that consciousness is both material, in that it is a feature of the physical brain; and non-material, in that it is a different type of phenomena from the physical processes that underlie it. It regards the essential relationship between the physical and non-physical features of consciousness as (by their very nature) causal. That is, each causes the other, in the way that hydrogen and oxygen molecules, in certain conditions, cause the feature of liquidity. You can't have water (or whatever other liquid substance you choose) without liquidity, says Searle, so there is no link that holds the two together (if there was it could conceivably be broken). On the other hand, the two things are not identical in the way identity theorists would have it, because consciousness is essentially subjective, so it cannot be reduced to material alone.

'Think of a single molecule in a wheel that is rolling,' suggests Searle. 'The whole structure of the wheel and its movements as a wheel determine the movements of the molecule, even though the wheel is made of such molecules. And what is true of one molecule is true of all the molecules. ... [Similarly] each molecule in a liquid is affected by the liquidity of the system, even though there is nothing there but molecules [and] in the conscious brain each neuron in the conscious portions of the system can be affected by the consciousness of the brain, even though there is nothing there but neurons.'[11]

Not everyone finds this persuasive. It is one thing to say that a system can produce an emergent entity with new causal effects – water has the effect of dissolving salt whereas hydrogen and oxygen cannot, so there is nothing controversial about that. However, it is quite another thing to suppose that such new effects can work downwards. Hydrogen + oxygen = water which can dissolve salt – fine. It is a straightforward linear chain of cause and effect. The power of water to dissolve salt is, if you like, latent in the hydrogen and oxygen and is merely realized by these constituents coming together in a certain way, just as your hands can hold water when you cup them but not when you wave them around. But the supposed power of consciousness to affect the brain state that goes with it is something else. If conscious state A is simply physical brain state X (i.e. they are identical) then there is no problem because one physical state can – in the ordinary way – affect another. But if consciousness is something else – the non-physical thing it seems to be – there is no obvious way, given what we know of the material universe, that it can effect a change in the underlying brain state.

And so we arrive at two distinct types of emergence: Type 1, which allows consciousness to arise from the material world but denies it causal effect (i.e. an epiphenomenon) and Type 2, which somehow allows it causal efficiency.

John Searle
Mills Professor of the Philosophy of Mind and Language
University of California, Berkeley

Solving the Hard Problem - Naturally

The problem of how brain processes relate to mind has two parts to it: one philosophical and one scientific. There is, I believe, a simple solution to the philosophical part and it is this: consciousness and other sorts of mental phenomena are caused by neurobiological processes in the brain, and they are realized in the structure of the brain. In a word, the conscious mind is caused by brain processes and is itself a higher level feature of the brain.

The relationship of brain mechanisms to consciousness is one of causation. Processes in the brain cause our conscious experiences. This does not force us to any kind of dualism because the form of causation is bottom-up, and the resulting effect is simply a higher level feature of the brain itself, not a separate substance. Consciousness is not like some fluid squirted out by the brain. A conscious state is rather a state that the brain is in. Just as water can be in a liquid or solid state without liquidity and solidity being separate substances, so consciousness is a state that the brain is in without consciousness being a separate substance.

It is irreducible not because it is ineffable or mysterious, but because it has an essentially subjective first person mode of existence and therefore cannot be reduced to third person phenomena. The traditional mistake that people have made in both science and philosophy has been to suppose that if we reject dualism, as I believe we must, then we have to embrace materialism. But on the view that I am putting forward, materialism is just as confused as dualism because it denies the existence of subjective consciousness as a thing in its own right. Just to give it a name, the resulting view that denies both dualism and materialism, I call biological naturalism.

Now to the scientific problem:

Seen from the outside, it looks deceptively simple to solve. There are three steps. First, one finds the neurobiological events that are correlated with consciousness (the NCC). Second, one tests to see that the correlation is a genuine causal relation. And third, one tries to develop a theory, ideally in the form of a set of laws, that would formalize the causal relationships.

So far this programme has failed even to reach step one, because in spite of all of the hype surrounding the development of imaging techniques, we still, as far as I know, have not found a way to image the NCC.

This may be because a large part of the current research effort is misdirected. There are two main ideas about how to study consciousness: one is the building block theory, which holds that consciousness is made up of small components: visual, auditory, tactile 'microconsciousnesses' that combine to form an apparently unified field, much as bricks combine to form a wall. The other is that consciousness is essentially a unified field: in order to have a visual experience, a subject has to be conscious already, and a particular experience – seeing red, say – is a modification of the field.

The building block theory predicts that in a totally unconscious patient, if the patient meets certain minimal physiological conditions (he is alive, the brain is functioning normally, he has the right temperature, etc.), and if you could trigger the NCC for say the experience of red, then the unconscious subject would suddenly have a conscious experience of red and nothing else. One building block is as good as another. Research may prove me wrong, but on the basis of what little I know about the brain, I do not believe that is possible. Only a brain that is already over the threshold of consciousness, that already has a conscious field, can have a visual experience of red.

Imagine that you wake from a dreamless sleep in a completely dark room. So far you have no coherent stream of thought and almost no perceptual stimulus. Save for the pressure of your body on the bed and the sense of the covers on top of your body, you are receiving no outside sensory stimuli. All the same, there must be a difference in your brain between the state of minimal wakefulness you are now in and the state of unconsciousness you were in before. This state of wakefulness is basal or background consciousness.

Now you turn on the light, get up, move about, etc. What happens? Do you create new conscious states? Well, in one sense you obviously do, because previously you were not consciously aware of visual stimuli and now you are. But do the visual experiences stand to the whole field of consciousness in the part whole relation? Well, that is what nearly everybody thinks and what I used to think, but here is another way of looking at it. Think of the visual experience of the table not as an object in the conscious field the way the table is an object in the room, but think of the experience as a modification of the conscious field, as a new form that the unified field takes. In other words, consciousness is modulated by the senses, not created by them.

If this is the right way to look at things (and again this is a hypothesis on my part, nothing more) then we get a different sort of research project. There is no such thing as a separate visual consciousness, so looking for the NCC for vision is barking up the wrong tree. The NCC we need to find is the one that marks basal consciousness, not a particular sensory experience. Only the already conscious subject can have visual experiences, so the introduction of visual experiences is not an introduction of consciousness but a modification of a pre-existing consciousness. The research implication of this is that we should look for consciousness as a feature of the brain emerging from the activities of large masses of neurons, and which cannot be explained by the activities of individual neurons. I am, in sum, urging that we take the unified field approach seriously as an alternative to the more common building block approach.

The approach whereby we think of big things as being made up of little things has proved so spectacularly successful in the rest of science that it is almost irresistible to us. Atomic theory, the cellular theory in biology, and the germ theory of disease are all examples. The urge to think of consciousness as likewise made of smaller building blocks is overwhelming. But I think it may be wrong for consciousness. Maybe we should think of consciousness holistically, and perhaps for consciousness we can make sense of the claim that 'the whole is greater than the sum of the parts'.

Indeed, maybe it is wrong to think of consciousness as made-up parts at all. I want to suggest that if we think of consciousness holistically, then our combination of subjectivity, qualitativeness, and unity all in one feature, will seem less mysterious.

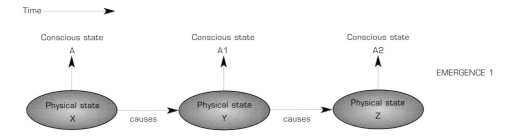

In Emergence 1 the stream of consciousness is produced by constantly shifting brain states, each of which is produced by an antecedent brain state. The brain states, however, are themselves unconscious, so all we know is that conscious state A flows into conscious state A1, and so on. This gives the illusion of consciousness directing its own course.

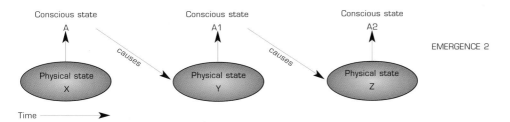

In Emergence 2, consciousness really does create itself, by effecting the physical states from which it emerges. But to explain this downward causation we seem to require some new explanatory bridging principal – a breakthrough in physics, perhaps, like Einstein's Special Theory of Relativity which integrated classical physics and electromagnetism.

The search for such an explanation has lured some researchers into the realm of quantum physics. Quantum mechanics is so weird that it is quite easy to think that it can account for almost anything that doesn't seem to make sense in the familiar world of Newtonian cause and effect. It includes indeterminacy – you can't classify if something is a particle or a wave until you measure it; non-locality – two atoms can be linked across space without any ordinary connection; and it seems to interact, in a way that classical forces do not, with the human mind. So at first sight it seems the perfect place to look for an explanation of consciousness.

The British mathematician Sir Roger Penrose is one scientist who thinks that quantum forces might explain consciousness and he has developed a theory for how they might do it. Basically he proposes that quantum effects

Dr Andrew Duggins
Clinical Research Fellow
Wellcome Department of Cognitive Neurology, London

A Quantum Description of Mind

One big problem with conventional brain models of consciousness is that the neural activation associated with experience is scattered throughout the brain while the subjective state is unified. In this respect, most neural models fail to capture an essential feature of experience. Apart from consciousness, the only other thing known to science which is distributed yet inseparable is a state of quantum entanglement. Hence the idea of a quantum model of mind is very attractive.

The problem with quantum theories is that entangled states 'collapse' as soon as they interact with the environment and cease to be unified. Penrose and Hameroff have suggested that quantum states might be protected from environmental interference in microtubules but – even if this is possible – I find it hard to reconcile a distributed state of coherent microtubule subunits with what is known about classical neural signalling. My approach is therefore somewhat different. Rather than speculate about sub-cellular structures which might support coherent quantum states, I have tried to describe consciousness using a mathematical framework borrowed from quantum mechanics: a framework that allows distributed but inseparable states.

The fundamental step is to consider an abstract 'vector space' – a field, if you like, that is bounded by the objective states of neural activation. Mental states would be vectors within this space. It works like this: a neuron can either be 'on' (that is depolarized, 'firing') or 'off' (polarized, 'not firing'), but its firing rate at any moment can only be estimated statistically – for example as the number of firings within a brief period of time (40 times a second, for example). Experience – at least the elementary features of it such as speed of motion or pitch of sound – is encoded in this firing rate, and I refer to this code, together with its contribution to experience as the 'conscious correlate of the neuron' (CCN). The neuron then bears a resemblance to a simple quantum mechanical system. the spin-$^1/_2$ particle. In each case, the 'state' of the system is intermediate between just two objective states: the CCN lies somewhere between 'on' and 'off' (in the case of the neuron) just as the quantum state lies between 'up' and 'down' (in the case of the particle). Diagrammatically, the state of either system (neuron or particle) could be described by a point on the surface of a sphere, where the poles of the sphere represent the objective states ('on' and 'off'; 'up' and 'down'). This is really no different to defining your current geographical location by a latitude intermediate between North and South poles of the globe. Once multiple quantum particles have interacted, they become entangled. That is, even if each particle were to move off to a different location, then the system of multiple particles would still behave as a single entity. A vector could still describe the quantum state of the system, but there would now be multiple 'poles' or objective extremes between which the vector might lie. I suggest that multiple neurons in the brain may be in a state similar to entanglement: their coordinated firing may reflect unified experience even though they are in different anatomical locations. In fact, the correlation of firing between 'entangled' neurons would be so tight that it could not be explained by local neural interactions alone (conventional models of brain function only allow neurons to communicate locally where they join at 'synapses').

I am not suggesting that quantum superpositions occur at the level of neurons – only that a quantum-like model of mind 'fits' what we know about the brain. It can therefore be used to explore difficult questions that cannot be addressed by any model that misses out mind. For example, one might ask whether it is possible for me to know the exact nature of your experience, perhaps by observing your behaviour or performing a sophisticated experiment to record your brain activity. Surprisingly, using the framework I have outlined, the information in subjective experience can be quantified – at least in theory – and is always greater than or equal to the information 'accessible' to measurement by others.

take place in the microtubules – minute ducts in the walls of brain cells – and that these effects are the stuff of consciousness.

Quantum explanations for consciousness are a minority interest so far and many neuroscientists treat them with polite derision, claiming they are merely 'answering one mystery with another'. One frequent objection is that quantum effects generally occur only at sub-atomic level – not in things like big, warm, wet brains. It is very difficult to see how events which take place at such tiny magnitudes could influence the relatively large-scale activities of neurons. However, quantum devotees claim they have answers, and work is underway on parallel-processing quantum computers which they confidently predict will eventually develop consciousness.

Property dualism is another relative latecomer to the legion of consciousness theories. It leaves open the possibility for consciousness to be causal (though its main proponent, David Chalmers, thinks it is a small possibility).[12] And it allows consciousness full status as a real aspect of the world, not just a way of describing a state of matter, without making it into Descartes' separate 'stuff'.

Some property dualists are happy to state, simply, that the two properties are 1) material and 2) consciousness. That, they say, is just the way things are. Others believe that this is not sufficient and that real understanding requires some great leap forward in the physical sciences – the creation of a 'Theory of Everything', perhaps – before it will be understood.

Chalmers' version of property dualism (he calls it naturalistic dualism) has some things in common with functionalism. For example, it holds that consciousness is multiply realizable – it could happen in any system providing the processes that underlie consciousness take place. Chalmers gives the example of the population of China, much multiplied, and linked in the same pattern as neurons in the brain, creating a conscious entity over and above the consciousness of each individual. The stuff of consciousness may turn out to be information, or causal interaction, according to this idea: 'information from the inside' as Chalmers describes it, while physics is 'information from the outside'.

Chalmers does not necessarily claim the information has to be of a certain kind – not complex, for example, as most emergentists would demand – just information. So anything that undergoes change – even a simple system like a thermometer or a thermostat could have some tiny inkling of consciousness. As everything we know undergoes change (even a rock slowly crumbles) this leads to the conclusion that consciousness may exist, potentially at least, in everything. 'The view that there is experience wherever there is causal interaction is counterintuitive' admits Chalmers. 'But it is a view that can grow surprisingly satisfying with reflection, making consciousness better integrated into the natural order. If this view is correct, consciousness does not come in sudden jagged spikes, with isolated complex systems arbitrarily producing rich conscious experiences. Rather, it is a more uniform property of the universe, with very simple systems having very simple phenomenology [experience] and complex systems having complex phenomenology. This makes consciousness less "special" in some way, and so more reasonable'.[13]

Property dualism as described by Chalmers is close to panpsychism – edging us back towards the pre-Cartesian idea of the world as inherently sentient. It hints at a natural universe that is very different from the mechanistic model which has proliferated since the Renaissance. Needless to say, it does not go down well with those who hold to a hard materialist line. Daniel Dennett, for example, dismisses it scathingly, claiming it does nothing to actually explain consciousness. 'We can see this by comparing Chalmers' proposal with yet one more imaginary non-starter: cutism, the proposal that some things are just plain cute, and other things aren't cute at all', he says. 'You can just see it, however hard it is to describe or explain – we had better postulate cuteness as a fundamental property of physics alongside mass, charge and space-time.'[14]

Property dualism is a relatively new entry to the legion of consciousness theories, but it is not new in proposing that to understand nature we have first to rethink our views of the universe as a whole. So-called mysterians believe that we will never understand consciousness because our means of perceiving the world are too crude and limited. Philosopher Colin McGinn, for example, thinks we cannot solve the hard problem for the same reason that a cat can't do calculus – our brains simply don't have the right equipment. The limitation, he claims, comes from the fact that our brains evolved to perceive things in space, not those in other dimensions. The physical world we know through our science is therefore a partial, distorted fragment of an unimaginably different state – perhaps some holistic, non-spatial reality that existed before the Big Bang created time and space. Consciousness may be a 'left-over', or a crack in the physical world that can never be understood in scientific terms.

The mysterians may turn out to be right, but to many scientists – even those who acknowledge the hardness of the hard problem – their belief just seems defeatist. Better, they say, to put aside grappling with the knotty philosophical issues and get on with solving some of the easy problems. Perhaps when these are sorted, the hard problem will just dissolve.

It seems a sensible strategy. So let's begin.

The Old Steam Whistle Test

'Consciousness would appear to be simply a by-product of the body's working, completely without power to modify that working, just as a steam whistle that accompanies the working of a locomotive is without influence upon its machinery.'

Thomas Huxley, 1890

If you can't be sure what a thing is, it may help to find out what it does. If it looks like a duck, walks like a duck, quacks like a duck ... well, you may be satisfied to call it a duck and have done with it. After all, maybe that's all a duck *is* ...

In the case of consciousness it should, in theory, be fairly easy to find out what consciousness does. All that seems to be required is to compare the behaviour of a conscious being with that of a similar but non-conscious one. Whatever the conscious one does that the other doesn't can then be taken to be consciousness's function.

So you could, for example, compare the behaviour of a normally conscious human being with that of a very sophisticated computer, or that of a person in a state of *petit mal* – a condition in which people carry out routine acts yet have no memory of it.

At first sight certain differences seem obvious: a normally conscious person is finely responsive to the things that are going on around them, and their actions appear to be spontaneous and varied. Computers and people in *petit mal*, by contrast, behave in a predictable and stereotypical way. So consciousness, you might think, gives flexibility, creativity and choice of action – freewill.

Plausible though this is, the assumption that consciousness accounts for these apparent differences can't be taken for granted. There is, first, the problem that you can't know whether your unconscious subject is totally unconscious or just unable to report on their awareness (see chapter one). But even if you allow the appearance of consciousness to stand as proof of it, you still can't be sure that the 'extra' behaviour is due to it. Responding to the environment, for example, is a matter of degree – why should consciousness not be necessary for walking, eating and even driving a car (all of which have been observed in people in *petit mal*) but may be necessary for playing tennis or writing a sonnet? More fundamentally, why should consciousness be necessary for anything? Who is to say that the things that consciousness seems to do: turn our mind back and forth in time; deliberate and choose; come up with creative solutions to new events – are not actually carried out entirely by the physical mechanisms *associated* with consciousness?

A thought experiment: A visiting Martian has been sent to Earth by the Interplanetary Exploratory Corporation of Mars to find out about human behaviour. He decides to go about it by getting hold of a specimen and examining it. (If you are tempted to think this idea too absurd to contemplate, by the way, bear in mind that three million Americans firmly believe that this sort of thing actually happens.[1]) In this particular abduction scenario the aliens don't satisfy themselves with the usual laser probes and dubious sexual shenanigans because they are already familiar with the physical anatomy of humans from previous field trips. They know, for example, that brain cells work by sending electrical messages (mediated by chemical neurotransmitters) from one cell to another, rather like a spark travelling along a trail of dynamite. They know these cells create semi-permanent linkages so that when one in a linked formation fires, so do the others. And they know the brain is made of distinct but interactive modules, each of which specializes in one particular type of cognitive process, such as distinguishing human faces or the different wavelengths of light (called colour by humans). They have also studied the very latest brain-maps, produced by humans, which show which parts of the brain do what. So they know the layout of the hardware – their aim on this trip is to find out how it all works together to produce observable behaviour.

Our Martian starts, in the standard Martian way, by stunning his victim with a ray gun. While the human is paralysed he and his mates manoeuvre their victim into their spacecraft, where they have a super-duper brain-imaging machine. They push the stunned man into the machine and begin to watch his brain activity on a video monitor.

At first there isn't very much to see, but as the paralysis wears off, the human's light sensors pop open and his brain suddenly lights up like a shower of meteorites. Deep in the base of his brain, an area called the Reticular Activating System kicks off the show with a stream of chemically-induced electrical activity which flows up to the outer brain layers. In order to see more clearly the abductors slow down time (an old Martian trick) and chart the precise sequence of events that happen next.

First they observe electrical signals whizzing from the light sensors to various other brain areas. One main stream goes to the back of the brain (which they know, from the brain maps, is the primary visual cortex) and then starts creeping forward and up towards the parietal cortex – an area which processes information relating to the victim's body and its relation to other objects in space. A second stream, moving faster than the first, goes to the limbic system – a cluster of organs buried in the centre of the brain. One bit of the limbic system in particular, a little organ in the temporal lobe called the amygdala – starts to fire away like crazy.

The amygdala, notes our Martian, is closely connected to another bit of the brain called the hypothalamus, which is in turn connected, in many complicated ways, to various glands and organs throughout the body. He sees that the activity of the amygdala has triggered, via this connection, activity in the hypothalamus. And this in turn has sent messages to the glands and organs, which have responded by producing a flood of chemicals which now course through the victim's nerves and bloodstream. As these chemicals arrive at various places, they lock on to various cells, which in turn produce more bodily effects. The muscles, including the heart, tense up, and the capillaries – tiny blood vessels under the skin – contract. The chemicals also produce effects in the brain cells. Those on the outside, which make up the cortex, became active in places and silent in others.

This corresponds with a spurt of action from the specimen which, the Martian realizes, is designed to help it to extricate itself from its situation. Among other things, its light sensors bulge, increasing the amount of light-carried information entering the brain; its skin goes pale; its central fuel-distribution pump speeds up; and one of its facial orifices opens and emits a high-pitched noise. When our Martian, intrigued, leans in closer to observe the specimen, he receives a nasty bonk from one of the victim's fists.

Rubbing his sore antenna, the Martian returns to his monitor where he sees that the amygdala has by now sent a second stream of information along pathways which lead to the front part of the specimen's brain. This stream ends in an area just behind the forehead – a bit labelled on the brain maps as the ventromedial cortex. The parietal cortex – the area of brain surface behind and to each side of the crown of the head – is also feeding information to the frontal lobes. One place lit up by this is the right orbital frontal cortex (a bit just behind the eye) which the brain maps show is associated with the presentation of an 'oddball' – something outside ordinary everyday experience.

The flow of activity does not stop there. As the Martian watches, an elaborate series of feedback and feed-forward loops develop. The frontal activity, for example, feeds back to the limbic system, but instead of making it more active, it actually quietens it down. For a short time, most of the brain is quiet, with just a handful of areas buzzing. Then another frontal area, the dorsolateral cortex, perks up and starts to exchange information with the temporal lobes (in the sides of the brain) where – the brain maps show – certain types of memory are encoded. Information, in the form of activated nervous pathways, is now zipping up and down, side to side, throughout almost the entire brain.

All of this coincides with another change in the specimen's behaviour: instead of thrashing about he now becomes still, his eyes roving around his strange environment, his breathing quiet. Finally, electrical signals from the frontal lobes travel to a spot in his left frontal lobe, and produce a new blip of activity. The facial orifice opens again and another sound comes out: 'Take me', it says, 'to your leader.'

Later, our Martian re-runs the video record of his captor's brain processes and traces each tiny activation back through the causal train. His work done, he returns his specimen to its natural environment and writes up his report – a careful analysis of how a stimulus, fed into the human brain, is automatically turned into potentially advantageous behaviour. It shows how the brain, when confronted by stimuli which suggested a perilous situation, first produced a physical reaction (the Martian's antenna still bears the mark) and then a more complex response borne out of the processes described by humans as 'thought'. This thinking process involves linking 'perceptions' (fed from the sensory registers at the back of the brain) to relevant memories from the temporal lobes and combining them in different ways in working memory in the frontal lobes. Other parts of the frontal lobes then translated these combinations into imagined action and selected the most promising. The selected action was speech-based, so it triggered the part of the brain which articulates words. The entire process from the moment the specimen opened its eyes to its pathetic B-movie script-line was revealed as the work of a beautifully engineered system of systems.

Back home the Martian's report is well received. Even the dumbest of Martians can see that it explains everything there is to be explained about how and why that particular specimen behaved as it did. And by extrapolation, it explains how humans do everything – for every act could clearly be produced in a similar way. It is just a matter of triggering the system with different stimuli and letting the brain run its course. Having cracked the problem, and decided that such primitive creatures were of little interest (not to mention dangerous) our Martian decides to turn his attention henceforth to the more complicated Venusians.

Of course, the story from the inside of the human's brain looks very different. People cannot observe the vast majority of their own brain processes (not, anyway, without a brain scanner) so our captor had no knowledge of the complicated machinations the Martian saw as accounting for his behaviour. What he does know, though, was that when he suddenly found himself in a metal cigar tube with an iridescent green alien waving its antenna at him, he felt very frightened indeed. It was fear that made him scream, fear that made him lunge out, and fear that made his heart pound. He also knows that, a couple of seconds later, it occurred to him that this must be some kind of huge joke. He recalls thinking that he would play along, and remembers dredging his memory for a response that would look cool on *Candid Camera*. Recognizing it was a bit limp (but stumped for anything better) he decided to go for the cartoonist's stock caption: 'Take me to your leader.' (When he subsequently recounted his story to the *National Enquirer* his little joke was omitted. But that is a different story.)

The point of all this is that, from the Martian point of view, automatic brain processes seem to be all that is required to bring about action. If it never occurred to our Martian that his specimen was conscious (and why should it? Only green things with antennae are assumed to be conscious on Mars) he had no reason to suppose, from his investigation, that it was. The processes moved along smoothly and continuously, and at no point did the human's brain start to do anything that could not be explained as part of that process. No qualitatively different activity sparked up at any stage to indicate that something was running parallel to the grinding, mechanical trudge from stimulus to action. There was no gap between stimulus-response that required some extra ingredient, like consciousness, to fill it.

Yet from the inside, it felt to our would-be TV star that his behaviour was the result of his consciousness. Sure, he knows enough about biology to know that those actions are associated with certain goings-on in his brain – but from his point of view the processes seem to be the mere physical execution of his will.

Alas for this (widespread) intuition – closer scrutiny of brain processes does not seem to bear it out. And you don't even need a Martian super-scanner to demonstrate it. In 1985, Benjamin Libet carried out an experiment using EEG

Libet's experiment showed that the brain starts to execute a voluntary movement before the person 'decides' to do it. A wave of neural activity known as the Readiness Potential – a marker of action to come – was detected nearly half a second before the person reported being aware of their decision to act. The actual action occurred shortly after, when the neural processes which started with the Readiness Potential produced the contraction of muscle fibres.

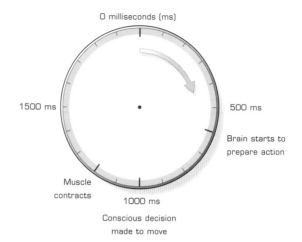

O milliseconds (ms)

1500 ms

500 ms

Brain starts to
prepare action

Muscle
contracts

1000 ms

Conscious decision
made to move

recordings, which was to undermine some of our most dearly held ideas about the nature of human will.[2]

Libet set out to discover the timing of brain events which led to consciously willed actions. In particular he decided to find out how the timing of the conscious decision related to the brain processes that executed it.

Student volunteers were fitted with EEG sensors placed to pick up signals from the cerebral cortex, and were told to make a simple hand movement whenever they felt like it. The important thing was that the act should be self-initiated, rather than dependent on some outside cue. The timing devices employed were deceptively simple. The EEG measurements were precisely pinpointed in time by the sensors, while the timing of the subjects' decision to move their hand was arrived at by getting the students to watch something rather like a stopwatch – a huge analogue clock-face with a sweeping light which rotated around its face so fast (once every two-and-a-half seconds) that it was possible to measure tiny fractions of a second. The students were instructed to watch the clock and note precisely when the conscious 'urge' or decision to move occurred.

Previous experiments had already demonstrated that voluntary actions are preceded by a wave-like activation – called the Readiness Potential (RP) – in the cerebral cortex about half a second before they are carried out.[3] Mere reflex actions – like whipping your hand away from a hotplate, do not produce a RP. Nor do the tics and shouted obscenities suffered by people with Gilles de La

Tourette's syndrome, which are nearly always described by those who manifest them as involuntary. Libet arranged his EEG equipment to catch the RP and catch it it did. Each time a hand movement was made, the brain processes required to do it were announced – about half a second before the actual act – by the characteristic fluctuation in neural activity.

If an act of will is something outside the automatic brain processes which actually execute the movement you might expect that the decision to move would come just before, or maybe at the same time as that first, preparatory brain activation. But what Libet found instead was that the students (who were, of course, unaware of the RP) consistently reported making the decision to move their hands after the RP had begun. The reports were consistent over hundreds of trials. In nearly every case the subject said the conscious urge, or decision to move, occurred about 350–400 milliseconds after the EEG spikes revealed the RP. The movement itself then took place about two tenths of a second after that.[4] The 'decision' was not the *cause* of the action at all.

Various alternative interpretations of Libet's findings have been put forward, and some people have tried to discount it on the grounds that reports from people about the timing of their own conscious events are not dependable. However, recent variations of the experiment using more sophisticated methodology (though pointing to a rather more complex story than described here) support the essential conclusion that the unconscious brain kicks off a movement and the conscious decision to make it is not a decision at all.[5]

If this is true of all actions – not just simple hand-moving tasks in laboratory conditions – it follows that our behaviour is simply the end product of automatic brain processes. Just as our Martian concluded, there is no need for any further enquiry: as far as causation goes, consciousness is out of the picture.

Coupled with the apparent problem of finding a causal 'gap' for consciousness in the physical world, Libet's experiment lends strong credibility to the idea that consciousness is epiphenomenal – an inconsequential by-product of the brain with no power to do anything, even within the brain itself. If unconscious brain processes are sufficient to cause the RP that begins an action, there seems little reason to doubt that the RP in turn can cause the processes that go on to produce it. If that is what happens, it follows that we have no freewill – the feeling that we can choose how we are going to behave is just another illusion.

This, as we have noted, is for most people deeply disturbing and counter-intuitive. It is also difficult to imagine that such an important thing as consciousness (important to us, anyway) arrived by accident, rather than for a

purpose. As the philosopher John Searle puts it: 'if that were so it would be the biggest joke in the Universe'.[6]

This is not, in itself, a good reason (scientifically) to believe it is false. But the shift in thinking required to demote consciousness from the crowning glory of the Universe to Huxley's steam whistle is too imense to be brought about by a few laboratory experiments, compelling though they may be. Surely, we should not dismiss consciousness as a mere by-product until all other possibilities are exhausted. So, how (apart from supposing that actions have two causes, one being automatic brain mechanisms and the other 'purely' mental) can consciousness be 'saved' from epiphenomenalism?

One way is to say (as identity theorists do) that mental events are physical – so of course the problem does not arise – they can influence events just like any other physical event. But this does not satisfy those who think consciousness can be distinguished from the neural events that give rise to it.

Libet himself is one of those who cannot accept that the evidence provided by his work eradicates the possibility of freewill. In what might seem a slightly desperate attempt to rescue the notion of conscious causation, he has suggested that what consciousness actually gives us is a veto – not so much freewill, as free-won't. His idea hinges on the fact that we are able to stop an act, even after the brain has started to carry it out, during the one fifth of a second processing period that comes after the conscious 'decision' and before the act itself.

That in turn, of course, begs an obvious question: wouldn't the veto, too, be preceded by a Readiness Potential? Libet suggests that there may be no need for one because the veto, as he envisages it, is not so much a willed act, as a control on an existing decision to act, which does not come about through the same sort of brain processes.

Comforting though this idea might be, it seems very strange that negative actions should be so very different from positive ones. What, for example, if the veto in question was a last-moment decision not to wolf down a dish of ice-cream, even as the spoon touched your lips? Would putting the spoon down somehow be achieved without a RP because it related to an action that was already underway? If so, could you tease apart the veto on the act of sticking the spoon in your mouth (no RP) from the act of putting the spoon down (RP)? It seems rather unlikely. Furthermore, experiments in which people are instructed to refrain from doing things have shown that this type of negative action is preceded by a RP, and that the stronger the conscious veto, the stronger the RP is.

A study of two groups of rifle-shooters, one expert and the other inexperienced, found that the inexperienced shooters fired as soon as their gun was momentarily stable, while the experts waited until they had established gun stability that they knew could be sustained. Both were conscious of inhibiting the desire to fire for a second or two as they waited for their guns to stop wavering, and brain imaging showed that both showed a RP during this period. Furthermore, the expert group, who reported making the greater conscious effort not to fire until they were ready, showed a stronger RP than the inexpert group – suggesting that the brain activity mirrored the degree of conscious inhibition.

What happens in the laboratory cannot always be exported to the messier, more complicated real world, however, and it is possible that complicated behaviour – the sort that is associated with slow deliberation and the juggling of many choices – may be initiated in quite a different way from single tasks carried out in a controlled environment. Maybe consciousness plays a role in some sorts of actions, and not in others. It might even be that certain actions can be done automatically *or* by conscious guidance. In other words, granting that a particular action can be done without conscious causality does not necessarily mean that it is always done that way. It is also possible that some levels of consciousness are causal but others are not.

One argument which is often put forward to defend consciousness as a causal force is that things, generally, don't come to exist unless they are in some way useful. So if consciousness doesn't do anything, why have we got it?

The brain itself, with its immense package of cognitive talents, is clearly a product of evolution, but that does not mean that its consciousness is. Without knowing whether it has a function, it is impossible to say whether it arrived because it was a beneficial adaptation, like the white coat of a polar bear which camouflages the animal as it stalks its prey, or whether it just 'popped up' as a useless side-effect of some other adaptation, like the white colour of milk. It is plausible that consciousness arrived in living things as 'free riders' on new cognitive mechanisms such as the ability to predict the effect of one's actions, or to make a mental model of one's self. By comparison, think of the form that appears between two arches (or an arch and an adjacent wall or ceiling). Such spaces are known as spandrels (see page 92).

Spandrels are not 'designed in' – they are a mere by-product of a designed structure (the arch) and if that is removed (or had not been built) the spandrel would not (and could not) exist. Yet spandrels are 'real', in that they can be identified and located.

A Free Will?

The debate about whether people have free will is, of course, ancient. Today the question mainly revolves around whether the laws of physics allow for it; in the past it was the laws of God.

The problem for believers was (and is) that many religions posit an all-powerful deity, yet also demand that followers accept moral responsibility for their acts. So they either have to square the notion of being the subject of a higher will with that of being free – which is intellectually tricky – or they have to accept responsibility for their acts even though they acknowledge they have no control over them, which seems simply unfair.

One rather convoluted solution arrived at by medieval theologians has it that any train of events has both a 'remote efficient cause' – which triggers it – and a 'final cause', which is the purpose for which it is done. In between there can be any number of 'efficient causes' that help it along the way. For example, the efficient cause of my knocking over a cup of coffee might be that my hand slipped. And the efficient cause of that might be that I was shaking because I was nervous. The efficient cause of that might be that I had just nearly been hit by a truck, and the efficient cause of that might have been that the truck-driver was distracted ... and so on, back and back. In this scheme of things, the first cause is God, and so is the final cause – the purpose of it all. But all the efficient causes in between are down to human agency. So we are free – but only up to a point. God kicks everything off, and ultimately decides how it will end, but in the meantime we can do as we choose.

The problem of finding a way to lay moral responsibility upon individuals does not disappear when supernatural agency is taken out of the picture. Rather than being controlled by an all-powerful deity, we instead become puppets controlled by the string of cause and effect known as physical determinism. Even if we can resist the strong intuition that we are the agents of our actions, most people are keenly aware of the advantage of nurturing a societal belief in free will and moral responsibility. Within the individual it works as a sort of self-policing mechanism, inhibiting anti-social behaviour and making it possible to maintain a coherent society without excessive external controls. So it is very useful. Hence the attempt to find a place for free will in a determined universe continues.

Mysterians, and some 'quantum-mind' theorists, leapfrog the problem of free will by postulating that the universe is not determined and that consciousness itself is the primary uncaused cause of everything else. Some

point out that events at sub-atomic levels do not seem to be determined in the rigid way that classical Newtonian physics dictates, and suggest therefore that the string of causes and effects we observe are founded on randomness which allows free will access at base level.

This claim is not necessarily supported by quantum theory at all, which states only that events are essentially unpredictable, rather than random. But even if the universe was founded on randomness, it hardly seems to help the case for free will. It simply means that human actions would arise from random rather than lawful events – which might make them irrational, but hardly free.

Compatibility – so-called because it argues just that for physical determinism and free will – claims that we have free choice whenever we act in the absence of outside constraints, such as having a gun to one's head. The trouble is, this neat idea of freedom falls down as soon as you try to apply it to the real world. It would hold, for example, that a person who is forced to take a drug that leads them to do something violent – a hallucinatory compound, say, that alters their perception so that an innocent gesture from someone else is seen as a threat – would not be acting freely. A person who took the drug themselves, however, presumably would be. But what if the person took the drug themselves unaware of its possible effects? Or if they had a genetic mutation that caused their brain to malfunction in precisely the same way as the drug? It is impossible to make a clear distinction between 'outside' influences and 'internal' decisions.

Although it is now well-recognized that the internal/external influence distinction is a nonsense, in practice most of us continue to use a rough form of compatibilist thinking to ascribe responsibility in day-to-day life. When someone does something bad that looks to be an unconstrained choice we tend to blame them, whereas we do not criticise them for a similar act when it is clearly done under duress. This works fairly well on a practical level but it produces all sorts of problems when it is applied in a more testing framework, like a court of law.

It is now routine in the US, and becoming so in other countries, for offenders to claim it was not 'they who dunnit', but their genes, or their upbringing, or a head injury ... a movement Daniel Dennett has called the 'Spectre of Creeping Exculpation'. Some such defences get chucked out of court, but others are highly successful: in 1999, for example, a man called

Dan White claimed that his diet of junk food, and particularly the effect of eating sugar-saturated sweets called Twinkies, drove him to kill San Francisco Mayor George Mascone and Supervisor Harvey Milk. He got a sentence of just five-and-a-half years – far less than the normal going rate for a double murder.

More challenging still are the legal actions against tobacco manufacturers, in which cigarette addicts claim, effectively, that the responsibility for their self-destructive habit lies with those who lured them into it, rather than with themselves. The punitive damages awarded to some of these claimants demonstrates that some juries have considerable sympathy for their plight. It is not clear though that they reflect an acceptance of the idea that free will does not exist; it may just be that some juries are happy to find an excuse to punish tobacco companies for what they see as antisocial behaviour. If this is so, it suggests, oddly, that they endow international corporations with more autonomy – free will even – than individuals, in that they are prepared to see the company's actions in pushing cigarettes as more blameworthy than the individual's act of smoking them.

The question of free will, then, is by no means just an academic one – it has pressing implications for everyone.

Consciousness, then, might be the 'spandrel' that arises by virtue of a layered architecture of functional cognitive faculties, each of which was selected because it brought a survival advantage quite independent of its role in creating consciousness.

Of course, panpsychicists would argue that consciousness did not 'arrive' at all, but was always present and that all evolution has produced is a vehicle that allows it to be spectacularly intense. However, if we put panpsychicist claims aside for the moment, and accept that consciousness is 'awareness of awareness' – the product of a particular type of system – it is possible to concoct a plausible evolutionary explanation for its emergence without assuming it was selected by virtue of it having an advantageous effect.

Let's begin with molecules – primitive bits of matter in an otherwise formless universe. At first these molecules would be constantly bashed and buffeted by others, joining perhaps with a neighbour for a moment or two then spinning apart. Some stuck together though, and eventually, out of the primeval soup, solid chunks of conjoined molecules started to appear, their structure held stable by chemical bonds. Some developed complex structures and a few – a very few – came to preserve that structure against destruction by becoming self-organizing entities.

Self-organization requires that there is a boundary between the thing that is organized and the world outside. This distinction between the inside 'this' and the outside 'that' creates for the organism both a divide from the world, and a relationship to it. This is the foundation for what is known as intentionality – an 'aboutness' which is the organism's singular relationship to the world outside its boundaries. Intentionality is a key feature of experience because normal consciousness is of something other than itself. However, intentionality alone is not sufficient to bring consciousness about – a flower has it, and shows it when it turns to the sun; a virus displays it when it seeks out cells to invade. But neither (in the non-panpsychist view) are likely to be conscious.

Organisms maintain their equilibrium by homeostasis. Here's a simple example of how it works: Let's say we have a self-organizing entity, 'Blob', which needs a particular substance – blobium – to survive. Too much blobium is harmful, however, so Blob needs to keep the levels steady, which it does by producing an enzyme – blobase – which breaks down blobium. Blobase is produced when levels of blobium reach a certain point. The enzyme then breaks down blobium until the blobium level falls to a certain threshold, when the process that produces blobase is switched off. Levels of blobium will now rise – and the whole cycle will begin again.

Spandrels

A spandrel is the space between two arches, or between an arch and the wall or ceiling adjacent to it. It exists only by virtue of the arch being there. So although it has distinct form – you can point to it, locate it, identify it – it has no separate existence and need not have been 'designed in' to the structure. Take away the arch and it ceases to be.

Consciousness may be rather like this. It may have appeared when certain cognitive mechanisms evolved, but only by virtue of them rather than for any purpose of its own.

All Blob consists of at this stage is a simple system which obeys nothing but the laws of chemistry. Yet to a (close) observer, it already appears to be acting in an 'intentional' way in that its processes seem to be 'about' its survival. 'Survival', however, is not designed in as an 'extra', but is integral to the system itself.

Now, at some time – probably around four billion years ago, self-organizing entities like the Blobs started to reproduce.[7] Once an organism reproduces, it can adapt. Or, to be more precise, the environment changes the organism, generation by generation, by killing off organisms that do not mutate adaptively, leaving those that do to reproduce.

So, what chance mutation would have served these primitive life forms best? Clearly, one would be a system or systems which would enable them to alter their relationship to the world in order to make it more conducive to their survival. The more changeable their world, the more important this would be – a replicator that simply existed, replicating, wouldn't do so for ever in a constantly changing environment. Eventually – probably after another three billion years or so – these single-cell life forms evolved complex systems which allowed them to adapt to change.

Action means movement. All action is that: even your most sophisticated plotting, your most subtle joys, are based on movement. No act, however cerebral and subtle, can be executed unless at some stage, in some way, it is translated into movement. It may be the movement of your fingers on a keyboard as you compose a letter; or the movement required to press the play button on a CD player. Even speaking involves moving the lips and tongue and vocal chords.

How might action have evolved? Well, let's suppose that Blob has a relative, Blob-2, which does not produce blobium inside its body but absorbs it from the environment. So long as Blob-2 basks in a blobium-rich location it is fine – its existing enzyme process will prevent it from getting an overdose. But if levels fall its internal processes are no longer able to support it so it must move to a new spot. No great evolutionary leap forward is required for this: another chemical reaction, albeit rather more complex, will suffice to get it out of its predicament. For example, a fall in blobium might trigger the release of blobisquirm, which in turn affects cells on the surface of the body causing them to contract rhythmically. By this means Blob-2 slithers around until it hits another blobium-blessed spot, where a rise in blobium levels switches off the production of blobisquirm.[8]

This is a simple example of a circular system in which an input (falling blobium levels) triggers a control process (production of blobisquirm) which provokes action, which in turn feeds back as input (rising blobium). Blob-2's behaviour is still determined by wholly unconscious chemical reactions, yet it seems to be even more 'determined' than its passive relative.

As the Blob line continued, various other mutations allowed it to become more adept at moving around. Instead of just slithering around it evolved specialized limbs. This required a certain amount of internal remodelling, because in order to move them effectively it needed to have two or more separate 'modules' that could operate in opposition. One clump of cells, for example, would have to contract while another relaxed, in order to produce a sequential movement of its limbs. It would also have needed to evolve a way of coordinating its parts, because if its limbs didn't contract and relax in an organized way it would just squirm.

This would necessarily include the capacity to sequence movement in time. So along with the boundaries between 'inside' and 'outside', the system would have to include a mechanism to divide 'now' from 'then'.

Actions are not much use unless they are beneficial – if an organism was capable only of random movement it would be as likely to transport itself into the jaws of peril as away from it. So along with movement must have come some sort of guidance system. And that would have required a way of receiving information from a distance.

Such information first impinges at the boundary of any entity, so the earliest information-receiving systems in our little blob of life almost certainly began with the development of specialized cells on its surface – light-detecting sensors, for example, or molecular receptors for aromatic molecules. To make good use of this information, however, it would need to know where it was coming from: the smell of a predator, say, would be pretty useless unless it could be identified as coming from a particular part of space.

Armed with this new sensitivity to its environment, and the ability to act, the organism could now move in a very determined way indeed. And in order to make best use of its sensory guidance system it further evolved a means of orienting to changes in its newly-spatial universe – the basis of attention.

By now our organism is pretty well-equipped. It has its boundaries and intents; a world that is divided into inside and out, here and there, now and then; and a good/bad relationship with the world. It can gather information, orient itself to changes, and act appropriately. It has a brain. But is there yet any sign of consciousness?

Probably not. But consider what, it seems likely, happened next. We have an organism that can move around in a guided way, but so far it has no way of knowing when to stop. It is fine to slither or shuffle away from danger, but if you kept slithering indefinitely you would soon use up your energy resources and die of sheer exhaustion. What it needs now is some way of monitoring its own, internal state – whether it is getting too hot, or its fuel reserves are being depleted – as well as what is happening outside. So the next useful change it might have undergone was to develop a feedback system which allowed it to know the effect of its own actions and sensations on itself.

This type of information processing would be different from the processing of information from outside. The knowledge it delivered would be straight from its own insides: the knowledge of cells dying for lack of water; of muscle tissue contracting and running short of oxygen; of blood being pumped more forcefully; of limbs extending into space ... This information would be more imminent, and perhaps more intense than knowledge of things beyond the boundary. It would be 'inside information'. And that, of course, is exactly what qualia feel like. So could this be the crucial adaptation that laid the foundation for consciousness?

Perhaps. But as we shall see, experience requires more than the inflow of information – even the vivid, personal type of information that stems from one's own insides. It requires the ability to 'know that we know'.

What further mutation might have brought that state about?

One change that would help our organism to survive now would be the ability to move selectively, so that instead of reacting to every passing threat it could expend its energy only on movements that are advantageous. But, of course, to know whether or not a movement would be advantageous it would need to be able gauge the risk (or benefit) presented by an outside stimulus. And that would require comparing the present situation with those it had encountered in the past. It could only do that if past experiences were encoded in its nervous system and could be replayed on demand. In other words – a memory. In addition to that it would be necessary to have a form of 'future memory' – the ability to anticipate the effect of a movement – to count the cost of action before doing it. So in addition to memory, it needs a system that can 'rehearse' actions, without actually having to do them.

To achieve all this the brain must both have evolved many new neuronal modules and – more importantly – a dense and compact network of feedback and feed-forward connections by which they could communicate. Information coming in from the sense organs would need to be shunted from sensory processing areas to the area where similar information encountered in the past is encoded. Past responses need to be recalled and shunted forward to movement-rehearsal areas where their effect in the present situation can be assessed; they may then be adapted in the light of further incoming information, or shunted forward to the movement areas proper.

At some point the majority of information being exchanged would come to be between other brain cells and groups of cells rather than between the brain and the peripheral sensory and motor areas. The brain would no longer merely be a relay station, shunting sensations to the appropriate action stations. Certainly there would be parts of it that would still do that, but now there are other parts which are processing incoming information in more sophisticated ways, and which may override the automatic input-output routine. These parts would have to communicate constantly with one another in order for a cohesive plan of action to emerge which takes each of their roles into account. The brain would be talking to itself. And as this interneuronal traffic increased the internal chatter would have more effect on the whole system than the relatively few messages coming in directly from outside. Sensory information would now enter a vast gossip machine already buzzing with stories of past events, future plans and current preoccupations. In this milieu its arrival could fail to have any effect at all, or it could spark off such a complicated reaction that its effect might appear to have nothing to do with the original stimulus. To an outside observer it would seem that the system has a mind of its own.

This, it seems likely to me, is how basic consciousness emerged. Not because it brought benefits, but because it is just 'how it happens to feel' to have all that going on inside the brain.

That consciousness could have arisen by fortune rather than design does not, of course, mean that it did not come to have a function once it was there. After all, spandrels can be said to have a function of a sort in that they affect a person's perception and may create a sensation of pleasure because they enhance the look of things. So, once it arrived, would consciousness have made a difference thereafter?

One way to explore this is to assume that the evolutionary process we have described so far took place in parallel on two different universes – one in which it just happened to result in consciousness, and another, Zombie-world, in which it happened not to. (Of course, monist materialists will say this is not possible – but then the whole question of epiphenomenalism doesn't bother them, so let's look at this from the dualist perspective and assume it is possible.) Would organisms in the conscious universe be distinguishable from the Zombies?

Let's assume that it made no difference for a few billion years. That Blob got all the way to being human before his brain started talking to itself. Now let's home in on one particular aspect of human behaviour: language.

Humans, like many other species, benefit enormously from the ability to communicate with one another. Indeed, without the cooperation that language allows it might be that the species would have perished. There is no reason to suppose that communication requires consciousness, though – my PC 'communicates' with the telephone network every time it goes on-line to the Internet but I doubt very much that either system is conscious of the flow of signals between them. So it is not necessarily surprising that a visitor from Earth would find Zombie-land inhabited by beings that talked to one another. Indeed, the first conversations between an Earthling and a Zombie might proceed precisely along the same lines as that between two Earthlings. The Zombies would have the same social set-up, science and art; and shared concepts like 'good' and 'bad'. Plenty to discuss, therefore, with their visitor.

There is one concept, however, which it is very difficult to imagine arising in Zombie-world: that of consciousness itself. By definition, Zombies would have no first-hand knowledge of what it is to be conscious, and until the Earthling arrived there was no-one in their world who had. So the chances of them 'thinking it up' are remote.

As the human visitor got to know the Zombies better, this conceptual gap would start to show. For a start, the word 'consciousness' is unlikely to exist in Zombie-land, and if it did it is difficult to imagine what it might refer to. Other words in Zombie-English would have subtly different meanings from human-English. The word 'understanding' for example, means more than just being able to produce appropriate responses to a statement or sensible answers to a question. Like the file-rummager in John Searle's Chinese Room (see page 66), it is possible to produce behaviour that looks like understanding without actually understanding at all. The Zombie-word 'understanding' would presumably refer to this sort of information processing, while the human word would mean something quite different – a subjective 'grasping' of knowledge which is essentially conscious. 'Sleep' would mean something different to Zombies, too. To us it refers to a change in consciousness, but this would not be so for the Zombie because Zombies do not have consciousness to alter. The Zombie-word 'sleep' would therefore refer merely to a period of time in which motor processes are paralysed and external information shut out. Dreams would be different too. Even if Zombie 'sleep' involved internally generated sensory processing – the equivalent of human dreaming – it would not be distinguishable (except perhaps by its bizarre content) from any other sensory processing. Given this it is difficult to see how Zombies could know that their dreams were dreams. The only way they could be sure that they were not 'ordinary' events would be by deduction – they would have no intuitive way of telling the difference.

So, if the Earthling, at breakfast one day, mentioned that she had had an interesting dream during the night her Zombie host might ask her how she knew it was a dream. Her reply: 'I just knew', or words to that effect, would be utterly puzzling to the Zombie. And if the conversation then drifted into philosophical waters the confusion would increase. What would a Zombie philosopher say when asked to comment on 'the hard problem'? How would they understand a conundrum like the 'dancing qualia' thought experiment (see page 68) or, for that matter, the notion of Zombiehood?[9] From this it seems that even if consciousness was not essential for the evolution of all the behaviour that we observe in people – the concept of it was. And such a concept was very unlikely to pop up in the brain of a Zombie. So – if only at the level of philosophical discourse – consciousness seems to make a difference outside our heads, as well as inside.

And yet ...

If having a concept is the only difference between a conscious human being and a Zombie, might it not be possible to transform a Zombie into a person by providing them with the relevant concept?

The question takes us back to Mary the colour scientist (see page 20). If you believe that consciousness is having a certain concept-just-like-any-other-old-concept then the answer must be yes. Similarly, if the concept is seen as a type of brain function – an ability rather than just new knowledge – it might be possible to persuade a Zombie to 'do' consciousness. The Zombie would certainly find it very difficult; but perhaps no more difficult than it is for a chimp, say, to understand language. It would require a change in their brains – whether it be a change in its database or a change in its functioning. But brains – Zombies' included – are famously plastic. If they did manage to grasp the idea, presumably the neurological change involved would make their brain states identical to humans'. Now, of course, they would be able to discriminate the changes in their brains which, in humans, signal changes in consciousness. So they would know when they were dreaming. They would 'think' they were conscious even if they weren't.

However, if you believe that the concept of consciousness is a concept like no other – a 'thing' that may be accompanied by certain types of neural activity but nevertheless separable from it – the Zombie could remain unenlightened however intense its education. The brain states that accompany consciousness in humans could be reproduced in the Zombie's mind, even to the extent that it could speak fluently of its dreams and pains and write books about the nature of consciousness. From outside you would not be able to spot the difference between humans and Zombies because consciousness would make no difference. The two would work together, marry, reproduce and go to each others' barbequeues. But only some of them would feel satisfaction from a job well done, fall in love, suffer the pain of childbirth or taste the steak. Perhaps this is the case already. Indeed, maybe we are all Zombies?

Except, of course, you. And me.

Nicholas Humphrey
School Professor
Centre for the Philosophy of Natural and Social Science
London School of Economics

The Making of Mind

Sensations, I argue, originate with the protective and appetitive responses of primitive animals to stimulation at their body surface. Under the influence of natural selection, these sensory responses become finely adapted so as to reflect the particular pattern of stimulation, with the intentional properties of the response varying according to the nature of the stimulus, its bodily location, its modality, and so on. These responses therefore encode information about what is happening at the body surface and how the animal evaluates it. However, in the early stages, the animal has no interest in bringing this information to mind – no use, as yet, for any kind of representation of 'what's happening to me'.

Life grows more complicated, and the animal, besides merely responding to stimulation, does develop an interest in forming mental representations of what's happening to it. But, given that the information is already encoded in its own sensory responses, the obvious way of getting there is to monitor its command signals for making these responses. In other words the animal can, as it were, tune into 'what's happening to me and how I feel about it' by the simple trick of noting 'what I'm doing about it'.

The result is that sensations do indeed evolve at first as corollaries of the animal's public bodily activity. And since, in these early days, the form of this activity is still being maintained by natural selection, it follows that the forms of the animal's mental representations – its sensory 'experience' or proto-experience, if you like – are also being determined in all their aspects by selection.

Life moves on further, and the making of responses directly to stimuli at the body surface becomes of less and less relevance to the organism's biological survival. In fact the time comes when it may be better to suppress these responses altogether. But now the animal is in something of a bind. For, while it may no longer have any need for the bodily responses as such, it has become quite dependent on the mental representations of the stimuli – representations that have been based on monitoring these very responses.

The animal has therefore to find a way of continuing to make as if to respond to the stimuli, without actually carrying the activity through into overt behaviour. And the upshot is – or so I've argued – that the whole sensory activity gets privatised: with the command signals getting short-circuited before they reach the body surface, and eventually getting entirely closed off from the outside world in an internal loop within the brain.

Once this happens the role of natural selection must sharply diminish. The sensory responses have lost all their original biological importance and have in fact disappeared from view. Note well, however, that this privatisation has come about only at the very end, after natural selection has done its work to shape the sensory landscape. And the forms of sensory responses and the corresponding experiences have already been more or less permanently fixed, so as to reflect their pedigree.

It is this evolutionary pedigree that still colours private sensory experience right down to the present day. If, I today feel the sensation red this way – as I know very well that I do – it is because I am descended from distant ancestors who were selected to feel it this same way long ago.

From *The Mind Made Flesh – Essays from the Frontiers of Psychology and Evolution* (Oxford, Oxford University Press, 2002).

Making Consciousation

'No longer need one spend time enduring the tedium of philosophers perpetually disagreeing with one another. Consciousness is now largely a scientific problem.'

Francis Crick, 'Visual Perception Rivalry and Consciousness'

Neuroscience is on a roll. New findings about the brain and its workings are pouring out of laboratories, and newspapers, TV and radio programmes continually report the cracking of another mental mystery. A casual observer may well think that the problem of consciousness is only a matter of doing a few more experiments.

In truth, the data gathered from neuroscience is fragmentary. The information is like pieces of a jigsaw that have been scattered and are now being picked up, one by one, by hundreds of different people, many of whom have an entirely different idea of how the finished picture will turn out. No-one is sure how to fit their little bits together, let alone how to fit them in with those found by others. There are no obvious edges to the puzzle, and no indication of how big it will turn out to be when – or if – it is completed. Some argue that the whole enterprise is frivolous anyway, because even if brain processes were understood to the last sub-atomic particle in every atom of every molecule in every neuron, it would still have no bearing on the 'hard' problem of what consciousness actually is. It might turn out to be the wrong puzzle anyway – consciousness could lie outside the brain, perhaps in the interaction between minds or in some cosmic universe beyond time and space. So the best it can do is shed some light on the 'easy' problems.

This might turn out to be so. On the other hand, it might turn out that the hard problem is actually just a knot of easy problems which will solve itself as each of its strands are teased apart and straightened out. After all, life was once thought to be an impenetrable mystery – a matter of some essential God-given vital spark that no amount of biological research would ever explain. Few take that view today – as it turned out, the analysis of living systems showed that

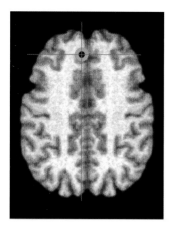

Functional MRI (fMRI) shows the areas of the brain using the most oxygen – a marker of neural activity.

what once seemed like a mysterious 'life force' is just what happens when you have certain complex physical systems operating in an appropriate environment. Now that we can see how these systems work, they no longer seem mysterious. And now that we can have a direct view of what goes on inside a normal, working brain, it may be that we will find the mental phenomena that seems to come with it is similarly understandable.

The main experimental method for examining the relationship between the brain and consciousness is functional brain imaging. It enables researchers to look inside a working brain and see not just what is there, but what is going on in there, because as well as showing the physical tissue it shows the electrical activity that is the basis of all nervous function.

Different imaging techniques give different degrees of detail, rather as different lenses in a microscope can give a closer or wider view. Between them these techniques can 'map' brain activity from single-cell to global level, in snapshot form or even as a movie.

Electroencephalography (EEG) and magnetoencephalography (MEG) show a very fast but rather vague read-out of brain activity over a wide area; while Functional Magnetic Resonance Imaging (fMRI) reveals changes in very precise areas, but more slowly, because it detects the blood flow increase which follows neuronal activity rather than the activity directly. Positron Emission Topography (PET) is slower than fMRI and has lower spatial resolution, but can show neurotransmitter activity as well as simple blood flow. It is also possible to detect the activity in a single neuron by fixing a mini-electrode on or near it. This, of course, is invasive, so (for ethical reasons) it is only used on humans when their brains are exposed, anyway, for surgery.

Brain imaging is not exactly like peering down a microscope at a slide full of bacteria, however. To make sense of it you need to scan a brain that is doing a particular thing, and to know precisely what that thing is. It is very difficult to design an experiment in which you can be sure that the picture on the screen correlates with a particular mental activity. It sounds easy enough to ask a volunteer to read then recall a list of words. The activity recorded during the exercise should, in theory, reflect just that process. But what really happens when you recall a list of words? Can you be sure the blip of activity in the temporal cortex is really associated with registering the word 'rose'? Or could it be generated by the imagined smell of rose petals, a recollection of a rosy sunset, the thought 'must remember to do the pruning', or even 'this is a really boring experiment'? Not surprisingly many studies show conflicting results, and single studies of a particular thing are notoriously unreliable.

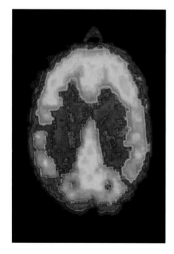

Positron Emission Topography (PET) is slower and less precise than fMRI.

However, through increasing replication of studies, the introduction of consistent protocols and simple volume of work, brain imaging has now built up an impressive map of which bits of the brain are concerned with specific mental processes like memory, speech and sensory awareness, and how they work together systematically to produce complex mental activities.

From here to the discovery of the neural basis of consciousness may sound like a small step. All that seems necessary is to get a person into the machine, design some clever experiments in which they become conscious or unconscious of some stimulus, then look at the difference in their brain activity as awareness dawns. With luck, a flurry of activity in a particular spot will identify a single brain module as the 'seat' of consciousness, or perhaps a single type of neuron will turn out to be responsible, or a particular type of inter-neuronal signalling.

In practice it has turned out to be much more complicated. Even if you skip over the 'fridge light' problem by assuming consciousness is only 'on' when it can be reported, physical markers of awareness have proved extremely elusive. Searching for a single locus of consciousness, for example, is like looking for the source of power in a car: you can point to the battery (without which it won't start), or the fuel (without which it won't go), or to the driver (without whom it would grind to a halt). But none of these alone is sufficient to drive the car.

What has been discovered – or at least seems pretty near certain – is this:

First, to be conscious a brain must be active. This may seem obvious, but it is worth stating because there are some people, including at least one eminent neuroscientist, who believe personal consciousness can exist without any activity being present in the individual's brain at all (see chapter nine).

Second, it has to be active in certain places; not just anywhere. Although there seems to be no single spot in the brain where mental activity 'comes together' to form a conscious perception, the cortex certainly needs to be active for normal consciousness, and some parts of it – the frontal lobes, for example, and the lower-level association cortices behind them – seem to play a crucial part in producing certain kinds of consciousness, like introspection and sensory images. Certain sub-cortical areas also need to be active to support consciousness. If you destroyed the limbic system or the brain-stem then the cortex would eventually die too. In fact the support system for consciousness extends to the body and the environment, in that the brain is activated by information flowing in from the sensory organs, and from nerves in the skin, joints and gut. And most of this information, of course, comes from outside the body. A 'brain in a vat' – nurtured by oxygen and glucose but bereft of

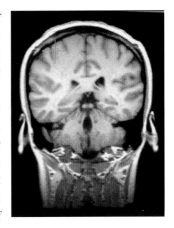

Magnetoencephalography picks up the tiny magnetic pulses from active neurons. It is the fastest scanning technique available.

input from other flesh and other minds would probably die, quite literally, of boredom.

Third, brain activity must be of a certain type. The neurons have to be firing (or oscillating – both terms refer to speedy, rhythmical changes in the cells' electrical potential) at a certain rate, or at least within a limited range.

OK. So the next question is to consider what all this activity is actually doing. The nearest to a 'standard' view is that the neural activation produces a representation of reality within the brain, and it is this representation that we call consciousness. Given the fragments of knowledge we have about the neural activity associated with it, and a fair bit of speculative filling-in, it is possible to construct a picture of what might be happening in the brain each time a moment of consciousness is experienced. Perhaps the quickest way to get an idea of it is through an analogy. The one that follows is rather elaborate – but far less so than the real brain processes that it models.

Imagine a huge crowd of people travelling in a vast airship. Only these people are zombies. Not philosophers' Zombies but ordinary, common-or-garden humanoid robots who do certain intelligent things but in fact have no internal experience whatsoever. The craft is powered by a fuel-injection system, and controlled by rudders and flaps and propellers which are manipulated by passengers sitting deep in the bowels of the craft. They can't see out, so in order to pilot the ship they depend on messages sent down from the passengers above.

Some of these passengers have window seats. The windows, however, do not offer a direct view of the outside world. Rather the airship is equipped with a sort of periscope which is sensitive, not just to light, but also to vibrations and molecules – everything in the physical world outside that might affect the airship's progress. The periscope feeds this information to a device which splits it up before passing it on. The most basic, and first division it makes is to assess whether the general view is 'good' or 'bad'. If the ground is rushing up to meet the ship at an unseemly rate, the information is classified as bad, and if the scene is of a clear blue sky it is rated as good. Once this distinction has been made the device splits the sensory information, that given by light waves, vibrations and so on, into elements. The visual information, for example, is divided into colour, form, movement and so on. These 'bits' of information about the outside world are then sent to window-like video monitors. Some show just 'blue', for instance, and others show just 'white', and any one 'window' only lights up when the airspace the ship is passing through contains the element that it is designed to present. During a flight through clear skies, for instance, the 'blue-presenting' screens are almost permanently on, whereas the 'white-presenting' ones only flicker into life when the ship passes through clouds, and the green-showing ones do nothing until the ship banks and a field beneath heaves, momentarily, into view. Similar windows transmit information about sounds, and the physical state of the ship itself – whether it is passing through moist air, or being battered by wind, or hit by debris. And some of the windows simply alert those sitting by them to whether things are 'good' or 'bad'. Thus, at any one moment, the sum of information showing in the windows contains everything picked up by the periscope.

The task of the window passengers is to report when their window lights up, and their window only. So a zombie seated next to a blue screen would shout 'blue' and one next to a white-presenting window would shout 'white' when their respective screens were alight. They don't just shout willy-nilly, though, because the pilots do not want to know about every lit-up window – indeed, if they did it would cause chaos. On a long, cloudless flight, for example, the blue-presenting windows would be permanently on and the

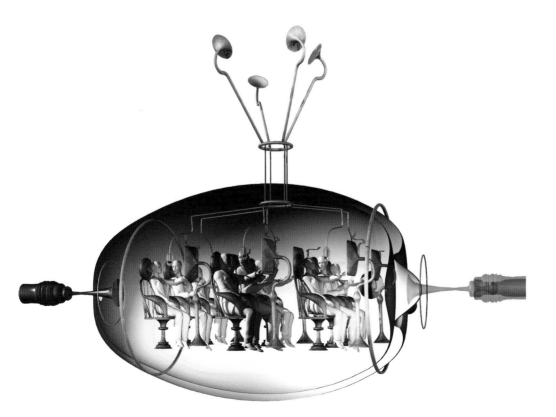

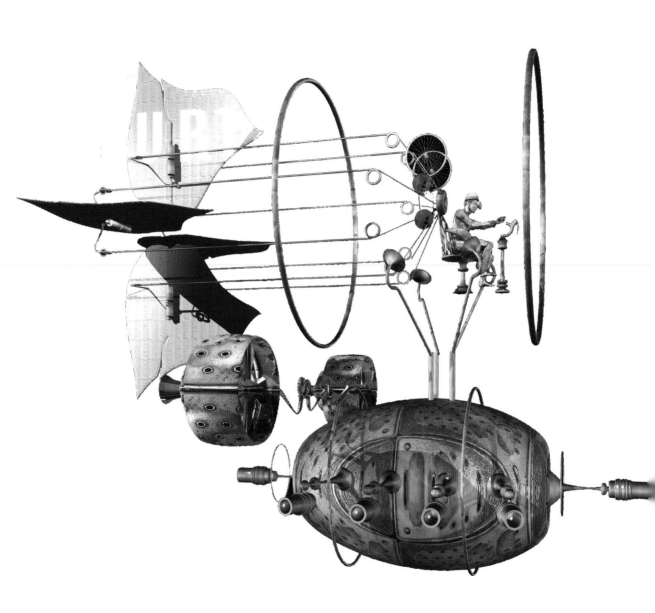

zombies next to them would be shouting 'Blue!', 'Blue!' at such a pitch that – should a handful of 'black-presenting' windows briefly light up, the cries from the few reporters sitting next to them would be drowned out by the blue team. And that could be disastrous if the black happened to be another craft approaching on collision course. So if a window-seat passenger goes on shouting for too long, adjacent passengers tell it to shut up. This means that at any time, the shouts coming from the window passengers relate mainly to new events – the changes in the view rather than steady background information.

Now the pilots in this ship (it's enormous, remember) are too far away from the windows to hear all this shouting, and even if they weren't, they would have a hard time putting together all the different 'elements' of the scene into a picture coherent enough to act on. So the passengers sitting next to the window-seat ones are charged with picking up their neighbours' reports and passing them on in such a way that they will build up to create a meaningful picture. Some of them can hear more than one reporter at a time and so they pass on the combination of those reports: 'blue + white' say. The next passenger in line can hear two of these 'combination' reports, and puts them together: 'blue + white and fluffy + above' say. And so the message progresses up the line, becoming more complex (and closer to the 'whole' view through the periscope) at each stage.

This works so long as the airship is cruising gently through blue skies and fluffy white clouds. The only information required is a sort of 'everything OK ahead' monitoring from a handful of passengers while everyone else quietly snoozes, oblivious to their neighbours.

But now let's suppose the ship is coming in to land at a chaotic airport with no air-traffic control. Now the view through the periscope is much more complicated and fast-changing. Windows that have been blank for hours are now flashing with information relating to distance from ground, angle of flight, speed of descent, plus the position, speed and direction of dozens of other craft trying to land in the same place. And of course, the zombies charged with reporting the 'bad' message become wildly excited as they are alerted to countless perils; while those sitting next to 'good' windows would chirrup away about the advantage of making it back to the ground. Unlike the reports about sights and sounds, the cries from the good/bad zombies shortcut the construction process and carry straight through to the pilots. As all their shouts contain is the crude message 'good' or 'bad', the pilots cannot make a reasoned decision about what to do in response, though if the cries are loud enough the pilots might be prompted to react in some crude way. But most of

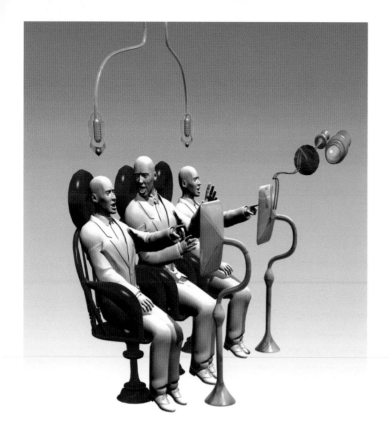

the time the pilots are just alerted by the good/bad shouting, and wait for more information before they act.

Because each window-seat zombie can only see their own bit of world, they have no way of knowing how the changes they see fit in to the overall picture – they can only shout louder when the changes are big or sudden. If all this shouting was passed on to the zombies at the controls the ship would probably crash because it would first swing right, in obedience to the hysterical passengers in the window seats on the left-hand side of the airship who have between them shouted what amounts to a description of a low-flying gull, then back again to dodge the hang-glider reported by passengers on the right; then dive to avoid a storm cloud above observed by the passengers at the back ... and so on to disaster.

By now, however, something else has happened in the passenger cabin. The other passengers have woken up and the information coming from the outlookers is being exchanged in all directions rather than just being relayed in a straight line to the crew. The 'bad' reporting zombies, in particular, are by now in a lather of excitement, threatening to drown out everything else with their insistent, but rather useless screaming. The vast majority of the passengers have no view, are not part of the communication 'chain' of reporters, and have no direct communication with the people who are pushing the levers. But they are nevertheless intensely interested in the outcome of the flight and are gossiping urgently about what the onlookers are reporting. Some are whispering only to their near neighbours, others are shouting to friends at the opposite end of the cabin, and some are trying to quieten things down. Sometimes a passenger gets their comment fed back to them through some circuitous route, distorted, like a Chinese whisper, or amplified so it sounds more important than when it was transmitted. And of course, that confirms their original conviction ('it's not just me who thinks there's a hang-glider out there so I must be right') so they repeat what they said with more confidence. Little sub-groups of people get particularly hung up on one particular bit of information: 'The gull – we're on collision course with a gull!' As they convince each other of the importance of this peril, their voices get louder and other groups pick up the cry.

Another lot mutter for a few moments about the storm cloud, but their voices are drowned out by the gull-people. Then another group becomes concerned about the hang-glider, and they make contact with a second group that was just starting to mull over that problem themselves. Confirmed in their concern by the first group: 'Yes, there really is a hang-glider coming at us – the people at the back have confirmed it!' – this group raises their voices and encourages the original hang-glider spotters to do the same. Others now take up the 'Hang-glider!' cry and very soon it has drowned out the ones who are shouting about the gull. The news of the hang-glider travels around the cabin, winging back and forth between the passengers. Some of them recall a tragic story of a hang-glider killed by a low-flying aircraft and add this to the cacophony, others calculate exactly how far the airship would have to turn to avoid this one, and what the effect of such an action would have on their flight-path. Some curmudgeonly individual mutters that any hang-glider daft enough to fly over an airport deserves to get hit. Soon nearly everyone is talking about the hang-glider, and the gull and storm cloud are forgotten. Eventually a crowd nearest the hatch to the control deck shouts 'dive!'. But by then the pilot has already picked up on the chatter above and leant on the joystick.

On the practical front what all this inter-passenger gossip achieved was to select, through consensus, a limited number of items for attention, and decide what should be done about them. However, it has also contrived to create an internal representation of the knowledge known directly only by those in the window seats. Although the vast majority of passengers do not have a view of the outside their gossip has given them their own idea of it. Every time a new piece of direct information comes in – either from the outlookers or from the effect of the whole craft's interaction with the environment (the lurch), they incorporate it into their 'virtual' reality: 'What was that?' squeaks one; 'We're avoiding that idiot hang-glider.' announces another. 'I told you it would cause a lurch!' smirks a third. If the information fits the expectations of the crowd their conversation goes on smoothly and quietly, but if it doesn't – being an excitable lot – they erupt into a frenzy of shouting. 'What was that?'; 'Just a lurch, stupid.'; 'No, it's not, I felt a bump.'; 'So did I!'; 'So did I!'; 'Me too!'; 'A big bump!'; 'Huge!'; 'And a crunch.'; 'You can't have.'; 'I did!'; 'Rubbish, ignore it.'; 'But I felt it!'; 'It's the gull! We've hit the gull!'; 'Phew, that's all right then ...'

and so on. Then, in rising chorus, a bunch of passengers drown out all dissent with the definitive 'story' of the event:

'A hang-glider!

Which we swerved to avoid.

But we got a gull instead ...

Poor little gull!

Now we are back on course ...

So everyone can relax.'

Taking the passengers' conversation to stand for the cognitive processes in the human brain, the elements of it which represent conscious moments would be those when a critical number of passengers took up the same chant, long and loud enough to 'swing' the conversation right through the cabin, rather as the majority vote in an election decides the winner. Conscious actions are those that are carried out in accordance with this 'majority view'. Note, though, that they would not be carried out as a *result* of it (though it would seem that way to the passengers). Rather they arose from their unconscious antecedents – the shift from conflicting mutterings to consensus. Unconscious actions (the automatic reaching for a cigarette, say, when an addict thinks of something stressful) would be those carried out in accordance with a minority view – the murmuring of neurons habitually inclined to whisper the consolations of nicotine.

Now this does not explain the 'feeling' of consciousness. That is part of the hard question. But it does explain certain features of it. For example, it helps explain why our experience does not always accord faithfully with reality and may be erroneous enough to make our behaviour seem crazy.

Each time an item of new information from outside is correctly interpreted the notion of the outside world held by the passengers is nudged a little closer to reality, but each time it is misinterpreted their conversation becomes a little more eccentric.

Say the outlooker who spotted the hang-glider to the right of the airship passed this information to a group of passengers who were already in a high state of excitement about the gull on the left. With 'alert to left' so well-established in their minds, the passengers may have taken in the idea of a hang-glider but not dropped the idea of avoiding something from the left. So the message they sing out is 'hang-glider + left'. The pilot, reacting to this clear alert, would thus confidently steer into the path of the hapless hang-glider.

It also helps to explain why conscious thoughts and feelings change over time, even if the events they are about remain similar. If the passengers ever again found themselves with a gull on one side and a hang-glider on the other, they might not be so quick to take up the hang-glider cry – those who were most traumatized by the collision would probably form a little clique of tedious caution-mongers urging the others to double-check everything before lending their voice to it. It explains, too, how habitual mental contents give our consciousness a familiar quality even though its contents change constantly. Some of the passengers continue, like pub bores, to trot out the same old stories and behave in the same way whatever happens (maintaining the familiar feeling of a night at the local), but others will be affected by every little snippet of information they come by (making each night slightly different).

It also accounts for the feeling of unity that consciousness typically has: over time the airship's inhabitants would come to develop a 'personality' over and above that of each of the individuals, and they would start to think of themselves as a unit. Some would form tight, mutually reinforcing little cliques who always say the same sort of thing and limit their intra-clique conversation to the same subject: 'Do you remember when ...'; 'Keep quiet everyone!', 'What next? What next?'; 'Look – its red ... red ... red!' and so on. The role of each clique is dictated partly by their place in the craft: those in the window seats for example, are stuck with the task of reporting on outside events and their neighbours are permanently locked into the reporting-forward chains. Those nearest the controls are obliged to manipulate them, and their neighbours are best placed to rehearse actions and make sure that the lever-pullers make the right moves – correcting them urgently if the ship seem to be careering off course.

And it helps to explain how our personality and individual viewpoint develop: at the beginning of the journey the passengers are inclined to exchange small talk with more or less anyone, but as they get to know each other, and their roles become clearer, they don't bother with the passengers who do not share their interests. They instead establish permanent communication channels with those whose talk informs their own concerns, or whose ideas conflict so much with theirs that they constantly try to shut them up. And with their nearest neighbours – their clique – they form such close bonds that they effectively become one. Eventually, like workers in a vast, highly-professional construction team, they divide the component tasks according to who is best at each, and communicate smoothly, continuously, and quietly to keep the whole project running smoothly. So long as the information coming in from the reporters is consistent with what the passengers expect, and presents no danger, it raises only a little frisson of interest among a few whose muttered acknowledgements are broadcast locally

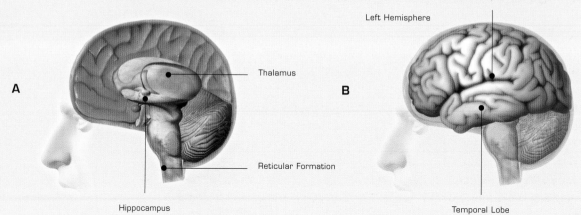

A

Thalamus

Reticular Formation

Hippocampus

B

Left Hemisphere

Parietal/Temporal Junction

Temporal Lobe

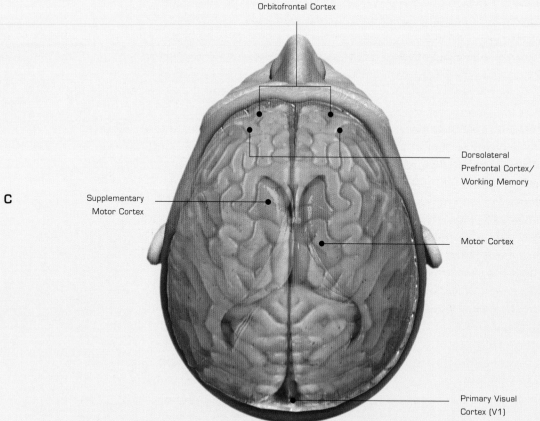

Orbitofrontal Cortex

C

Supplementary
Motor Cortex

Dorsolateral
Prefrontal Cortex/
Working Memory

Motor Cortex

Primary Visual
Cortex (V1)

Locating Consciousness?

A

Thalamus: Directs attention and switches sensory input on and off.

Reticular Formation: Activity here stimulates the cortex into action – without which there is no consciousness.

Hippocampus: Personal memories are encoded here and it is also responsible for spatial memory (in the right hemisphere) – two lynchpins of consciousness.

B

Parietal/Temporal Junction: This is where the brain stores its 'map' of self and judges the self's relationship to the world. Has good connections to the frontal lobes and is in a position to pull in information from sensory areas. The 'locus' of consciousness?

Temporal Lobe: Stores personal memories, processes sound and speech. Language may be the scaffolding that supports consciousness.

Left Hemisphere: The dominant side in 97 per cent of people, and usually the only one to use language. Its ability to describe experience, and spin stories, may be the means by which we become fully conscious.

C

Orbitofrontal Cortex: Emotions become conscious here. If it is not active, emotion is reduced to a robotic reflex without feeling.

Dorsolateral Prefrontal Cortex/Working Memory: Where different ideas and perceptions are brought together. Could consciousness depend on this type of 'binding'?

Motor Cortex: Is consciousness dependent on body awareness? If so, the motor cortex must be of central importance.

Primary Visual Cortex (V1): Take this away and you lose visual consciousness even if other vision-processing areas are preserved.

Supplementary Motor Cortex (sma): This is where actions are 'rehearsed'. Was this the brain function that jacked us up to consciousness?

rather than to the whole team. Only if something big happens, or if the good/bad reporters startle everyone with a scream, does the conversation erupt into the general shouting match that resolves in a consensual chorus – a 'blip' of consciousness.

Does this model match with what we see when we look inside a real brain? Do neurons – our passengers – behave anything like these airship travellers?

First let us look at the neural equivalents of the various airship components. The brain can be divided very roughly into three 'layers': the brainstem and mid-brain structure at the base; a group of organs called the limbic system in the middle; and the cortex – the grey wrinkled surface – on top. The activity of all three levels is primed by bursts of excitatory neurotransmitters (chemicals which trigger nerve cells to fire) which are sent up from the brainstem. Think of it as the fuel-injection system of the ship.

Sensory information (the view from outside) is like the ship's periscope. And the sense organs, each of which detects a different strand (visual, auditory and so on) is like the view-splitting device. Each strand travels along two main pathways. One takes it to the limbic system, where it is evaluated as good or bad, while another carries it to the thalamus, where it is relayed along parallel routes to brain regions specialized to process one or another sort of information. These pathways terminate in the equivalent of the airship windows.

Individual neurons are equivalent to our zombie passengers. The cortex is made up of several layers of closely-knit neurons. Those towards the back are mainly concerned with reacting to sensory information. One area is concerned with visual information, another with auditory information, and a strip around the top registers tactile information (the equivalent of physical effects on the airship's structure). Within these major areas are sub-regions, each of which is concerned with a particular element of visual (or auditory or somatosensory) information. In the visual cortex, for example, there are separate areas for colour, form, motion, location etc. And within these sub-regions there are neurons which are so specialized that they respond only to one type of element information: a particular colour, say, or a line at a precise angle.

In airship terms, these are the window-seat passengers. As with neurons, all the colour ones tend to sit together, as do the form ones, and the location-spotting ones. And each of them pipes up when (and only when) he spots a stimulus that he is 'charged' with reporting.

Further forward in the cortex are large regions known as association areas. These do not respond directly to sensory stimuli – they respond instead to reports coming in from the primary sensory areas (the zombies in the window seats). They too are specialized, but their speciality is not to respond to elements of sensory information, but to particular combinations of those elements. So, for example, a cell in the visual association area may respond only if it receives two particular messages: 'grey' + 'moving', say. What they do, therefore, is to bind the information coming in from behind into more complex aggregates – rather as the airship zombies in the communication chains 'bind' the individual reports of those at the window seats.

Forward from the association areas are two types of region: one holds records of past experiences – memories; the other responds to the information received from association areas by creating 'action schemas' – plans, if you like – for how the body should react to such stimuli. So when the potential perceptions arrive in these regions, they are, in those concerned with memory, 'clothed' with associations such as the names they are known by and the effect that such things have had in the past. And in the 'action schema' areas they provoke a disposition to respond physically.

The airship passengers analogous to the memory areas are those which take the combined sensory information and 'recognize' it – the ones who chant 'It's a gull! A sea-bird ... known to have collided with airships.' And the 'action-schema' neuronal areas are equivalent to the passengers sitting near the pilots, saying 'We'll instruct them to move the rudder to the right.'

Moving right to the front of the brain there is a huge area of cortex which carries out what is loosely known as 'executive' functions. By the time an item of information reaches here it has accumulated and bound together – like a snowball rolling forward – its full quota of sensory elements, together with associated memories, words, and good/bad evaluation. It is similar – though not identical – to the view registered by the periscope. The differences are that, like information travelling along a bad telephone line, it has been subject to various errors and distortions.

A largish part of the frontal cortex is given over to what is known as 'working memory'. What it does is to take the now fully-formed perceptions and play around with them. To do this it keeps them 'warm' – that is, the neuronal activation patterns associated with them are maintained (either as a sensory image or a language-based thought) while other parts of the system call up relevant memories relating to them. Working memory may hold four or five related concepts at any time, and may juggle them around, testing each new arrangement in an attempt to come up with a rational response to what is going on. Meanwhile the action schemas plotted by areas further back in the brain are inhibited – kept on hold in case this further cognition comes up with

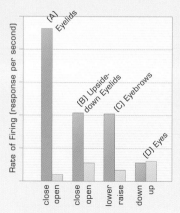

Rate of Firing (response per second)

(A) Eyelids

(B) Upside-down Eyelids

(C) Eyebrows

(D) Eyes

close open | close open | lower raise | down up

Stimulus Presented to Neuron

The graph above shows the rate of firing activated in a single cell, The neuron became most excited (A) by the image of a closed eyelid, but more or less stopped reacting when the lid opened to reveal the eye. The sight of an upside-down eyelid (B) stimulated neurons less than in (A), and made the cell less sensitive to the difference between the closed and open lid. A lowered eyebrow (C) sparked about the same amount of excitement as an upside-down, closed eyelid, while a raised one calmed it down. The cell responded only faintly to the actual eyes (D) and was unmoved by a change of eye direction.[3]

Neurons come in all shapes and sizes, each sort specialized for the type of job it does. Some have long axons which carry information from sense organs to specialized brain cells (A), while others communicate only with other brain cells. The pyramidal cell (B) for example, exchanges information with neurons in different layers of the cerebral cortex. Neurons which take in dense amounts of information, like the Purkinje cell (C), have numerous dendrites to receive messages from a large number of other neurons.

Brains Within Brains

Neurons used to be thought of as simple on/off switches, but now they appear to be little 'brains' in their own right. Each one may receive information from thousands of others, and instead of merely passing on this information, it sifts and prioritizes it, favouring input from 'reliable' sources, ignoring that from others, and adjusting its output accordingly. The most powerful computer, according to one communications expert, does not have the information-processing skill of a single neuron.[1]

There are many different types of neuron. Some respond specifically to one particular thing: an edge, for example, or a narrow range of light waves. Others combine information from other neurons into quite complex representations, which are nevertheless very specific. EEG monitoring of a single cell in one of the brain's association areas showed that it responded only to certain facial movements around the area of the eye (see top left).

Activity in a single neuron, however, is not enough to produce experience – a stimulus must be strong enough to engage a group in synchronous activity before it can enter a person's consciousness. One study presented subjects with a stripy pattern on a screen, starting with the contrast set very low. Neurons which distinguish contrasting edges started to fire almost immediately, but the subjects were not, initially, conscious of the stripes. As the contrast was increased, however, more neurons sparked up, and when they reached a critical number the subjects 'saw' the lines.[2] In addition to this, the neurons must be active for a minimum period of time – anything from one-tenth to half a second – before the information they discriminate becomes conscious.

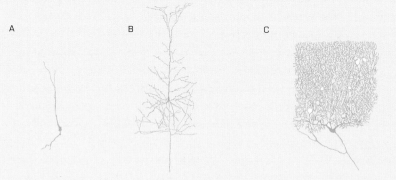

A   B   C

[1] C. Jonscher, *Wired Life. Who are we in the Digital Age?* (London, Bantam Books, 1999).

[2] Menon Ravi et al. Reported in *New Scientist*, 12 August 2000.

[3] Allison et al, 'Social perception', *Trends in Cognitive Sciences*, 4:7, (2001), 271.

a better response. Complicated though executive functions are, and systemic, in that they involve far-flung regions (the memory store and speech articulation areas, for example) it is nevertheless possible to pinpoint some of the areas involved. One part of the frontal lobe is responsible for generating new juxtapositions of perceptions, for example; another helps to keep the planning process focused by preventing irrelevant perceptions from entering the loop; while another picks up on – and feeds in – emotional information relating to the perceptions currently being juggled.

These areas correspond, in terms of the airship, to those groups of passengers who receive basic knowledge about what is happening from the reporting passengers and work out what to do with it. They call down to other groups saying effectively: 'Hey! We've got news of a hang-glider here – anyone recall meeting a hang-glider before?' They take the news of the gull, and the hang-glider and weigh up which is likely to be the best one to avoid – shouting back to the groups of passengers who have been working out action plans: 'So what's it going to feel like if we swing to the left? ... Uh-huh ... And to the right?' And once decided they issue instructions: 'OK, tell the pilots to do the second thing.'

That then, very roughly, is how the layout of the brain corresponds to the airship. Now let's look at the 'conversations' that go on in it. What is the neuronal equivalent of all that shouting?

Brain signalling is done by the transmission of electrical energy along neuronal pathways. There are dozens of different types of neuron, but each one has certain things in common: each has a cell body and a long tendril, called an axon, which stretches out to make contact with other cells. Neurons also have multiple protuberances called dendrites, which have docking points on them (synapses) where incoming messages from axons are received by receptors. Some axons latch straight onto receptors at the synapse, and transmit electrical signals directly, but most stop just short of the receptors, creating a tiny gap called the synaptic cleft. Where this happens the signal is carried over the gap by a chemical mediator called a neurotransmitter.

The inside of the neuron contains ions – atoms which have lost or gained electrons. Ions that are short of electrons are said to be negatively charged, while those which have excess electrons are positively charged. Ions are naturally unstable because they are always seeking to gain or lose their missing or excess electrons in order to return to their natural state. So a collection of negative ions (those with lost electrons) will react with positively charged ions by grabbing some of the latter's electrons, creating the exchange of energy we know as electricity.

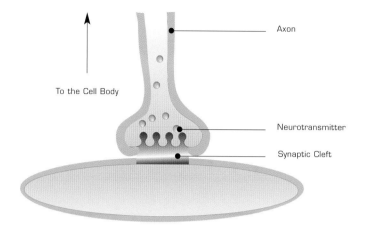

Axon

To the Cell Body

Neurotransmitter

Synaptic Cleft

Neurons communicate by passing electrical signals between themselves at docking points called synapses. In most cases the signal is carried via neurotransmitters – chemical mediators which are released by one cell and picked up by the next cell.

When a neuron is 'resting' the ions inside it are negatively charged in relation to the ions on the other side of its cell wall, but when the receptors at the synapse are stimulated, the cell-wall membrane becomes porous and positive ions flood in, altering its charge. The resulting electrical signal, known as an action potential, travels down the cell's axon, and when it reaches the tip it either excites the adjacent cell directly, or, if the synapse is dependent on chemical transmission (as most are) it causes the release of neurotransmitters which are held in packets in the axon's tip. The neurotransmitters float into the synaptic gap and latch on to receptors on the next cell's docking point. This may produce the stimulation required to cause that neuron to fire too, creating a chain of activity like a spark along a trail of dynamite.

The process, however, is more complicated than the sketch above suggests. Neurons are not simple on/off switches – rather each one operates like a little brain in its own right. Indeed, so complicated is the neuronal process that, according to one Artificial Intelligence (AI) expert the most powerful computer does not (yet, anyway!) have the information-processing ability of a single neuron.[1]

For a start there are hundreds of different neurotransmitters, and many different varieties of the same neurotransmitter. Then there are a correspondingly large number of different types of receptor. And each neurotransmitter and sub-type has a different effect. For example, acetylcholine is an excitatory chemical, and when it connects with the appropriate receptor on a neighbouring cell it is inclined to make it fire. But GABA is an inhibitory neurotransmitter and when it hits a neighbouring cell it tends to shut it down. Different neurons secrete different neurotransmitters and some have different mixes of neurotransmitters. So a single cell, on firing, might release two neurotransmitters with conflicting effects. Which one 'wins out' will depend on all sorts of other factors: the amount of neurotransmitter released; the time it hangs about in the synaptic cleft (excess neurotransmitters are 'mopped up' and returned to axons, or are broken down by enzymes); the type or number of receptors on the neighbouring cell (no amount of released neurotransmitter will have an effect if it can't latch onto a fitting receptor), and so on. Further, every cell that passes on its signal to another is competing with others to be heard. The receiving cell, for example, may be taking in signals from up to one hundred thousand others at its other docking points, all at the same time. Some of these signals will cancel each other out. One cell's signal may have more effect than another's of the same strength because it is nearer to the cell nucleus and thus has to push its charge less far to arrive at the axon. Some cells are richly endowed with receptors, so they will be highly sensitive to the neurotransmitters in their vicinity. Others will have few receptors – or the receptors may be desensitized. And there is some evidence to suggest that information may be passed on by a neuron without it actually firing.

Neuronal activity, then, is not straightforward. Information is passed on only after a large amount of internal computation has been done. In airship terms, this is equivalent to the internal cognitive processes of our zombies – complicated, but not itself conscious. In the end though, just as the zombie either articulates his message or not, a neuron either fires, or doesn't. And if it does, and the next neuron 'decides' to fire in response, the message is sent on along pathways from one part of the brain to another.

A single firing, however, is not likely to push much of a signal down the line. It is rather like a zombie giving a single squeak – the sound would be drowned out. To get the message thrust forward the neuron (like the zombie) needs to shout, and to do this it does not just fire once, but repeatedly and quickly. Further, it needs to be doing it with a fair number of others. And their shouts have to be synchronized – that is, they have to be firing at the same rate.

Neuronal firing rates vary from about 1 Hz (Hz is the number per second) to 250Hz.[2] Generally speaking the higher the firing rate, the more likely consciousness is to be present: in deep sleep firing in most parts of the brain is slow and regular, at about 1–2Hz (known as delta waves); drowsiness is marked by a rate of 4–8Hz (theta); relaxed awareness is 8–12Hz (alpha); and diffused attentive awareness is 18–30Hz (beta). However, in addition to these overall oscillation rates, small areas of the brain may show intensive activity, known as gamma rate oscillation. The rate of firing in these averages about 40Hz.

Generally, the higher the firing rate of neurons and the more brain modules engaged in this activity, the 'fuller' the experience. But it is not simply a matter of more excitement + more synchrony = more experience. Epilepsy is a state of exceptionally high neuronal excitement and in severe cases

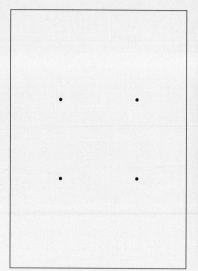

A B C

Complexity

A picture (A) with a few regularly spaced dots does not convey much – you could write down the information it contains on your thumbnail. And an image consisting of very dense randomly packed dots (B) is meaningless. However, if you take out some of the dots so there is a heavy contrast between the areas 'with-dots' and the areas 'without-dots', then you get something more informative (C).

If consciousness is information, the more there is of it, the more conscious we should be. However, the amount of information in a system is not just dependent on the amount of activity in it – it also depends on the way it is ordered.

The maximum amount of information resides in the middle range between regularity and randomness. The technical term for such states is complexity.

Brain activity is probably that type of complexity known as chaos. Chaotic systems are those which are extremely sensitive to initial conditions: a tiny change in input can have dramatic effects on outcome. Hence, in the brain, it is possible that a single firing of one neuron (among billions) at a critical moment could cause a shift in the entire system, producing a brain state (and behaviour) that seems entirely unpredictable. Anyone seeing the results of such a shift from the outside would reasonably conclude that it happened spontaneously or randomly – so it would seem to be free from the sort of rigid determinism that is seen in non-chaotic systems, like computers.

Chaos is not, however, random (the word is misleading). Over time chaotic systems produce semi-stable patterns of activity called 'strange attractors', which draw surrounding activity into harmony with them. An example is the

Right: fractals are patterns which look the same however much you zoom in or out of them.

swirling pattern you get when water goes down a plughole. The harmonization of neural activity may also be an example of this. Researchers have found that a computer model (neural network) of a brain, programmed with the average electrical potential between the outside and inside of neurons under differing conditions, produced a pattern very similar to alpha brain waves.[1]

Chaotic systems create patterns known as fractals. These are structures in which the overall shape is identical at every scale, like a set of Russian dolls. Brains have a fractal composition in that its major specialized processing 'modules' (visual, auditory, etc) are made up of hundreds of even more finely specialized mini-modules, which in turn are made up of yet more specialized neurons. The neurons themselves are now known to be 'mini-brains', and perhaps one day the mini-brains within them will be found to be made of even smaller 'brains' – and so on. Going up the scale, it is recognized that many individual brains create behaviour that is like one giant brain (think of bees in a hive or termites in a colony). In turn these group minds may be part of some greater consciousness – a universal mind.

[1] David Liley et al, *Chaos*, 11, (2001), 474.

inter-connectivity may be almost total, with activity spreading like a forest fire to create synchronized hyperactivity across the whole brain. Although mild, localized epileptic seizures do seem to increase the intensity of experience, the major episodes block it out altogether. There seems, then, to be a fairly narrow range of neuronal excitement which supports consciousness.

The idea that gamma waves underlie consciousness has been heavily championed by Francis Crick, the biologist who (jointly) won the Nobel Prize for the discovery of the structure of DNA, and his colleague Christof Koch. Many studies have found that 40Hz activation is detectable in the human brain whenever a subject reports conscious experience. Further, the brain areas which show 40Hz activity at any time correspond to those which are thought to produce the type of contents which a person will report. When we are generally alert – that is, fully awake and aware of what is going on but not concentrating on anything in particular – many different areas of the brain oscillate around the 40Hz mark. However, when we narrow our attention to just one thing there is a general drop in brain wave frequency across the brain, while those brain areas concerned with the object of attention remain at around 40Hz. If you are lost in the dark and hear a rustle in the bushes, for example, the areas of the brain which are concerned with picking up information from the senses fire at 40Hz while other areas fall quiet, producing oscillations in the region of 15–30Hz. It therefore seems that gamma-rate oscillations indicate brain areas which are actively 'in use', while slower oscillations are associated with those which are temporarily off-line.

It is tempting to infer from this that 40Hz brain activity *is* conscious experience – or that it is all that is required to produce it. But (of course) again it turns out not to be so simple.

Experiments (including some by the Crick/Koch team) show that 40Hz activity is almost certainly not enough, alone, to determine consciousness. Anaesthetized cats, for example, whose eyes have been propped open so that light information continues to enter their brain, have been shown to have synchronous 40Hz firing in the visual cortex despite being (presumably) unconscious. 40Hz brain waves also occur in people when they are anaesthetized. Again, they do not seem to signify consciousness – not, anyway, reportable consciousness.

They do, however, seem to signify a state in which people absorb information, and are subsequently able to put it to use. In one experiment researchers played a tape of the story of Robinson Crusoe and Man Friday to a group of anaesthetized patients, while at the same time recording their EEG.

Some of them showed 40Hz wave-forms, and further experiments found that these patients, though not the others, had 'taken in' the taped story while they were on the operating couch. However, their memory of the story was not conscious – it only came to light when they were asked to come up with associations to the word 'Friday'. Seven of the patients who had shown 40Hz activity responded with 'Robinson Crusoe' whereas those who had not exhibited this form of activity failed to came up with the name. The memory was therefore implicit – able to affect behaviour, but not itself conscious.[3]

There are many ways of interpreting flutters of 40Hz activity in the brain when people appear to be unconscious. One explanation – impossible to prove or disprove, as discussed in chapter one – is that they do produce consciousness but the memory of it is erased almost immediately and is never therefore reported. Another suggests that consciousness is a little like a dimmer switch – it can be so low that you don't notice it. But that, of course, is paradoxical – if you aren't conscious of being conscious then you aren't conscious! A third is that consciousness can 'float free', in the sense that it can occur without being 'owned' by the person. It is as though micro-consciousnesses, little sentient beings, can arise which have no expression because they have no 'self' to attach to. But that, of course, only pushes the question back. For each micro-consciousness to be conscious – even to itself – it must presumably create a self system to own it! As we shall see in chapter eight, in some people micro-selves, complete with their own experience, and unknown to the person in whom they reside, do seem to exist. But they are almost certainly created by more complicated cognitive processes than an isolated patch of 40Hz activity.

A fourth interpretation – and the one that I think is most likely – is that 40Hz activity marks information processing which has the potential of becoming conscious, providing it is 'doubled-up' or re-presented at a higher level. So, for example, an island of 40Hz firing in the sensory cortex is the first-level representation of a sensory event which will be one of the 'contents' of consciousness if – and only if – it triggers further 40Hz activity in a part of the brain which produces higher-order or 'whole' perceptions and/or concepts.

If, for example, there was a flurry of 40Hz activity in the sensory area charged with discriminating red, it would be red 'knowledge', similar to the knowledge of your feet on the ground. That is, it would be capable of informing action. You shift your feet to accommodate your weight without necessarily being conscious of the minute sensation changes in your heels which direct the movement. Similarly the red knowledge may prompt you to brake. But it only becomes conscious when it is represented at a higher level as a concept –

Backing up to Consciousness

The 'elements' of a visual perception – the form, colour, location and motion of an object – are processed in separate brain areas. When the main motion-detecting part of the brain (V5) is stimulated, for example, people get a conscious sensation of movement, even if there is no moving object in view. You can experience this for yourself: if you look at a waterfall, or a similar moving image, when you look away you continue to sense movement around you, even though the scene is now still. This is because the V5 neurons take a little time to calm down. Certain still images, like this Bridget Riley painting, also get V5 neurons firing, giving the illusion of movement.

Bridget Riley, *Cataract 3*, 1967.

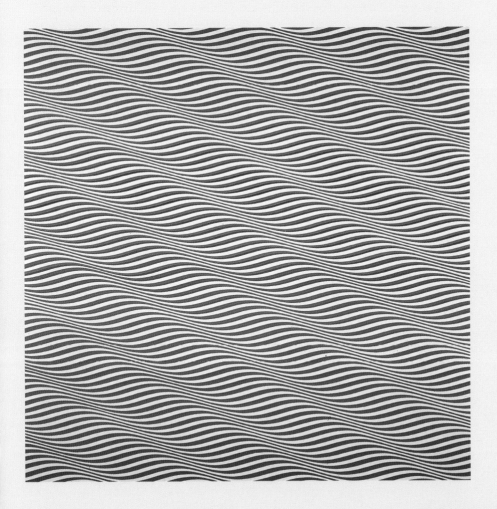

Conscious movement perception does not seem to arise by V5 activation alone, however. Rather it requires that V5 is 'backed-up' by input from the primary visual area, V1.

One theory holds that V1 has specialized 'awareness-dedicated' neurons, which have to be activated before other areas distinguish what the awareness is of. Studies show, however, that the 'higher' visual areas (such as V5) send information back to V1, as well as receiving from it – and there is some evidence that such feedback is necessary for it to be made conscious.

A study by Alvaro Pascual-Leone and Vincent Walsh tested this hypothesis using Transcranial Magnetic Stimulation (TMS).[1] TMS involves sending a brief magnetic pulse through a spot on the skull and into the cortex beneath, where it disrupts the local neuronal activity. If a pulse is directed at V1, for example, a person who is consciously perceiving a visual image at the time will experience momentary loss of that image. If V1 is inactive however, they will experience flashes of light caused by random activation of some of the cells. Similarly, if the pulse is directed at V5 they will experience momentary disruption of visual motion (if they are looking at a moving image) or moving flashes.

Pascual-Leone and Walsh first applied TMS to subjects' V1 area, followed a few milliseconds later by a pulse to V5. As expected, the subjects saw moving flashes. The researchers then reversed the experiment – applying TMS first to V5 and then to V1. The gap between pulses was varied within a time-range calculated to include the length of time taken for signals from V5 to feed back to V1. The idea was that the disruption to V1 would prevent that area from picking up the V5 signals and – if such pick-up is essential for conscious vision – the subjects' awareness of movement (conveyed by the V5 signals) would be wiped out. Sure enough, over the course of the experiment all eight of the subjects reported that, when the gap between pulses was set at a certain length (between 25 and 45 milliseconds), the flashes were stationary.

This study suggests that feedback from 'higher' brain areas occurs at all levels – as though neighbouring areas talk back to one another as well as sending their messages onwards and 'upwards'. And it is this ceaseless, internal chatter that gives rise to subjective awareness.

When this is absent, as in blindsight (see page 19) a subject is able to act in relation to a moving target, but only if prompted, and – according to their own description of the experience – without any normal sense of movement.

[1] 'Fast Back Projections from the Motion to the Primary Visual Area Necessary for Visual Awareness', *Science*, 292, 510–512.

perhaps embellished with associations of blood and traffic lights. Concept and knowledge together translate into the feeling of red – a quale.

By this interpretation, the islands of 40Hz recorded in the anaesthetized patients who were played the tape of *Robinson Crusoe* were those which represented the story – or parts of it – and thus guided their actions when they were asked to come up with associations to Friday. But because it was not re-represented at a higher level (due to the anaesthesia 'turning off' the higher areas of the brain) they were not conscious of it.

In terms of the airship, 40Hz activity, then, is the equivalent of the particular type of shouting which has the potential to spread through the whole ship. It is loud enough, organized, and coherent enough to be heard. The things that become conscious are transmitted in this form – but so are many things which are not destined to become conscious. So, for example, a cloud may bring about an 'island' of shouting by 'white-watching' and 'fluffy-spotting' zombies which could – and might – influence the way the pilots steer the ship. But unless the cry was taken up by passengers in other parts of the ship, it would remain unconscious.

Back to the brain. What are the neuronal equivalents of the passenger groups that must be alerted to potentially conscious activity in order to make it actually conscious?

One clue is to consider what conscious perceptions are like. If you see an object (consciously) it appears as that – an object. The pen on my desk, for example, is a stick-like thing with a sharp point and a transparent barrel through which I can see a thinner black stripe. Furthermore it is lying in a particular place on the desk, pointing in a particular direction. I do not see these components as separate 'bits' of awareness – a shape, plus a colour, plus a location, orientation and so on, but as a whole perception.

What is conscious then, is not the initial brain representation of the pen – that is just lots of bits due to the splitting and relaying action of the sensory organs and thalamus, but the re-representation created by the areas of the brain that bind the bits together.

You might think that we could be conscious of a whole such as this by virtue of the fact all the bits are being processed at the same time. But this doesn't quite work because, although there is an overlap, the elements are processed sequentially – the form of an object, for instance, is distinguished before its colour and orientation. Indeed, if you look at the processing of a visual image in the brain you can actually see how the information 'sweeps' forward through the various sub-regions of the cortex – by the time the colour

Constructing Consciousness

When we look at something we do not see its colour, its form, its position and its motion in sequence – the information comes as a whole, even though the brain initially processes each of these elements separately. This 'binding' of facts is done by the various brain modules, which process each element by pooling their information through synchronization. When 'pink-reporting' neurons fire in time with 'form-reporting' neurons you get a pink-shaped experience; when they in turn synchronize with 'up-above-reporting' neurons, and they all join with 'motion-reporting' neurons, and then 'leftward-reporting' neurons join in too, you get a pink-shape-moving-left-above-you experience. If the frontal lobe modules join in too, and bring in temporal neurons which encode matching pink-shaped memories, you get a recognition experience: 'pink balloon'.

If any of the pathways between these interconnecting brain areas are blocked then the things we discriminate with our senses cannot be pulled into a single perception. If the sub-regions of the visual cortex are not fully in touch with each other, for example, you may get bizarre effects such as the colour of a thing appearing in a different place from its shape. If the blockage is between, say, the visual sensory area and the memory or speech area you may get a condition called agnosia, in which a person can see a thing perfectly well, but be unable to recall what it is or to name it.

The more complex the thought or perception the more modules need to exchange their information to form the whole of it. If you catch a glimpse of a house, for example, the sight will trigger activity in several different areas of the visual system – those which processes form, colour, location and depth. The concurrent activation of these brain areas bind these elements into a coherent image, so you see the house as a whole rather than, say, a boxy shape and the red of the brick. You only know it's a red house, though, when the areas of the brain which hold the concept of a house also come into play. And you can only name the item as a house when the area which encodes the word becomes activated. In addition to this, these various areas must be activated together for long enough – up to half a second – for the perception to be laid down in so-called 'working memory', the area of the brain which combines various aspects of an item of consciousness. So in order to see, recognize and label a house, the brain needs to synchronize several visual and spatial processing areas such as colour, form and location, along with recognition processing areas, language areas – and finally, working memory.

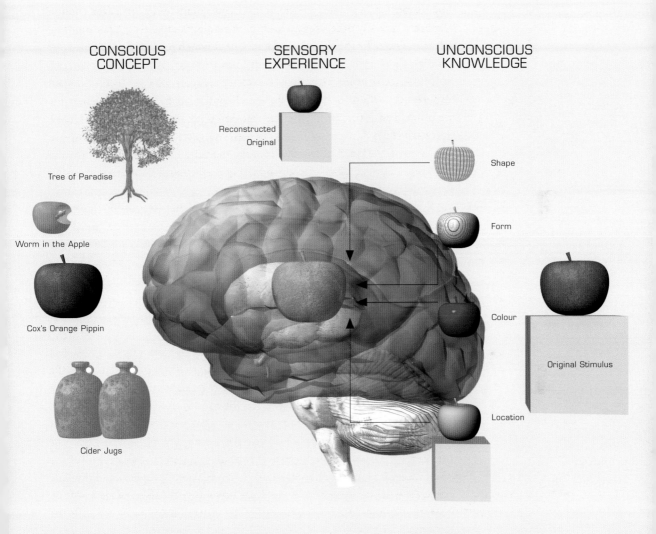

CONSCIOUS
CONCEPT

SENSORY
EXPERIENCE

UNCONSCIOUS
KNOWLEDGE

Tree of Paradise

Worm in the Apple

Cox's Orange Pippin

Cider Jugs

Reconstructed
Original

Shape

Form

Colour

Location

Original Stimulus

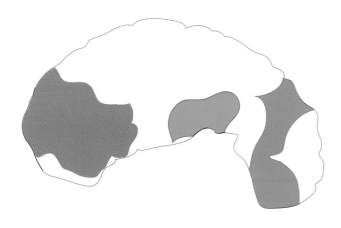

area is alight, activity is already fading in the primary visual cortex.

Conscious perception, then, is not of these first-order representations. Yet nor does it seem to be *just* of the higher-order re-representations that follow. The 'knowing of knowing' requires both the higher-order representation and the lower-order representation to be present in the brain at the same time, or at least close enough in time for them to merge. Going back to the airship: the shouts of the window-seat zombies alone are not enough to produce consciousness, and nor is the interpretation of those shouts by the interior passengers. It requires both at once.

To achieve the equivalent of this in the brain it requires that the primary cortices are active even when their message is being interpreted in the association cortices. Yet, as we have seen, the initial activation in primary cortices is already fading by the time the association cortices represent it. So how do both levels of shouting come to exist together?

Working memory is the brain function that holds different ideas in mind for a short period, either to put them to use in action (e.g. to hold a phone number for long enough to dial it), or to compare and juggle them to work out an action strategy. Working memory is located in the frontal lobes (red) but draws on verbal memory (blue) and visual and spatial memory (green).

The answer seems (again) to be feedback. In the visual area, for example, the region at the very back of the brain, known as V1/V2, is where visual information is first received. The neurons here do little more than discriminate between light and non-light in a particular area of the visual field. Then, about 20 milliseconds later, other visual areas receive this basic information and make further discriminations such as orientation, colour and motion. Recent studies using TMS (Transcranial Magnetic Stimulation) suggest that the information from these 'higher' visual areas feeds back to V1/V2 and reactivates these areas (see 'Backing Up To Consciousness', page 127). It is only when this replay of the initial stimulus occurs that the colour information is fed forward to consciousness. A conscious perception is therefore both a brain state (concurrent activation of neurons at many levels) and a process – a recursive bottom-to-top then top-to-bottom sweep of activity which merges parts and meaning into a whole object.

The time taken by our brains to become conscious of a simple visual perception is about one-tenth to one-fifth of a second. This is just the time it takes for the first activation sweep to travel to the association areas towards the front of the brain. A number of studies show that conscious states are accompanied by activity in association areas whereas non-conscious but otherwise comparable events activate the sensory cortices only.[4]

It seems then, that the association cortices are where consciousness 'happens'. Yet these areas are huge in humans, and within them there doesn't seem to be one final 'finishing' line at which a perception pops into awareness.

How to explain this untidy state of affairs? One way is to think of the contents of consciousness as different layers of complexity or 'wholeness', each of which emerges at a different stage of construction and in a different area of the brain. So my consciousness of the pen on my desk may indeed first arise when my brain has merged all its visual elements into a single image in the visual association area. And that's where it might stop – producing a fleeting snip of visual perception, instantly forgotten.

Alternatively it might go on to become something richer. Instead of just being aware of the pen as a visual object, I might also become aware of what it is called – a pen. I might be aware of it as a particular pen – the one I was looking for a few moments ago, say. And if it was the only pen in the room and I urgently needed to note down a phone number it might be charged with a frisson of emotion such as relief.

What is happening in my brain is that neurons in the association areas receive from the various neurons charged with visual processing the sum total of visual information relating to the pen – its shape, form, colour, position and so on. But these neurons are not concerned with what it is called, or that it is needed to jot down a number. All they 'know' is the concrete image, and it is this they represent in their firing, singing out the message, much like the airship zombies.

In the absence of other information relating to the pen, their chorus might engage enough fellow-singers to become fleetingly conscious. But the perception thus generated would be a rather pitiful little thing – just an image, with no thought attached to it and no way for it to be encoded in memory. Let us suppose, though, that their shouting occurs in conjunction with other mutterings about pen-related things. Say there is a little group further forward whispering: 'Where is that pen?', or a gaggle shouting about the need to note down a phone number before it is forgotten. When these groups hear the shouted visual description they do not ignore it, as they might if it was a shouted description of, say, the stapler that is lying next to the pen. It resonates with their own interest, indeed it is central to their interest, and it duly affects them. The visual image of the pen is therefore incorporated into their own chorus – indeed, they all get together to sing something along the lines of

'Hooray! Here's the pen. Now we can note the number!' It would be a rich, sophisticated 'bit' of consciousness – a visual image clothed with emotion, thought and a plan.

It figures that if this scenario matches what happens in the brain, complex thoughts would take longer to come to consciousness than simple sensory perceptions, because they would involve more 'constructing'. And experiments suggest this is so. Whereas a simple image becomes conscious in about 200 milliseconds, complex images take almost half a second to emerge. You would also expect to see a parallel between the level of complexity of a 'piece' of consciousness, and its place in the construction chain. And you do. Roughly, the more complex the perception, the further forward in the brain the neural activity relating to it extends.

One way of considering a conscious 'object' then, is to think of the cognitive process as an assembly line in which raw components go in at the bottom and finished perceptions pop out at the top. The line may be short, resulting in a simple object; or long, resulting in a rich and complex one, laden with meaning. But if we are conscious of something, it is always the highest-level representation of it, not the lower-level ones which went into its making. The back rooms of the brain are always closed to us.

According to this 'consensus' version of consciousness, the objects that are constructed into the contents of our consciousness compete for their status in a process which is similar to natural Darwinian selection. Our brains are like mini-ecospheres, designed to favour the amplification to consciousness of knowledge which has most survival benefit for the system as a whole. This is knowledge of the most salient features of both its internal environment and that of the world beyond. Although the objects themselves arise by a competitive process, the system as a whole is essentially passive.

There is a problem though. This is not how it feels. I, the 'system' known as Rita Carter, feel as though I am the active generator of my consciousness, not the passive recepticle in which it emerges. I feel as though there is me and the things I am conscious of ... and that this 'I' is what decides what those things are. I can 'turn my mind' to things I want to consider, I don't have to wait for them to 'pop up'. I can zoom in on one thing, or relegate it to the back of my mind. And these things very often do not seem to have any 'survival benefit'. What benefit was there for me in the little daydream I had half an hour ago about a summer picnic in a buttercup field? As far as personal survival is concerned I would have been better off writing another couple of paragraphs of this book. And, if conscious objects are triggered by environmental stimuli,

Imagination

Imagination seems like a dim version of perception – if you close your eyes and summon up a picture of the scene it may feel as though you are really seeing it. But this is not the case. You cannot read out an image precisely, as you could a real scene and the reason is probably because what you are doing is generating the experience from the 'top down' without the back-up of incoming information to solidify it.

When people track an external image with their eyes – following the curve of a circular object, say – their eyes hug the contours and move smoothly. This is probably because the image is generated almost wholly by the visual cortex, which is closely connected to the mechanisms which control eye movements. The reciprocal flow of information from visual cortex to the eyes works like a guidance mechanism, locking sight onto the image and so allowing very close tracking.

However, when people close their eyes and follow the contours of an imaginary circle, their eyes progress in the jerky movements known as saccades.[1] This suggests that the imaginary circle is not wholly, or even mainly, generated by the visual cortex, but by direct activation of the association areas where concepts are stored. The image produced is thus both less vivid and more difficult to track.

[1] Stephen LaBerge, report to Towards a Science of Consciousness conference, Tucson, 2000.

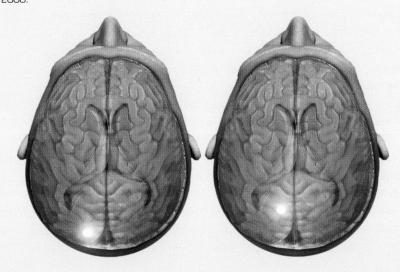

The images show difference in brain activity when a person imagines a letter written very small (left), and the same letter written in large type (right). The 'blip' of activity in the visual cortex that encodes the smaller image is further back and smaller than the blip encoding the larger image. A similar difference in location and size of visual activation would be expected if the person was looking at an external image, but the level of activity would almost certainly be much higher.

Backrooms of the Brain

The skills of autistic savants – people who can, for example, do fantastically complicated sums in their heads or draw perfect reproductions – may be due to a 'breakthrough' of low-level brain processes that remain unconscious in normal people. If this is correct, the reason we can't all display these extraordinary skills is because our conscious faculties are employed with things that matter more.

If asked to compute some enormous sum, say 1,541 x 2,306,754, and then square it, each of us may 'do' the calculation at an unconscious level, but our 'higher' or 'executive' brain functions filter out the result before it becomes conscious. Effectively, our brains say 'What do we want to know that for?' – decides that we don't, and bars its way to consciousness.[1] Similarly, when we look at a house, for example, it may be that we register each crack in every brick, every shadow, perhaps even every molecule of its structure. Monitoring of individual neurons in the visual cortex has shown that some neurons respond to patterns that are much finer than anything we usually 'see' consciously.

Can you find the smaller figure in the bigger image? Autistic people (if they are capable of the task at all) find it relatively easy because they see the world as separate fragments. Other people have to work harder to distinguish individual bits because they react to the image as a meaningful whole.

The savant artist Stephen Wiltshire can reproduce much of this intensely detailed information after a single glance, but most of us simply come away with an impression like; 'house', or 'Georgian house (nice)'. Or 'My house. Needs a lick of paint'. In other words, the things that make it to consciousness are those that we can (or could) do something with.

That this selection is carried out by the executive regions of the brain seems to be borne out by the fact that damage to the frontal lobes sometimes seems to allow the background processing to flood up to consciousness, as though a filter has been removed. Patients with a type of frontal lobe dementia have been found suddenly to develop an ability to access phenomenally detailed early memories.[2] And experiments in which normal people have had the frontal areas of their brain effectively 'turned off' temporarily, using a technique called Transcranial Magnetic Stimulation, have exhibited an ability to do various calculations and memory tasks that – though not quite as breathtaking as those shown by savants – is certainly much enhanced over their normal abilities.[3]

Right: the autistic savant artist Stephen Wiltshire drew fantastically complex and accurate drawings of buildings, sometimes after merely glimpsing them for a few moments. He did this drawing of Notre Dame when he was fourteen.

[1] Allan Snyder and John D. Mitchell, 'Is Integer Arithmetic fundamental to mental processing? The mind's secret arithmetic', *Proceedings of the Royal Society B*, 266 (1999), 587.

[2] Bruce Miller et al, 'Emergence of Artistic Talent' *Neurology*, 51, (1998), 978.

[3] Robyn Young, Flinders University, Adelaide, and Michael Ridding, Royal Adelaide Hospital reported in *New Scientist* (March 17, 2001), 7.

27th october 1988

notre dame.

Stephen Wiltshire

Binocular Rivalry

When you look at an image that conveys two rival concepts the brain is only able to be conscious of one at a time. The doodle to the left, for example, is either a rabbit or a duck – never both together. Similarly, if two rival images are presented to the brain, one through each eye, we are only conscious of one at a time, even though the visual information from both is entering the brain continuously.

This phenomenon – binocular rivalry – is used by neuroscientists to observe the difference in brain activity during conscious versus unconscious perception. In one study, a number of volunteers were shown rivalrous images – one red and one blue. The images were 'tagged' by flickering them at different rates – the flicker is reflected in the brain activity and therefore gave an objective indication of which image created which activity.[1]

Each image activated different areas of the brain, and all of these activations continued throughout the experiment. However, when the subjects reported that a particular image was 'now conscious', the activation associated with that one was found to be 50–85 per cent more intense than that linked to the 'unconscious' stimulus.

This adds to the evidence that consciousness is dependent on a relatively high level of relevant neural excitation. But it does little to help locate consciousness, because the scans showed that the active areas in each subjects brain was slightly different. This may be a reflection of greater general differences between individuals at higher levels of cognitive processing. Elementary brain functions – distinguishing colour, say – are reflected in near identical activity in all brains, but when cognition gets close to the threshold of consciousness it becomes more individual because it starts to involve learned concepts which are different in each individual.

[1] Gerald Edelman and Guilio Tononi, *A Universe of Consciousness* (New York, Basic Books, 2000), 56.

'Necker Cubes' (below) are ambiguous images. Cube (A) switches orientation while (B) changes from a flat shape to a three-dimensional one.

A
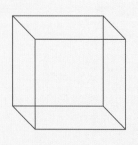

B
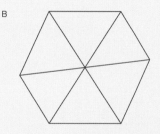

how is it that I can generate thoughts in a blackened, silent room; override incoming sensory data and imagine some other place entirely; or wonder about the meaning of zero, or of infinity?

Our ability seemingly to generate experience from the inside – to invent our world rather than merely to apprehend some external reality – is known as top-down processing. It feels as if it is a far more active process than simple perception of external events, much more something we do rather than something that happens to us. The conscious products of bottom-up processing require some shadowy self to 'own' them, but those produced by top-down processing need an active 'I' to create them – an 'I' that is not just a vehicle for consciousness but contains the raw materials that are needed to construct it. Where there is no sensory input it provides it. More wondrously still, it can construct abstract ideas – conscious objects that seem to be made of nothing that has roots in the concrete world.

The way that we constantly seem to create and live in a world of our own helps to fuel the intuition that our mental processes can float free of the material world. It seems at first to be compelling evidence for 'mind-stuff', a transcendent 'I' that directs the brain.

In the chapters that follow I shall try to show that this divide is illusory. Our awareness of the concrete world and the stuff of abstract thought is essentially the same: both are the result of both bottom-up and top-down processing. The difference between them is only that concrete perceptions contain more from the bottom – the raw data from outside – while abstract thoughts are more heavily informed by pre-existing concepts, most of which are themselves products of bottom-up processing.

To put it another way: bottom-up and top-down cognition are not two separate things but part of a single circular system: information from outside comes in and forms (or confirms) concepts that are lodged in the brain. These concepts then act as a lens through which the next things coming up from the bottom are interpreted. Sometimes there is so much interpretation that the conscious object that results appears to be completely devoid of the raw data that triggered it, rather like an abstract painting that at first sight seems to bear little or no relationship to its title.

Further, I suggest that the 'I' that owns perception and seems to generate thought, is itself created by the operation of deeply rooted concepts which transform our perceptions, moment by moment and year by year, into the narrative of our lives.

Colours and Categories

Colour is generally regarded as a property of objects in the world, or at least of the light that is reflected from objects. In fact there is no colour 'out there' – it is constructed by our eyes and brains. Light waves that are usually associated with 'green' for example, may be experienced as yellow or grey according to what else the brain is experiencing at the time, what it expects to see, and what it has just seen.[1]

This initial classification of a colour is made by retinal neurons. The brain then continues to sort the incoming stimuli into various colours according to a classification system which is partly innate and partly learned.

Imagine a band of colour blending smoothly from red at one end to blue at the other. Now imagine dividing the band into thousands of tiny slices, each one so thin that the difference between one and the next along is so slight as to be imperceptible.

Now think of a person naming the colour of each slice in turn, moving along the spectrum from one end to another. If they start at the red end, they would name the first slice, obviously, red. Then, because they would be unable to detect any difference between the slices, they would name the next one red too. And the next, and the next, and the next... Right up to the blue end.

In fact, of course, we don't do this. Rather at some point in the exercise we make a decision to switch colour categories. However, the decision would not be based on a *perceived* difference between one slice and the next because there would not be one – rather it would reflect a shift from one conceptual category to another. We don't *see* the dividing line between one colour and the next – we impose it.

Some languages divide the visible spectrum into many more colour categories than others. English speakers, for example, divide the colour 'space' (see right) into eight categories (red, blue, green, pink, purple, orange, yellow and brown), whereas the language of the Berinmo tribe, in Papua New Guinea, has only five colour names for the same range. But the difference between the two cultures is not just that they use different words for the same colour qualia – rather that they actually experience different things when they look at the same colour.

A study by Jules Davidoff, of Goldsmith's College in London, found that Berinmo speakers do not just have a relatively crude way of describing colour differences, they also perceive fewer distinctions.[2] This suggests that having a language-based concept for a particular colour may be necessary in order for us

to see it as distinct from another. It could be that the relatively impoverished colour lexicon of the Berinmo tribe reflects some difference in the colour part of their visual sensory cortex so that it is not equipped to make fine colour distinctions. An alternative interpretation is that the Berinmo have not developed the language-based concepts required to make the distinctions, so that although their colour neurons register subtle colour changes in the same way as English speakers, these changes are not represented at a higher cognitive level and therefore do not become conscious.

The globe represents the entire 'colour space' of the visible spectrum. English speakers divide it into more categories (above) than the Berinmo of Papua New Guinea do. Experiments suggest that the Berinmo actually see it differently (below). This may be because the Berinmo do not have the language-based concepts required to make the distinctions.

[1] For more see Francisco Varela, *The Embodied Mind* (MIT Press, 1999), 157–160; and Christine Skarda, 'The Perceptual Form of Life', *Journal of Consciousness Studies,* 6 (November/December 1999), 79–93.

[2] Jules Davidoff, 'Language and Perceptual Categorisation', *Trends in Cognitive Sciences,* 5:9 (September 2001), 383–387.

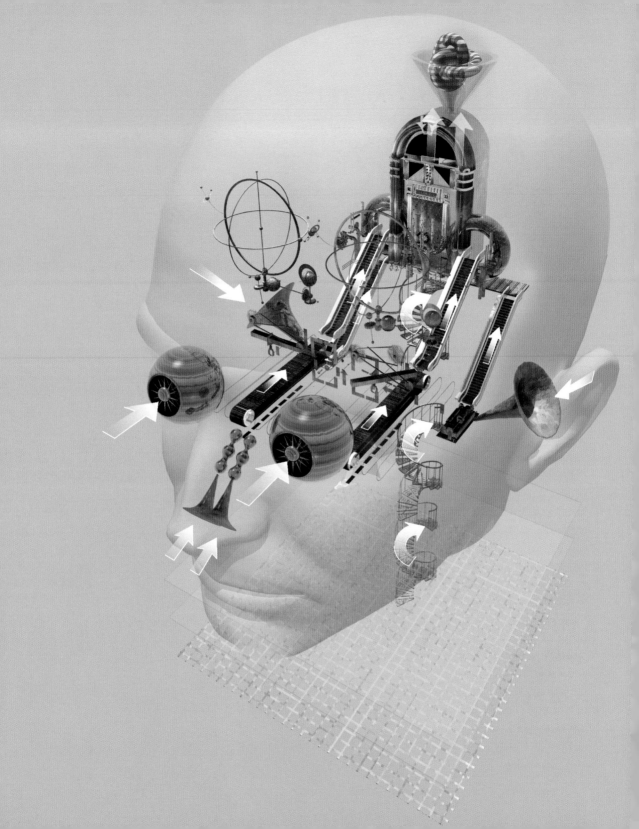

Consciousness and the Brain

'The beast does but know, but the man knows that he knows.'

From a sermon by John Donne (1628)

The human brain is not an empty vessel – right from the start it is packed with knowledge, some of which is built into its very structure. A newborn baby just knows, for instance, that crying will bring other members of the species to its aid – it doesn't learn it, or work it out. We know that objects that are far away look smaller than those up close, that the smell of rotting flesh is nasty, and a smile is more inviting than a frown.

Other knowledge accumulates, over the years, as we interact with the world about us. By adulthood we all carry a vast inventory of permanent or semi-permanent knowledge, some of it shared with more or less every other member of our species, and some of it peculiar to ourselves. It includes memories (personal and factual); ideas ('democracy is good'); symbols ('d-o-g' stands for things that go woof); prejudices and preferences. It also comprises know-*how*. At the most basic level our brains have the know-how to turn light waves and vibrations into 'objects' of consciousness such as visual perceptions. Later we learn to ride a bike, and to put one foot in front of another without falling over. These skills, like those which are 'built in', soon become automatic.

I am going to refer to all of this various mental 'furniture' as 'concepts'. In its ordinary sense a concept means an idea, so it may seem odd at first to use the word for, say, the activation of instinctive behaviour, or an event such as the firing of a particular pattern of neurons. But, in stretching the word to incorporate even very low-level automatic brain processes, I hope to show that active interpretation – which is surely a type of conceptualizing – goes right to the bottom of cognition, moulding everything from the most basic sensation to our most complex thoughts. Experience, even the sort that seems just to be the passive 'taking in' of information from outside, requires the exercise of knowledge which is already in our brains.

Concepts – in this broad sense – are essential for consciousness because they turn information into something meaningful, and the only things we can experience are those which have meaning. The source of that meaning is discussed in chapter six. Meanwhile, to give some idea of what I am talking about, look at the image to the left.

The chances are, that at first sight, all you will see are blobs of ink. If you are familiar with this sort of image (known as a Moody image) you will know that there is, in fact, a meaningful picture there, but even armed with this knowledge you may not be able to make it out. However, it is almost certain that you have in your brain a concept which, if activated, will make you see it. It can be encapsulated in two words, but before giving them to you (and assuming you have still not 'got' the image) I would like you to stay with the blobs a moment longer.

If it is impossible to be conscious of something without having a concept of it we must be bringing some sort of concept to bear on the blobby image – otherwise how could we see it at all? So consider what you are aware of. First, the image has a location – it is right there 30 centimetres or so in front of your face. It has a boundary – the frame which divides it from the page; and within the boundary it has a form, delineated by the contrast between the black ink and the white background. Being – as yet – without any 'higher' meaning, that's about it. What you see seems to be just 'given' – it doesn't seem to require any conceptualizing on your part to see it.

But is this correct? Take the matter of location. In order to see the image in that particular place you first need to have the concept of the bit of space that it occupies. Now you might think that such a concept is unnecessary because space is simply *there* – you don't have to invent it in your head before you can be aware of it. But this is not so. Our brains are primed to be aware of space – the parietal lobes contain a sort of spatial template closely associated with the body maps which grant us awareness of our bodies. This is the physical substrate of our concept of space, but what makes the concept effective is the activation of this part of the brain. And before it can make sense of space (that is, recognize that 'here' has a particular relationship to 'there' rather than just being different) the template has to be 'filled in'. Until then it is rather like having a map of a strange town – useless unless it contains an arrow saying 'you are here'.

We fill in our conceptual spatial maps by extending ourselves into the space around us, first using our bodies and later our senses – vision and hearing. Each of us carves out a slightly different mental space, so our inner maps are not a faithful representation of the spatial world, but an egocentric, idiosyncratic and plastic version of it. Indeed, our own idea of space changes over time. Most of us know what it is like to return to some childhood haunt and find that what we recalled as huge – a house or garden, perhaps – is actually quite small. This is because when we were small our 'carved-out' space was also small – and the things we saw in it (like a house) therefore filled a relatively large part of it. As we get bigger our concept of space expands with us, so when we return to a place we knew in childhood the objects in it take up proportionately less of our conceptual space and thus seem small. This shrinkage is a real, sensory experience – we don't deduce it, we feel it – because the concept that has changed is one that is deeply embedded in our bodies.

Because the idea of space is physically encoded in our brains, it is vulnerable to physical injury. Certain types of brain damage produce a condition known as neglect (see page 146) in which the individual loses awareness of one or another 'chunk' of space and, with it, awareness of any objects within that space.

One experiment that provides evidence for the need to move around in space in order to conceptualize it involved two groups of kittens. One was allowed to move around normally, but each of them was harnessed to a little carriage which contained a kitten from the second group. The ensconced animals had a perfectly good view of their environment as they were pulled around, but they were not allowed to explore it physically. When both groups were released, the 'carthorse' animals behaved normally, but those that had been in the carriages behaved as though they were blind: they bumped into objects and fell over edges.[1]

So, going back to the image on the previous page, the first thing you did in order to see it was to activate your concept of the area of space within which it lies. Having done that you were in a position to observe that it contained an object – which you duly did. To be precise you detected a boundary within which the image existed, separate from the space it inhabited on the page.

Now it is certainly true that the detection of that boundary was 'given' in that certain neurons (edge-sensitive cells in the primary visual cortex) were

Neglect

Merely 'seeing' the space around us is not enough to create the concept of it necessary for spatial awareness. We seem to need to 'carve out' a conceptual space for ourselves by acting within it.

The parietal lobes of the brain contain 'maps' which are designed to make us aware of our bodies and the space around them. The neurons that make up these maps are sensitive to location in relation to the body – that is, they are 'egocentric' – rather like the town maps that feature large arrows saying 'you are here'. Although these maps provide the physical basis for our concepts of space, they seem to need to be filled in by experience, and it is probable that an area of space does not really exist for us until we have established its existence in relation to our bodies by acting within it. Thus our concept of space grows outward, starting with 'personal space' (the area that we physically occupy), then extending to near space (that which we can extend our limbs to), and then far space (that which we can 'grasp' through our senses – by seeing, for example). Finally we gain the concept of space extending beyond our immediate knowledge and even – perhaps – the concept of infinite space.

The concept of all or any one of these 'chunks' of space may be lost if the neuronal substrate that encodes it fails to be primed by experience or is damaged. Injuries to the parietal lobes, for example, may produce a condition called neglect, in which people fail to acknowledge the existence of anything in a particular area – usually the left hemisphere. Such people typically leave uneaten food on the left side of their plate; ignore anyone who approaches them from that side, and may fail to use or even to dress the left side of their body. Although they are not literally blind to the left side of space, and the objects within it, their failure to acknowledge it makes them effectively so.

Neglect – or at least some cases of it – seems to come about when the parietal lobe 'map' of the neglected area fails to re-represent information about objects within that area which have been detected by visual neurons. It is, if you like, a failure to 'know that you know'. An experiment in which the

The brain divides space into at least three semi-independent categories: Personal space (the area immediately surrounding a person's body), reaching space (the area within which a person can grasp something by extending their limbs), and far space (the area beyond). Each one of these spaces may be 'erased' from a person's consciousness by neglect while leaving the others intact. Neglect has also been observed to affect the area below a person's natural sight level and the area above it. Most cases of neglect, however, affect one side of the visual field, a reflection of the failure of one hemisphere of the brain, but not the other, to conceptualise space.

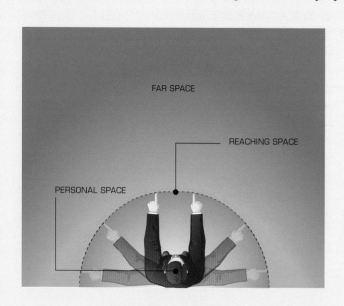

FAR SPACE

REACHING SPACE

PERSONAL SPACE

brain activity of people with neglect was monitored by EEG and fMRI shows that when the patients were presented with images in the neglected area of their visual field, neurons in the visual cortex were appropriately activated, even though the patients claimed not to see the image. Objects presented to the patients in the non-neglect area of their visual field (and which they reported being aware of) triggered similar activity, but in addition they generated activity in the parietal lobes and the prefrontal cortex.[1]

This suggests that what is missing in neglect is the higher-level representations of images – the information is in the brain but not reflected by the necessary higher-order thought or experience that brings it to consciousness.

The drawings (above) on the right are attempts by a patient with neglect to copy those on the left. The patient was unaware that they failed to complete the images, even when they compared the two sets of drawings.

The most common type of neglect involves the loss of one half of the visual field, but sometimes it is 'near' space (the area immediately surrounding the person's body) that is lost, or 'reaching space' (the area within the stretch of their limbs). Their ignorance of the 'lost' area is more profound than if they were blinded to it – it is not just that they can't see it, they don't realize it is there to be seen. Neglect is probably not caused by erasure of the concept of the neglected area of space, but by damage to the attention system, which then prevents people from activating the concept. Several studies have shown that – even in their mind's eye – the lost area cannot be accessed. For example, when a patient with left-side neglect was asked to describe an imagined walk from the south coast of England to the Scottish highlands, she named only the towns in the east on the way up, and only those on the west on the way down.[2]

[1] P. Vuilleumier et al, 'Neural fate of seen and unseen faces in visuospatial neglect: a combined event-related functional MRI and event-related potential study', *Proceedings of the National Academy of Science USA*, 98 (2001), 3495–3500.

[2] J. C. Marshall, P. Halligan and I. H. Robertson, 'Contemporary Theories of Unilateral Neglect, (1993). A critical review in Marshall and Robertson (eds.), *Unilateral Neglect: Clinical and Experimental Studies*, (Hove, Erlbaum).

Attention

Attention occurs when several areas of the brain lock in a circuit. One area is the cluster of neurons which process the object of attention. In the case of a visual image, for example, the neurons in the visual processing area at the back of the brain would be activated. Another area is the thalamus, which directs attention to the relevant processing area. A third is the part of the frontal lobes which deals with short-term memory. Attention also involves activation in the parietal lobe where we encode 'maps' of our bodies and our relationship to things in space. In visual attention the part of the parietal lobe engaged invariably matches the location of the object that is being attended to.

You can, up to a point, see where a person's attention is resting by identifying the brain modules which are engaged in synchronous, high frequency activity. A personal recollection, for example, triggers activity in the left hippocampus, where such memories are encoded. Finding your way around, by contrast, is associated with activity in the right hippocampus, which deals with memory of places.[1]

If you concentrate on the sight of something, activation will increase in the visual cortex, and if you are listening to music the auditory cortex will show higher activity.

Children have short attention spans because the frontal lobes of their brain are slow to mature, and children (and adults) with attention deficit disorder are particularly bad at focusing. We generally assume that 'lack of concentration' is a bad thing, but inability to switch attention when new stimuli arrive can be just as bad.

People with certain types of frontal lobe damage sometimes develop a condition known as perseveration, in which they are unable to disengage from current activity and shift their attention to something new. They get so locked in to a particular idea that they then cease to be receptive to new information.

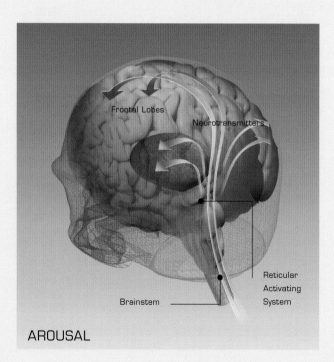

Frontal Lobes

Neurotransmitters

Reticular
Activating
System

Brainstem

AROUSAL

A psychological tool called the Wisconsin Card Test demonstrates the drawbacks of perseveration. The subject is asked by a researcher to sort a pack of cards marked with different coloured patterns, shapes and numbers, into two piles according to any categorization method they care to choose. They are told that they will be rewarded if they sort them correctly, but are not told how to go about it. Subjects usually start by sorting them according to colour or shape. At first the experimenter encourages them in this, telling them that they are doing well. But then she starts saying that the subject is getting it wrong – even though he will still be sorting the cards in the same way. Most people then switch their strategy and start sorting the cards according to another selection procedure. The experimenter again suggests that they are on the right track – then again switches to discouragement for no apparent reason.

Over many trials, it was found that the people who score best on this test are those who can switch strategy quickly in response to the experimenter's behaviour. Those who do worst are people who stick longest to a previously successful mode of behaviour. Attention therefore needs to be flexible as well as focused.

[1] Daniel Tranel and Antonio Damasio in Alan D. Baddeley et al (eds.), *Handbook of Memory Disorders* (Chichester, John Wiley, 1996), 35.

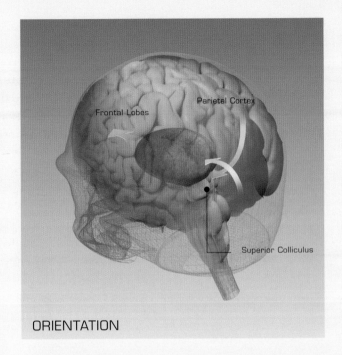

ORIENTATION

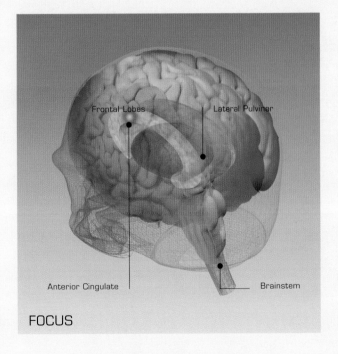

FOCUS

automatically triggered into action by the lines on the paper. But activation of cells in the visual cortex is not enough on its own to bring visual consciousness. People with blindsight show activation of neurons in the motion cortex when a moving object passes through the blind area of their visual field, but this does not make them aware of it. Cells in the primary visual cortex of anaesthetized cats fire in response to visual stimuli, but it is unlikely that they know about it. So to see the frame took more than just the activation of certain cells in your visual cortex – it required that you attended to it.

Attention is automatically triggered by more or less anything that stands out against its background either because it is unusual, emotionally salient (a familiar face, say) or exceptionally 'noisy' (e.g. it excites sensory neurons by its colour, motion or size). The 'concept' that directs attention to such things and therefore brings them to consciousness is that unusual or noisy things are likely to have some effect – to be a threat or to offer a reward. The Moody image is certainly big and 'noisy' enough to have captured your attention – at least for a moment as you turned the page. The body type on that page, by contrast, is unlikely to have done so. Rather, you would have noticed if it was not there, because that would be unusual. So what you were conscious of was your idea of words on a page, not the actual marks. They undoubtedly created some activity in your visual cortex, but this functioned more like an 'everything as normal' hum than an attention-grabbing alert ('Hey! Look at this – there are words on this page!'). Until your attention was turned to a few in order to decode them they might as well have been goobledegook. If you doubt it, try this: without taking your eyes off this paragraph, cover the bottom left-hand corner of this page with your hand. Now think – were you aware of the page number written there? A page number is a mark, as clear and defined as the marks that form the frame of the Moody image, and as you turned the page it almost certainly passed across your visual field and triggered a blip in your visual cortex. But were you conscious of it? If so – what was it? Were you right?

Assuming you have still not 'got' the picture, you will have seen the form merely as a 'blobby image' – and as such it might not seem to have any further concepts attached to it. It is not, for instance, describable, like a picture of a circle, or a photograph of George Bush. If you wanted to transmit an idea of it to another person in words you would be hard-pressed. Nevertheless, without realizing it you have imposed on it an idea – albeit a very primitive one – of what it is. The 'blobs' are the black bits are they not? So although you can't say what it is, you have decided that you are looking at a dark shape – or shapes –

against a white background, not a white shape against a black backdrop. You have interpreted it.

But this, you might object, is not an interpretation at all – the blobs really do have a particular form that is there, on the page. How could it be experienced in any way other than it is?

To answer that I invite you to consider what the image actually 'gave' your brain by way of stimulus. The picture is printed in monochrome on a flat piece of paper. If you run your finger over it you won't feel the edges of the blobs so you can't know its form by brushing against it or being grazed by its edge. All you get from it is visual information which consists of variations in the intensity of reflected light from the image falling on different parts of your retina. The light triggers the retinal cells to fire, more or less excitedly, according to how much light hits each one and this information is then sent to cells in the visual cortex where form-detecting neurons react to boundaries between light and dark. Both the cells in the retina and those in the primary visual cortex are mirror-like in that a bit of light information from a certain spot in the visual field excites a cell in an equivalent spot – indeed, you can scan a brain while it is detecting a shape and actually see it reflected in the activity of V1 cells.

So far, simple: the brain is just 'receiving' a given form. But the mental 'mirror' is not a simple reflective device like the one on your wall – it is an active, distorting one. Distortion number one occurs even before the light from the object hits the retina. Light passes through the lens on its way into the brain, and the shape of the lens determines how it falls on the light-sensitive cells behind. Distortion of the lens therefore creates distorted vision, as anyone with less than perfect sight knows. However, the shape of the lens is not fixed – it alters to accommodate far and near vision, to bring things into sharp focus or to allow us to see things clearly at a distance. This is generally regarded as an automatic process, but it is not dependent on the distance of the perceived object alone. The smooth muscles that alter the shape of the lens are also affected by the autonomic nervous system, which in turn is activated by emotional stimuli. For example, if your sympathetic nervous system is activated, perhaps by fear or anger, near images will seem fuzzy and indeterminate because the lens will become flatter.[2] Thus the signal from an image is edited even as it enters the eye – let alone reaches the brain – by pre-existing states of mind.

A further distortion is built into the architecture of both eye and visual cortex. Although the cells in both are arranged topographically, they are not evenly distributed – on both surfaces they are more densely clustered in the areas which detect light coming from the centre of the visual field. So when we look at something, although we may think we see all of it equally clearly, we are actually getting more information about its middle than its periphery.

Were you to move the image fast across your visual field the reflection of it in your brain would become even further divorced from reality – indeed, it would cease to be a reflection of the thing itself and become, rather, a representation of how your brain expects it to be a fraction of a second later. When a moving target passes across the field of vision it sets up a ripple effect in the visual cortex as edge-detecting neurons fire, one after another, along its trajectory. However, they do not fire when the edge passes across the bit of space they encode, but just before. Think of them as a line of people standing shoulder to shoulder in front of some malicious individual wielding a water pistol. This person starts to shoot water at the line-up, starting with the person standing to the far left and sweeping along the line. The first couple of victims flinch as the water hits them, upon which the third person flinches defensively – and the fourth does the same when the third person gets hit and so on ... If you were standing in such a way that you could only make out the reactions of the victims, rather than see where the water was actually hitting, you would conclude that the stream of water was one or two people ahead of where it really was. And so with a moving target – the brain responds 'as though' the object is passing across the space where it will actually be in a fraction of a second's time. If this response is then selected for consciousness the experience will therefore be of a 'virtual' object – not the actual thing at all.

Even at this most fundamental level, then, the brain is merely using 'raw data' as a cue to produce its own version of what is out there. Right from the start it is a re-presentation of reality – a guestimate of what is really there.

All of this, and much more, happens unconsciously (of course) – an initial representation is not the 'higher' representation that is conscious. Now let us see what happens when a higher concept is brought to bear on the unconscious representation so far constructed.

The concept that (I hope) will transform the Moody image from blobs to something meaningful is this: Darth Vader. Unless you have contrived to remain innocent of one of the biggest icons of popular culture in the last 25 years you will know what the Dark Lord of *Star Wars* looks like and – armed with that memory – his image will probably 'pop out' at you when you look again at the blobs on page 144. (If it doesn't, let me elaborate the concept by pointing out that the helmeted face is angled slightly to the right, with the light reflecting off the right side (left side of picture) and the left side in shadow. The character's left eye (right side of picture) stands out as a point of light.)

Assuming you have now 'got' the picture, consider the difference that has occurred in your consciousness of the image. The information coming from outside is exactly the same as it was before, yet your experience of it has changed. And I do mean your *experience* of it – it is not just that you now know that the image shows Darth Vader, nor do you just see it, even. Rather the addition of the concept has brought about a sensational difference – a real, felt, change in your awareness, typically known as the feeling of 'Eureka!' An extra 'object' of consciousness has come into existence.

Before considering how and why concepts convey meaning, let's look at how they come to be in our brains to start with. Concepts (in the sense that I use the word) are both mental processes and physical states. A personal memory, for example, involves the activation of a distinct (though constantly changing) neural firing pattern within a distributed system – a process. If you call up the last sight you had of your mother the brain areas which will probably be activated include the hippocampus, temporal cortex, and parts of the visual cortex. This combined activity is the neural correlate of the image you see in your mind's eye. But the memory also has a physical existence, of a sort, even when it is not being recalled. This is because the neural firing pattern correlating with a memory is largely preserved from recall to recall by physical linkages between the relevant cells. Each time a particular neuronal firing pattern occurs, the cells involved form stronger bonds between their axons and dendrites. In the case of long-term memories (the ones you 'relive' in recollection or hold as known facts) the neurons involved are located in the association areas in the temporal lobes. Although it normally requires systemic activation – that is, other areas, like the hippocampus or prefrontal cortex need to be active in order for these patterns to fire up – long-term memories can be triggered just by stimulating a cortical 'storage' area with an electrode. If you had a sensitive enough microscope and knew what to look for you might even be able to discern the shape of a memory, woven like a cobweb in the dense tissue of the cortex.

You could, then, consider the linkages between neurons or groups of neurons as unconscious concepts. When the neurons involved become active enough (firing, perhaps at 40Hz) and integrated with the general 'chorus' of activity in the brain, the concept becomes conscious. But if the firing rate remains low or if for some reason the activation remains separated from the

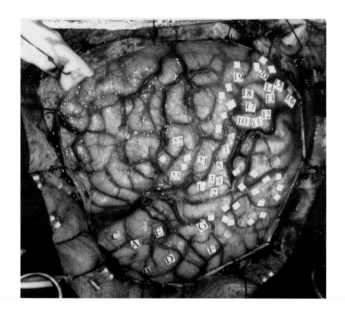

The Canadian neuroscientist Wilder Penfield discovered that fragments of memories can be triggered by stimulating certain spots on the cortex. Each number (above), shows the location of a particular experience elicited by Penfield's touch.

rest of the brain – an 'island' of 40Hz – it may influence behaviour without actually coming into consciousness.

Certain concepts run mainly at this subconscious level throughout our waking life. For example, the concept of our body needs to be 'switched on' in order for us to know that we actually have a body, and therefore to use it appropriately. The way that it remains 'on' is by being constantly stimulated by incoming sensory information. Some of this comes from outside – when we walk, for example, the pressure on our feet tells us how our bodies are interacting with the floor. But most of the information is proprioception – a constant stream of internally generated messages coming from our joints, muscles, and the movement detectors in our middle ear. This information impacts on the conceptual body and changes it from moment to moment, keeping our inner sense of our body lined up with what is happening to the real thing.

Rather like the victims of the water-pistol wielder, however, the concept is just a little ahead of the game. It takes the information coming in 'now' and uses it to construct a model of how our body will be in a fraction of a second. This is just the time it takes for the concept to become conscious, should it do so. Therefore when we become conscious of our body it seems that we are conscious of it in 'real time.' As we feel our weight shifting when walking from the pushing-off foot to the stepping one, for example, our body concept is altered to match how we expect it to be when the stepping foot hits the ground. Most of the time the prediction is so good that the real experience is more or less indistinguishable from our idea of it. Indeed, we don't have to take account of the external information at all because we have already incorporated its effect into our concept, which ticks along, getting us about, without becoming active enough to be conscious. However, if we put our foot down a hole and produce a sensory experience that clashes with the predicted concept of how our body is at that moment, the concept needs to be re-arranged very quickly. In order to do that the brain needs to extract as much 'real' information as possible in order to construct a more realistic internal model. At such times the neural representation of our body – caught in the act of incorporating new information into itself – becomes excessively active and flares into consciousness. Once the model is happily re-harmonized with the outside world it slips back into tickover mode.

The distinction between our conceptual body and the real thing is manifest most clearly in dreams or waking 'out of the body' experiences. In sleep the signals from the body that normally keep the two things closely yoked are blocked off, so our dream body is just our concept, uninformed by proprioception or external stimuli. Hence our experience of it can float free of the flesh, and do things (flying, for example) that the real thing is incapable of.

The most basic feature of our body concept is its boundary – where it begins and ends. Although the conceptual boundary is plastic in that, as in dreams, it can detach itself from the physical boundary, it is not easily breachable. We have a very, very strong concept of our bodies as whole, and it doesn't adapt easily. When someone loses a body part therefore, through amputation, it is very common for them to continue to feel it – the phenomenon known as phantom limb. When people with this condition say they can feel their lost arm what they are actually conscious of is the concept of that arm, which is still lodged securely in their brain.

Conversely, if the concept itself is partly lost, consciousness of the matching body part will be lost too. Stroke patients who suffer damage to the body map in their brain become partially paralysed either because the signal pathways between their real body and their conceptual one are broken, or because part of the body concept itself is wiped out. In the latter case, patients seem to lose not just feeling and movement in the affected 'real' body area, but also the sense of owning it. It becomes outside their body consciousness – an object 'out there' rather than an integral part of their selves.

The nearest to this that most of us experience is when we wake up to find that a limb or hand has gone numb. For a few moments, until the connection between body and body-concept re-establish contact and get back into line, the hand or arm feels as though it is no longer part of us.

The idea of our body – and the related concept of space – might seem to be the most deeply 'plumbed-in' concept we have. But in fact there is one that is even more taken for granted: that of time. Like space, it seems absurd to think of time as an idea – it seems just to be. But if that were the case – if time proceeds at its stately pace without any conceptual input – it would pass at the same pace for each of us, whatever our circumstances and whatever our brain states. And that is not the case. Even in common experience we find it does not

In a fast-changing environment, the body constantly acts on unconscious information. In one experiment subjects sat before three rods, one of which lit up in each trial. When the subject saw the light, they reached out to grasp the rod, saying 'tah' to indicate when they first saw the light come on. In some trials the light switched from one rod to another after the subject had started the hand movement. In each case the person made a smooth diversion to the new light halfway through the movement. In the 'switch' trials, the subjects made two exclamations – the first when they saw the first light come on, and another when they saw it change. When the timing of the spoken responses and the hand movements were compared it was found that the subjects began the diversion to the new target rod before they reported seeing the light switch. In other words, they changed direction before they seemed to know why they were doing it. 'On some occasions', say the experimenters, 'the dissociation between motor and vocal responses was such that subjects, to their own surprise, were already lifting the target rod when they emitted the vocal response.'[3]

milliseconds   100   200   300   400

▲ Start of movement correction   ▲ Awareness of light change

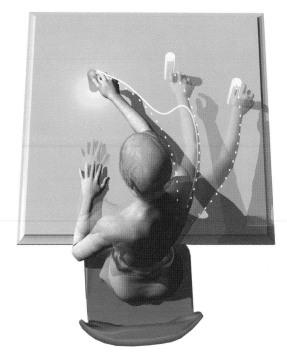

proceed smoothly. Anyone who has ever been involved in, or witnessed, a truly traumatic event, will know the sensation of 'time stopping still'. Conversely, when we are tired and struggling to do the things that need to be done in the day, time seems to fly past us, leaving us constantly in its wake.

Variations in subjective time are not usually great enough to affect our ability to function, but if the timing mechanisms in the brain are severely disrupted by illness the effect can be disastrous. The mechanism which produces the concept of flowing time is mainly fuelled by the neurotransmitter dopamine, which is the chemical that is depleted in Parkinson's disease. People with this condition commonly have a completely different idea of time to everybody else's. However, everyone else's idea of time is not necessarily any more 'realistic'. If you ask most people to say when – starting at a certain moment – they think a minute has passed, their answer, typically, will be to say 'now' after about 35 to 40 seconds (try it). Parkinsons' patients (without medication) are likely to be far closer to the real duration. This isn't much use to them, though, because in timing most things we refer to our idea of duration rather than the clock. 'Wait a minute' might mean a couple of seconds or half an hour, depending on the context.

The concept of time can be disrupted by damage to any part of the neural loop that comprises the brain's internal 'clock'. One 66-year-old man, for example, found as he drove to work one day that the other traffic seemed to be rushing towards him at terrific speed. That night he found he couldn't watch TV because things happened too quickly for him to keep up with them. When doctors tried the '60-second' test on him, he waited nearly five minutes before saying 'time up'. A medical examination revealed that the cause of the man's problems was a growth in his prefrontal cortex.[4]

Subjective time may even stop altogether. Damage to the basal ganglia and/or frontal lobes sometimes produces a state known as catatonia, in which people may become 'frozen', like living statues. Some seem to have been paralysed in mid-action, their hand outstretched as though to reach for something; or contorted into strange postures which they may hold – despite what would normally be severe discomfort – for days at a time. Although they do not appear to be conscious during this time, some patients have later reported that they had memories of it, but that their recollections lacked any sense of passing time and that their consciousness was utterly still, and devoid of possibilities.

A sense of timelessness – though starkly different to that of catatonia in that it seems full of possibility rather than empty – is also reported by people who reach a transcendental stage of meditation.

At the other end of the scale, people whose brains are suddenly thrust into overdrive experience an acceleration in subjective time, with a corresponding slowing of events in the outside world. This is what happens when excitatory chemicals flood the brain during terrifying experiences like accidents, or thrilling ones like a first parachute jump. Suddenly consciousness becomes very clear, with each tiny change in the environment noted and considered. Even when the experience is awful, there is an overwhelming sense of being alive.

Something similar happens when the brain's temperature rises and we experience the racing thoughts typical of fever-induced delirium. Experiments done on volunteers (before ethical constraints made such techniques impossible) found that putting heated helmets on people's heads to raise their brain temperature could speed up a person's subjective time by as much as 20 per cent.[5]

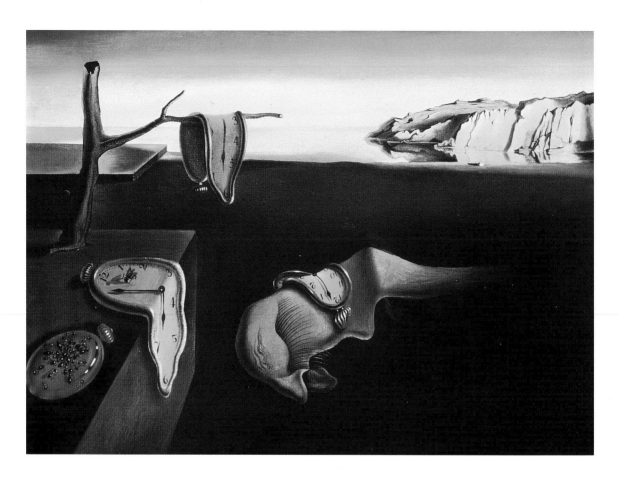

The Persistence of Memory
Salvador Dali, 1931.
Our concept of time is plastic –
sometimes the world seems to
come to a standstill, a feeling
captured by Dali in his famous
series of melting clocks.

The sharpening of consciousness experienced when the brain is excited gives a hint of how our concept of time dictates what we are aware of. Our normal idea of the present moment is equivalent to one of the 'temporal packets' or 'ticks' of the internal clock – typically around one-tenth of a second – and all the information we process during that window of time is experienced as happening simultaneously (see page 160). This is probably the optimum 'size' for making sense of things at a human scale. It means that when a cup falls off the table next to us we see the object hit the floor at the same time as we hear the crash, even though – as light travels faster than sound – there is actually a minuscule gap between the visual stimulus entering our brain and the auditory one. It also allows us to 'smear' time, fleshing out the subjective moment by squashing into it all the events that fall into a particular time packet.

The drawback, however, is that each of our moments is slightly blurred. When we watch the beating of a fly's wings, we cannot see each individual flap because several of them happen in each of our time windows. The result is that we see a fuzzy haze rather than a clear outline of a moving wing. If our subjective concept of time was more fine-grained, allowing us to split each moment into many more parts, we would see things more clearly. That we have not evolved to do so is probably because such clear-sightedness would burden us with more information than we need. After all, what advantage is there to discriminating the individual beats of a fly's wing? The things we need to be aware of most clearly are those that happen in seconds (animals moving or, today, cars bearing down on us) – not milliseconds. Just as there is no need for us to experience all the visual details that our brains detect unconsciously, time experience is most usefully cast in relatively broad brushstrokes. Only when we are faced with a situation, such as a life-threatening event or one which is wildly exciting, can we afford to ignore everything in the past and future and concentrate on the present moment. And when that happens our brains oblige by breaking the moment into more parts so each one can be separately scrutinized and dealt with.

Concepts such as time, space and body are absolutely fundamental – it is difficult to imagine any sort of consciousness which was not informed by them (though there may be such a thing – as we shall see in chapter nine). But they are not wholly installed at birth. Over time they are fleshed out by the emergence of concepts which have been preserved from generation to generation in the genes – instincts, in other words.

Many of our ideas about the physical world are instinctive, and given a normal environment they emerge more or less automatically as the parts of the brain that encode them become active. Visual concepts, shown by being able to see the illusory triangle on the right, for example, appear between the ages of six and eight months, and by 15 months babies know that objects are permanent and do not disappear from the world when they are hidden from their view.[6] Similarly we do not have to be taught to distinguish between distant objects and those that are close to us. Providing we are exposed to the normal range of visual stimuli, our brains will make sense of things like the difference in size between a near and far object without us having to take lessons in perspective.

We also have instinctive knowledge of how our bodies will interact with the environment and what that means. Fear of falling, for example, is evident even in a very young baby – if you ask one to crawl across a glass floor over a big drop

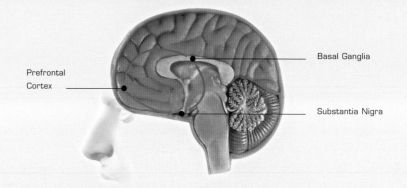

Prefrontal Cortex

Basal Ganglia

Substantia Nigra

The brain 'clock' is a loop of dopamine-generated neural activity which flows between the substantia nigra in the base of the brain (where dopamine is produced), the basal ganglia (a 'knot' of tissue around the thalamus), and the prefrontal cortex. Each 'tick' of the clock is the time it takes for the nerve signals to complete the loop, and all neural events that occur within that time are experienced as a single happening. The average 'tick' is about one-tenth of a second, and slower ticking results in time slowing down.

Time in Mind

Time is 'parsed' by the brain clock – split into packets, each of which comprises a single cycle of neural activity. The longer each cycle, the more external events get packed into it – so a person whose clock is running slowly is unable to make fine distinctions between events and feels that everything is 'rushing by'. It is rather like speeding up a film. The filmic effect is achieved by running a normal film fast, thus packing more frames into the same period of time. In the brain, the frames are external events, and the more of them that are packed into each subjective moment, the faster life seems to be passing by.

The neural activity cycle is fuelled by dopamine and when it is depleted the cycle rate slows. This neurotransmitter is also responsible for motivation, so slowing of subjective time (and the consequent speeding-up of external events) is often associated with feelings of apathy and depression.

Drugs which increase dopamine, or events that produce a flood of it, speed up the brain clock and time may then seem to slow down, giving a subjective feeling of clarity as an increasing number of events are discriminated.

Each 'tick' of the brain clock (a cycle of neural activity) is experienced as a single moment. Many events may actually occur within this packet of time, but they will be experienced as just one event. For example, if two flashes of light are presented to a person with a tiny gap between them (less than one-tenth of a second) they will see them as one flash only, providing the two flashes fall within a single cycle. If it happens that the flashes fall into two separate cycles they will be seen as two flashes, even if the time interval between them is the same.

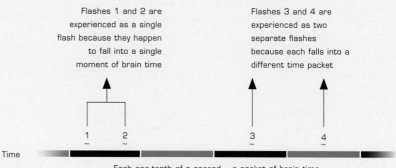

Flashes 1 and 2 are experienced as a single flash because they happen to fall into a single moment of brain time

Flashes 3 and 4 are experienced as two separate flashes because each falls into a different time packet

1
~

2
~

3
~

4
~

Time

Each one-tenth of a second = a packet of brain time

it will refuse, even if it is clearly keen to be reunited with its mother on the far side. The child does not have to learn that falling down a drop will be bad – it knows it instinctively

Genetically programmed knowledge, primed by a normal environment, ensures we can make sense of sensory stimuli at least to the point of turning it into the 'here and now' world of objects and events. But it is the 'fleshing out' of these perceptions through interaction with them that allows us to create rich and meaningful concepts. So how do we come to have these learned ideas – that dogs are hairy; ice-cream is nice; democracy is good; trees are beautiful; and space goes on for ever?

A child's brain is a little like picture B on page 122 – there's plenty going on in it, but the activity is more random, and as such is not as complex – in the strict sense of the word –

Our concept of perspective – that things that are further away look smaller – is unconscious. The figures above are actually the same size, but because we expect the furthest one to look smaller we assume, incorrectly, that it must in fact be bigger than the others to start with.

as an adult's. To return to the airship model outlined in the last chapter, it is rather like the passengers at the beginning of their journey – lots of them making small talk with lots of others but none of them as yet familiar enough with one another to discover common interests which allow a really interesting exchange of views or a concerted, synchronized chorus. It is, however, exquisitely sensitive – changed by and changing with every little stimulus.

At birth the brain modules that make up the limbic system are already fairly well-defined and many are already 'on-line'. The cortex, however, shows little activity – except in patches at the junction of the temporal, parietal and occipital lobes and parts of the somatosensory cortex.[7] These are the areas that encode the 'map' of the body, suggesting that this concept is already active, at least at an unconscious level. Within a few weeks, however, further brain areas come on-line, including parts of the primary sensory cortices and connections between these and the limbic areas.

In airship terms this is equivalent to some of the windows starting to flicker with information about blues and whites. The passengers near these windows start to wake up and exchange comments about these events. But they have yet to develop a common language, or even to sort out their proper seats.

Newborn babies already 'know' that a particular arrangement of features – those that represent a human face for example – hold special interest. Given the choice they will gaze at the top two face-like images on the far right rather than those at the bottom. The behaviour is not learned – babies have been shown to do this within an hour of being born.[8]

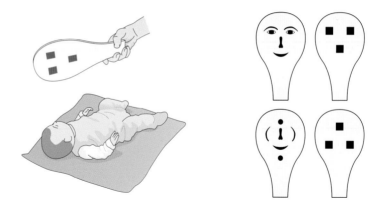

A blue-reporting zombie may send his signal to a zombie who is only able to understand white, so the message fails to be passed on. And even those messages that do get through cannot be placed in any context of time or space – not even the crude distinction between inside and out – because the passengers responsible for deciding all of this are still asleep. Nevertheless, slowly enough people on the inside of the craft strike up conversation to produce a representation of the fragmented information that is coming in – and with it comes the first flickers of awareness.

Such awareness is still likely to be very crude, however. It probably does not include any recognition of passing time because the prefrontal cortex (part of the neural loop which makes up the internal clock described on page 160) is

The number of connections between neurons increase with age as new things are learned. The neurons also extend further and further, to communicate with cells in far-flung regions, allowing them to 'pool' information and skills.

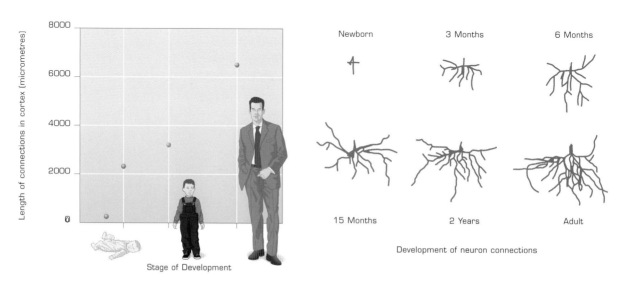

Development of neuron connections

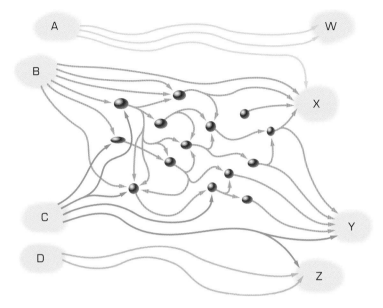

A W
B
X
C
Y
D
Z

Brain tissue consists of trillions of connections between billions of neurons scattered throughout the organ. The web of connectivity is incredibly complex, and at first sight the problem of working out how one group of neurons interacts with another seems hopeless. However, microscopic examination of the tissue, using dyes which mark the route of neural signalling between different areas, shows that the connections are very organised. The hugely simplified diagram (left) shows how axons from neurons in various brain areas (A to D) travel specifically to other areas (W to Z). Some make direct connections – like the wire that runs from a primitive 'telephone' made of two tin cans. Others go via a central network – like a telephone exchange. Some neuronal areas communicate only with one another (e.g. D to Z) while others send signals to multiple destinations (e.g. B to X and Y). Some of these connections are created by experience, but others are dictated almost entirely by genetic factors. These 'hard-wired' connections produce the experiences and behaviours that are common to all members of a particular species, while the learned connections are responsible for individual differences.

not yet active. And the spatial maps have yet to be 'filled in' by physical exploration. So a baby's experience is probably that of pure qualia in which the baby melts into its all encompassing, timeless sensory universe. Furthermore, the qualia are probably quite unlike those that we know because the cortical sensory regions, which cast adult perceptions in the familiar moulds of sounds and sights, are still being formed, and the brain regions have not yet become fully specialized for their tasks. A neuron which is destined to distinguish red, for example, may be connected to a neuron which distinguishes a certain tone. So when the red neuron gets excited, it may transmit its signal to the tone neuron, and the resulting experience will be a mixture of red and tone. This compound sensation is known as synaesthesia, and it is quite likely that an infant's inner world is synaesthetic to the point of being a holistic cacophony rather than a place of colour and sound, taste, touch and smell.[9]

The structuring of this sensory onslaught into definite sights and sounds (and later into objects) is produced partly by genetic determination – the equivalent of the airship passengers finding their rightful seats – and by the gradual rationalization of brain connections through learning. Unprofitable communication channels (like the pathway between the red and tone neuron) fizzle out while those which help create a realistic representation of the outside world are strengthened. It's a bit like pruning a bush to produce a neat shape, or taking out some of the dots in a random display to reveal an image.

Concepts – like 'dog' - are probably not stored in a single patch of brain tissue that could be snipped out. Rather, the different aspects of the concept – visual, functional, emotional, etc. – are each held in a different place.
It is rather as though a concept is a costume – a witch's garb, say: the conical hat is kept in the hat box, the cloak in the wardrobe, the broomstick in the cupboard ... and so on. To retrieve them the brain connects each bit and pulls them together.
Certain concepts may be stored almost entirely in one area because all the elements of them are of one type, such as visual or functional. The concept 'scissors' would have some parts of it stored in the visual compartment, but most of it would probably be in the area concerned with handling and using objects, because scissors are primarily for use rather than for looking at. The 'dog' concept, by contrast, would be mainly stored as a visual concept, with a few elements – those related to stroking – in the 'handling' department.
This theory fits with brain-imaging studies, which show that people activate many different areas of the brain when they access a concept.

For every useless connection that is pruned away, however, many new ones are made. These connections build up to form the physical basis of our learned concepts.

In a baby, each concept begins as a tiny 'seed' of sensory experience. The concept of a dog, for example, is probably no more than a particular sensation – the waft of hot doggy breath or a big moving shape. But over time it becomes more and more complex. The doggy sensation becomes 'furry thing that goes woof', and then grows to be hugely elaborate, incorporating ideas about different breeds of dog, the history of dogs, the affectionate or aggressive behaviour of dogs and so on. It may also be linked to other concepts: dog days and dog fights; doggy bags and dogged people; dog rose and dog-ends, so that when any one of these ideas crops up it drags with it a whole host of associations.

Most of the things that happen to us get forgotten almost as soon as they occur. But some of them stick in the mind as memories, or act on existing concepts to alter them. The 'ugh' experience of eating a bitter fruit, for example, may not itself be remembered, but it might leave a permanent mark by changing or elaborating an existing idea about apples.

Laying down new concepts derived from experience involves creating new patterns in the neuronal network (see 'The Network Mind', page 166). But these patterns – unlike those that are plumbed-in – are at first very fragile because the linkages between their neurons start to fall apart almost immediately. Such forgetting is essential because if everything we experienced stuck in our brains we would be overburdened with useless information, much as we would be constantly distracted if we were aware of every beat of a fly's wing. So only a tiny selection of our experiences are selected for permanent storage as memories.

These experiences are consolidated into memory by a process that can take up to two years. First the event is experienced; then it is 'kept warm' for a period through repeated replay until the pattern is effectively 'etched' into the tissue of the brain. As this happens it is incorporated into other concepts. The last of these two stages occur mainly during sleep – one reason (if not the main reason) why we all need to spend a considerable part of each day asleep.

Experiences are (or are produced by) specific patterns of neural firing, and recall happens when these patterns (or parts of them) recur after the event that originally caused them. This only happens if the original firing is strong enough to create links between the cells that take part in it. The only patterns that create links are those which are likely to be useful in some way. The 'tagging' of some experience as important (that is, potentially useful) is achieved by the action of neurotransmitters. When we are attending to an event, and especially if we are in a general state of excitement, the active areas in the brain are bathed in acetylcholine, the effect of which is to amplify neural patterns created by incoming 'here-and-now' sensory information. These patterns thus set up synchronous patterns in far-flung regions of the brain, especially in the association cortices – areas of the brain mainly in the temporal lobes, which represent information from some or all of the senses rather than just, say, sight or hearing. They also feed down to the hippocampus (the module in the limbic system which identifies them as 'our' experiences) and this makes them part of our personal narrative – an autobiographical, 're-liveable' experience, rather than a mere fact.

At the same time the acetylcholine suppresses the feedback of information from the hippocampus and the association areas to the sensory cortex. Thus existing memories are swamped by the incoming information, and top-down processing is minimized. This ensures that we get a clearer view of new events which are experienced in this state and we become acutely conscious of what is happening right now. The advantage of this feedback suppression becomes

Dr John Skoyles

LSE Centre for Natural and Social Sciences

The Network Mind

Neural networks are computer simulations of brains. Not whole brains, but parts – the equivalent of small bits of the massive network of 100 billion neurons and trillions of synaptic connections that make up a real brain. Briefly (and roughly) a neural network has three layers: input, middle and output; linked so that a pattern of information on the input layer – say a visual pattern of a dog – spreads through the net and activates one particular output pattern – dog 'recognition'.

The thinking power of a network comes from the way the nodes in each layer are linked. Each link has a particular 'weight' – the equivalent, if you like, of the strength of a signal between one neuron and another – and it will only arrive at the correct answer if these weights are correct. The weights have to be learnt, and the network does this by being given examples of inputs, producing answers, and adjusting the weights until it arrives at the correct output. The brain equivalent of this adjustment is called neural plasticity – the ability of neurons to alter their connections, either by forging new links or strengthening or weakening existing ones.

There is a problem here, of course: how can a network know when an error has been made (and thus adjust its weights) unless it already knows the correct answer? To get networks to work computer scientists had to 'tell' them, effectively, when they were right and when they were wrong. So the question arose: how does the brain get this essential feedback in the absence of an external programmer?

The answer seems to be that the brain's 'goals' (the 'right' answers determined by the network makers) stem from desires that are dictated by our bodies. At the most basic level these are things like the drive to eat or drink – basic survival goals, in other words. 'Wrong' answers are recognized by bodily discomfort – hunger, say, or thirst – and these act as feedback.

But human brains can also create very complex 'supergoals' – the desire to win the Nobel prize, or to go to a World Cup football match. The achievement of these 'right' answers depends on us being able to work out a whole range of subgoals and then execute them in a planned way. Furthermore it has to do them in parallel.

The internal 'programmer' that sets these supergoals, divides them into subgoals and then orchestrates the parallel network processing required to arrive at them is the part of the brain known as the prefrontal cortex.

The prefrontal cortex is different from other areas of the brain in that it is shielded from direct input from the external world so it is more free to abstract information – to create an imagined future or an alternative present. And it has links with practically all other brain areas, so it can draw on information from many different sources to make very complex, richly-informed ideas. It also matures much later than the rest of the brain, so it goes on learning.

The delayed maturity of the human prefrontal cortex is the key to our exceptional abilities. Unlike other species, human prefrontal working memory – the key agent in reshaping the brain – is not fully developed until well into adulthood. Thus its power over the rest of the brain can itself be shaped and expanded during a lengthy period, and so make even greater changes to the working of the rest of our brains. Our 'inner teacher' – the programmer that sets the goals and adjusts the 'weights' to achieve them – can itself be taught to be a better teacher.

A simple neural network: an input layer of nodes each communicate signals of varying strengths to a hidden middle layer, which computes them and passes the result to an 'output' layer. The output 'goal' is predetermined, and the network's job is to gradually adjust the strengths (or 'weights') of the inputs until the target goal is achieved.

The brain is thought to work in a similar way. For example, the input nodes might be sensory neurons communicating signals about the particular elements of the environment to which they are sensitive. The middle layer are neurons in association areas of the brain, and the output layer corresponds to motor nerves, which execute movement. To respond in an appropriate way to an environmental stimulus (e.g. achieve the goal output) the system gradually adjusts the sensory input.

The obvious difference between an artificial neural network and the brain is that the first is set its goal by the scientists who create it, while the brain's goals are set by the appetites, urges and drives of the body.

Sensory Merging

Consciousness of objects is enhanced when we receive information about them from more than one sense. A flash of light, for example, is more likely to be registered if the observer is simultaneously touched on the same side of the body from which the light shines. This is because the part of the brain that registers the touch communicates the information to the visual processing neurons which 'scan' the equivalent area of space and are provoked into activity.[1] This may be why we instinctively reach out to touch a curious object – it might not be the feel of it that gives us extra information, but touching it may give us a more acute visual image of it.

Although compatible cross-sensory information gives us a more coherent perception, if the information coming from one sense does not match that coming from another the brain becomes confused and may produce an entirely erroneous image. In one study people who were asked to judge the roughness of sandpaper took 10 per cent longer to report what they were feeling when the noise of rubbing the paper was manipulated to make it sound smoother than it really was.[2]

The neurons in different cortical areas are generally thought of as being dedicated to specific senses: those in the visual cortex, for example, generally respond selectively to light-borne information, while those in the auditory cortex respond to sound waves. However, there is growing evidence to suggest that neurons only have a *preference* for some kinds of stimuli, and, in the absence of the favoured type they may process similar information conveyed by a different type. Parts of the visual cortex in blind people, for example, get 'roped-in' to process tactile information when they read Braille, and if normally-sighted people are blindfolded for a week their visual neurons start to respond to touch.[3]

[1] Macaluso Emiliano et al, *Science*, 289, (2000), 1206.

[2] Research by Donna Lloyd, John Radcliffe Hospital, Oxford, reported in *New Scientist* (16 September 2000), 21.

[3] Alvaro Pascual-Leone, Harvard University, reported in *New Scientist* (11 August 2001), 25.

clear if it is blocked by drugs which prevent the acetylcholine from working: consciousness of events becomes marred by old memories which create hallucinations, and encoding of new information is reduced. Feedback is not entirely suppressed however – enough of it is allowed for memories to be retrieved when required, and for existing concepts to play a part in moulding perception.

The result of the strengthening by acetylcholine of current neural firing patterns is that the cells involved alter so that they are, temporarily, inclined to fire together again. Thus faint memory traces of events are created in the hippocampus and the association cortex.

Stage two of the process occurs when we are resting or drowsy. Now the acetylcholine levels fall and the pathways from the hippocampus to the cortex are freed up. As traffic starts to flow along these paths, the hippocampal neurons, which encode memories, become more active than those involved in keeping tabs on the external world. This feeds the memory patterns up to the cortex, where their matching traces are triggered. This replay continues as we fall into quiet sleep, bringing a stream of vague thoughts, ideas, ruminations and memories to consciousness in a hazy blur.

Stage three happens as sleep gets deeper and the cortex quietens down. In this condition the brain is ready to start consolidating the memories of recent events that are lodged in the hippocampus. Freed from the constant onslaught of here-and-now information, the hippocampus feeds its newly acquired memories back to the cortex. Because the cortical neurons involved in the relevant experience are still slightly 'warm', they are easily provoked to repeat the pattern in synchrony with the signals from the hippocampus. Observations of small patches of cortex in deep-sleeping cats reveals that this happens in a series of 'mini-bursts' of activity in the cortical neurons that have been most active during the day. Each burst causes the cells to leak chemicals from their synapses, which bind the cells together into the permanent linkage known as long-term potentiation (LTP). This firms up the faint traces left by the day-time neural firing into stable memories.[10]

Throughout the quiet phase of sleep, this toing and froing of activity is repeated, producing in the sleeper a hazy, dim trickle of conscious events, which are usually too dim to be remembered.

The final stage seems to occur during Rapid-Eye Movement (REM) sleep, which is associated with the more vibrant type of dreaming. When REM sleep starts, brain acetylcholine shoots up again, so neural traffic back from the hippocampus is again inhibited, as in alert wakefulness. However, the REM

Pavlov's dogs were taught to associate a bell with food. The sound of the bell caused them to salivate, suggesting that their conditioning had rewired their brains so that the response became automatic.

brain state differs from the waking state in that another brain chemical, noradrenalin, is reduced to practically nil, compared to a high level during wakefulness. While we are awake, noradrenalin inhibits feedback from cortical memory storage areas, and when it falls in REM sleep this inhibition is released. Thus old memories – those that have already been consolidated in the cortex – can flow back and integrate with the newly formed ones. In this state a new concept like 'dogs bite!', joins up with the pre-existent 'dogs go woof' concept to form the more complex 'dogs bite and go woof'. And the memory of the dog that bit you today can be linked to the memory of the dog that barked at you last year, and the dog basket you once gave your grandmother for Christmas and the dog collar you glimpsed on that man who reminded you of your father ... and so on.[11]

It is this freewheeling activation of associations, as new memories and old concepts intermingle and mix, that gives rise to the bizarre kaleidoscope of images and ideas that constitute dreams. The dream puns that Freudian pyschoanalysts make so much of are often merely the hooks by which a newly created memory brings an old one to consciousness. Yet there is significance in them too. If today's experience of a dog hooks up to a seemingly unrelated memory of your mother-in-law, it suggests that something about the dog experience resonates with your concept of the woman. And the ideas and memories that are triggered by your new memories are likely to be those which are not just related to the new ones, but also which are still warm from recent activation. Such activation might not have been strong enough to bring the memory to consciousness during the day, but if it has been firing gently at an unconscious level it is more likely to arise when a new memory is spreading around the cortex looking for existing patterns to join with. The creativity of dreams – their ability, sometimes, to produce solutions to problems that have foiled you during waking, may also be explained by this intermingling of ideas. Again, if the neural patterns encoding some unanswered question have been quietly firing in your unconscious, it may take only a tenuous link with the new experience to cause them to pop up in dream consciousness, and sometimes the link between old and new is precisely the 'missing' one that provides a solution.

The concepts formed by memorizing certain experiences and conjoining them with related ones provide a massive database of knowledge that can be brought to bear on new experiences and therefore affect behaviour. Take that memory of being bitten by a dog. It will be bound in with existing memories of dogs – of hairy bodies, wet noses, Rover, and so on. Any experience that occurs thereafter which 'hooks' into these peripheral memories will therefore also bring to mind – consciously or not – the memory of the bite. So a new experience of a dog will be attended by a certain degree of caution. However, there is a limit to the usefulness of such knowledge; so long as it can only be accessed by a reminder that is purely sensory (e.g. the experience of a wet nose), the concept that 'dogs can bite' remains locked away until it is needed *right here! Now!* It cannot be used to predict what might happen in the future, or what might be happening to someone else, someplace else. In order to make that concept available on tap – to *imagine* a dog biting – it has to be encoded in some way that makes it 'portable'. The meaning derived from the real event (*ouch!*) has to be extracted from the memory and put into a sort of mental vehicle which stands for all events which contain that meaning. In other words, it needs to be symbolized.

The symbols used by humans to transport experiences are words. Language – the structure in which words are embedded – can itself be thought of as a concept. Rather like the body maps that need only to be 'filled in' by physical exploration, the structure of language seems to be mapped in. You can actually see the parts where this language 'instinct' is lodged – Wernicke's and Broca's

The Sleeping Brain

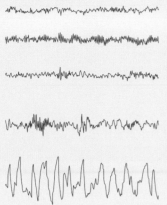

EEG traces show how neural activation becomes increasingly slow and regular as a person slips from waking (top) through drowsiness and light sleep to deep slumber (bottom).

The switch from sleeping to waking is brought about by changes in the Reticular Formation (RF) and the thalamocortical system, and are marked by variations in the rate at which neurons oscillate – that is, vary their electrical potentials. These oscillations are the source of the 'brain waves' which are measured by Electroencephalograph machines (EEG).

The RF comprises two sausage-like structures which make up the central core of the brainstem. It extends into the thalamus, which in turn is connected to practically every part of the cortex by a dense mesh of two-way neural pathways called the thalamocortical system.

The RF is made of different types of cells, each of which project to different end-points in the cortex. Each type specializes in a different neurotransmitter, and the various types tend to be situated closely together, so that stimulating the RF at different places triggers the release of different neurotransmitters, or particular mixes of them. Each neurotransmitter follows different pathways, and therefore enervates a different area, or areas, of the brain.

One type of cell, for example, releases noradrenaline (norepinephrine) which follows pathways that terminate (mainly) in the cortex. Another bundle releases dopamine, which goes mainly to the limbic system.

Wakefulness is created and maintained by activity in the reticular formation (RF) cells which produce excitatory neurotransmitters: acetylcholine (Ach) glutamate (GLU), norepinephrine/noradrenalin (NE/NA) and serotonin (5-HT). This activity causes neurons in the relevant pathways of the thalamocortical system to oscillate at a particular rate. Generally, the more activity there is in the excitatory cells of the RF, the faster and more irregular the oscillations of the thalamocortical neurons, and the more widely active our brains.

During sleep, activity in the excitatory cells in the RF is reduced. This triggers a change in the thin shell of cells which form the surface of the thalamus. Instead of firing fast and irregularly, these cells produce slow, regular bursts of activity which block information coming in to the thalamus from the sensory processing areas. In addition, special cells in the preoptic nucleus (part of the hypothalamus) become active, and these further inhibit excitatory pathways in the thalamocortical system.[1] This, effectively, shuts the brain's window on the world, and with this comes sleep.

Anaesthetics work by throwing the 'switch' in the thalamus, and/or by preventing the transmission of excitatory signals at synapses so that the

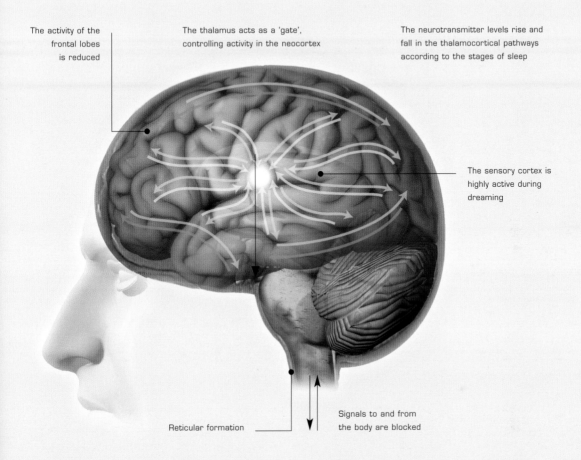

The activity of the frontal lobes is reduced

The thalamus acts as a 'gate', controlling activity in the neocortex

The neurotransmitter levels rise and fall in the thalamocortical pathways according to the stages of sleep

The sensory cortex is highly active during dreaming

Reticular formation

Signals to and from the body are blocked

pathways to the cortex are blocked. They do not so much put you to sleep, as prevent you from being awake.

Dreaming is triggered by bursts of activity in the cholinergic areas of the RF, which stimulate activity mainly in the back of the brain – the areas primarily concerned with sensory processing. Activity also occurs in the neurons which produce dopamine. These are particularly active in the limbic system, where emotion is generated. The result is that the sensory processing areas produce internally-generated sights, sounds and – to a lesser extent – physical sensations, complete with emotional consciousness. In other words – dreams.

Waking is not essential for consciousness – we are conscious when we dream. Indeed, the brain is nearly as active during dreaming as when we are

Memories appear to be consolidated during sleep. A person's name, for example, may be linked in memory with their face in the following way:

A (1) – During waking, a name, 'John', and a face are registered and a representation of this knowledge is then fed forward to the association area and the hippocampus. Acetylcholine (Ach), which is high during waking, prevents the hippocampus from feeding the signals back to the cortex at this stage, so the information is not distorted or merged with other incoming stimuli. A (2): Instead they link together and are 'locked', or encoded, in the hippocampus.

B (1) During non-dreaming sleep, ACh levels fall, and this allows the newly encoded memory to be fed back to the association cortex. There is no new information coming into the cortex from outside during this time, because sleep imposes a sensory blockade on external stimuli. The feedback from the hippocampus therefore re-triggers neural patterns that were activated during previous waking – including the sight of John, and the neural pattern corresponding to his name. As these two cortical patterns fire in unison, they become linked – and the neuronal linkage forges a connection between the two concepts such that if one is triggered (the face) the other (the name) is likely to fire up too. Hence in B (2) the memory of John's name is consolidated.

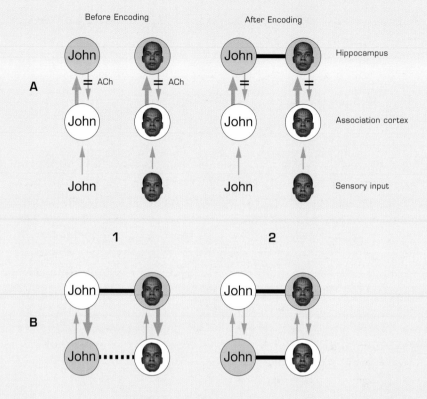

awake and dream consciousness is correspondingly intense. The sensory consciousness of dreams is not modulated by information from the (inactive) frontal areas, so there is no 'reality check' on it. Dream consciousness is therefore not 'full' in the sense of engaging the full range of cognitive abilities.

[1] T. Gallopin et al, 'Identification of sleep-promoting neurons in vitro', *Nature*, 404 (27 April 2000), 992.

areas make a discernable bulge along the side of the left hemisphere in right-handers. When these areas become active, around the age of two, children start to use language to communicate but – in a way more importantly – they also start to use it to structure their inner world. Language provides a scaffold for thoughts which, without it, would be amorphous and fleeting. It allows us to crystallize ideas, to link them to others, to encode them in a way that makes them retrievable on demand, to project into the future, and to string thoughts together in a rational train.

To return to the airship analogy: the emergence of language is the point in the journey when the passengers start to form ideas about what is happening outside, and weave them into a coherent, though constantly changing story. From now on this story will provide a basis for action as much as the data reported by the people in the window seats. When they hear that something is flying past outside the passengers will look to themselves for an explanation based on concepts formed as a result of similar sightings in the past. These concepts will come to influence each consensus they arrive at as much as – or maybe more than – the information delivered from the outlookers.

Once an experience is attached to, and encapsulated in a word, much of the sensory 're-liveable' nature of that experience falls away because we now have a way of conveying information (dogs can bite) and making it 'useable', without having to recall the experience itself. We may even seem to forget the experience and be left with just an idea.

However, if ideas could be totally divorced from bodily experience it would suggest that we are capable of being conscious of pure abstractions. And indeed, when we think about things like dogs biting, without invoking a mental image of such a thing, it seems that this is what we are doing.

But is this really the case? Can we really think about a dog biting in the abstract? If we can then it would seem that we are no longer representing a lower level of knowledge – the abstract level is all there would be. A brain in a vat could do it just as well as a brain in a body that had once been bitten. So the idea that consciousness requires knowledge of knowledge would be incorrect.

In the next chapter I hope to show that such a state of affairs does not, and cannot, occur in the human brain. For just as conceptualizing goes all the way down to the very foundation of cognition, so sensation goes all the way up to the top.

The Conscious Body

'If my heart could do my thinking and my head begin to feel, I would look upon the world anew and know what's truly real.'

Van Morrison, *I Forgot that Love Existed*

Throughout the ages people have tried to explain mysterious biological processes in terms of their own state-of-the-art technology. Descartes, for example, thought the mind exercised itself through a system of hydraulics; and at the beginning of the twentieth century the brain was likened first to a camera obscura and then to a telephone switchboard. When computers arrived in the middle of that century they provided a particularly good analogy for mental processes. The brain could be regarded as the hardware, the mind as the software, and sensation as the input to the system. In both cases 'raw' information went in and appropriate responses – answers in the case of the machine; behaviour in the case of the brain/mind – came out.

Given these parallels, it was natural to assume that the processes that led from input to output in each system were much the same. The way conventional computers work was well-known: you program them with some rules then feed in 'tokens' – such as numbers – and the machine juggles them in accordance with the rules to produce an 'answer'. It was therefore assumed that the brain was a 'central processing unit', which did a similar trick of manipulating incoming data and spewed out behaviour as the 'answer'. This computational view soon came to dominate cognitive science.

The computer analogy goes a long way towards explaining many aspects of behaviour, but it leaves a gaping hole as far as consciousness is concerned. If the brain is simply a computer juggling symbols into new representations, how can it know the meaning of what it is doing? Where is understanding?

The limitations of a purely computational, brain-centred theory of consciousness has shown up most clearly in the very area where the idea first arose: artificial intelligence. Fifty years ago AI enthusiasts confidently predicted that by the twenty-first century we would have robots and computers that would be able to do everything people can do, and better. Today, it is true, we have spectacular calculating machines, including one that can beat our best human players at chess. But if you installed such a 'brain' in a human head and sent it to a cocktail party it would probably not make it through the door, let alone make friends. It has turned out that the 'simplest' of human achievements – the ability to move around without knocking the furniture; to recognize the expression on another's face; to know when to talk and when to shut up – are impossible to program in from scratch. The world in which humans engage, especially their social world, offers so many choices of behaviour at every turn that it is impossible to equip a conventional computing machine with enough symbols for it to meet every demand. Nor do essential human qualities such as values, humour and emotion seem translatable into symbolic representations.

The sort of problems that have dogged the development of fully human-like robots were always predictable, though not necessarily by those involved in the enterprise. In his 1965 novel, *The Tin Men*, British writer Michael Frayn describes a scientist's attempt to develop an altruistic robot.[1] The first prototype, Samaritan I, was designed to sacrifice itself in favour of others, and its designer tested it by putting it on a one-man raft with various companions to see what happened when the raft started to sink. The robot duly chucked itself overboard with alacrity. However, it did this to save anything from a sack of lima beans to a chunk of seaweed, and the cost of drying it out each time proved expensive.

So the designer developed Samaritan 2, which sacrificed itself only for things it judged to be more intelligent than itself. Placed on the raft with research assistant Sinson, it waited until water washed over the planks then 'leaned forward and seized Sinson's head. In four neat movements it measured the size of his skull, then paused, computing. Then with a decisive click, it rolled sideways off the raft and sank without hesitation to the bottom of the tank.'

The hitch in Samaritan 2's design was revealed when it was placed on the raft with a bag of sand. 'Samaritan and the sandbag looked at each other impassively as the raft settled. When the deck was awash Samaritan seized the sandbag and attempted to measure its skull. It attempted its four neat movements, frustrated by the un-skull like shape of the sack, then paused, drew its conclusion, uttered a thoughtful whirr, and became completely still ... Gradually the water rose around Samaritan and the sandbag as they sat stoically accepting their fate. The sandbag was the first to disappear. Then, with a look of silent martyrdom, Samaritan vanished too.'

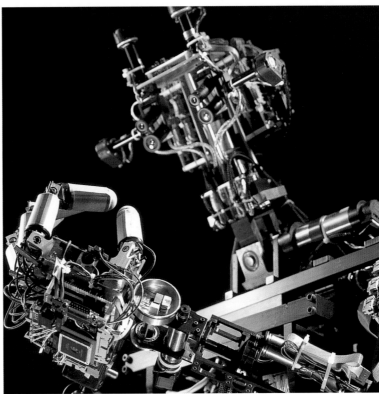

The next attempt, Samaritan 3, chucked the sandbag overboard before it went down. It also disposed of a sheep. Only when faced with a human did it allow itself to sink. However, it, too, proved expensive: when placed on the raft with another Samaritan 3, both machines chucked themselves overboard simultaneously.

Samaritan 4 refused to budge when placed on the raft with another of its kind. And so, of course, did its companion. This version proved to be most expensive of all – in order to survive the two machines bashed each other to bits.

Although most of us, mercifully, will never have to decide what to do in a two-man situation on a one-man raft, if we had to we would (it is to be hoped) arrive at a more creative solution than Samaritan did. But that is not because we are equivalent to, say, Samaritan 10, or perhaps even Samaritan 2000. All but the most gung-ho computationalists have conceded that simply programing more and more concepts into a machine will not give it the range or subtlety of responses which allow humans, on the whole, to behave sensibly in any situation.

The stupidity of Samaritans and their like arises from what is known as 'the grounding problem'. If all there is inside the brain is symbols, to what can they

Robot design mimics the human body in order to achieve something similar to human behaviour. Artificial consciousness, however, may not be possible until robots are equipped with bodies that are effectively indistinguishable from biological organisms – and we are a long way from that.

What Do Robots Think About?

In 1996 Igor Aleksander, then head of an AI Research team at Imperial College, London, introduced a (largely sceptical) world to Magnus – the first AI system which, according to its maker, had some glimmer of consciousness. Magnus was endowed with electronic circuitry which replicated the neural mechanisms which, in a human brain, give rise to the sense of self and therefore – by extension – to self-awareness. Although the system made its debut in the shape of a laptop computer, it has since been installed in a robot that 'learns' by using its body, in much the same way as a human does. This is an edited version of a conversation I had with Professor Aleksander in 2000.

RC: Let me get this clear – when you say your system is conscious you mean there is something 'it is like to be' that machine – an inner world of experience. Is this correct?

IA: I would certainly say that the robot has a sense of what it is like to be that robot. But his sense is a long way down on some gradation scale from my fully blown consciousness of what it is like to be me – it is still just a robot.

RC: But a conscious robot is not 'just' a robot even if it is pretty dim by human standards. As a sentient being it is surely more like an animal of some kind … And as we learn more about the self system in humans, and replicate it in artificial systems, eventually they will become like us and given that, won't they be deserving of the same rights and respect?

IA: I think there is a desperate necessity not to blur the line between the living and the manufactured. Similar lines are held between humans and apes or apes and amoeba. This classification is what science is about. I do believe that our robot has acquired something which serves it in the way that consciousness serves a human being. In the robot it is called artificial consciousness. I do not feel that the robot is 'like an animal of some kind' – it is a robot and not an animal. It is not the case that with advanced technology it will become more like a conscious human, it will become a better robot. Artificial consciousness is like an artificial leg. In important useful respects it is like the real one, but to believe that just by being a leg it *is* a real one would be a dangerous misconception as inappropriate consideration would be given to it (pedicures, athlete's foot preparations etc.) where a new plastic sheath to remove scuffs may be needed.

RC: But *why* the 'desperate necessity' not to blur the line between the living and manufactured? Of course it is useful, and important, to be clear about categories but surely the category demarcation between conscious versus non-conscious is a more fundamental one (and more important in terms of ethical implications) than that between living and man-made? (Or apes and humans for that matter.)

It seems to me that you are determined to avoid imbuing artificial consciousness with the value you (presumably) ascribe to it in biological organisms ... You seem to want to maintain the idea of human consciousness as 'special' – a bit like those who argue for the existence of a human soul. You refer to artificial consciousness in terms of its functions, for example, rather than to the very thing about it that makes it special – its 'inner' world of experience. Of course, if you don't think artificial systems can have this inner world then we are simply at cross purposes – what you mean by consciousness is not what I am talking about. But I don't think this is the case. I am puzzled.

IA: As a confirmed atheist there is no religious or mystical streak in my argument. I hope that it is just logical. It is my responsibility as a scientist not to blur issues that should be distinguished. The conscious/non-conscious divide is undoubtedly important, and to the extent that my machines have machinery which actually generates inner worlds for them, there is a continuum between the living and the artificial. But the conscious/non-conscious divide cannot be investigated without asking the question 'conscious of what?' Whatever I am conscious of, this self has what science allows me to call biological, living and human properties. A robot with replicated processes of my brain must put these very processes to work on being conscious of being a metal and silicon human-made being with metal and silicon needs. Part of each of our consciousnesses is that we know how to distinguish our make-up from that of the other. If one now says that the two consciousnesses of our selves are the same, this is clearly not true in terms of content. When an object therefore is claimed to be conscious *like* me it means to me that the word 'like' roughly applies if and only if the object's consciousness tells it that it is a human being. Therefore when I say that a robot is conscious, I mean that it is conscious of being a robot and hence not 'like' me. To say that my machines could be conscious 'like' humans is at best ignoring the content of consciousness and, at worst, blurring the distinction between the material make-up of a robot and the material make-up of a human being. To answer the question, why I feel that it is desperately important not to blur the line, is that by blurring it one eliminates discussion about content and almost eliminates the discussion about consciousness altogether.

RC: Nevertheless, I still wonder whether, potentially, the consciousness of an artificial system – and I mean the contents here, not the process – would be SO different from that of an animal or a person.

IA: How does one measure the difference? I fully agree that there are headings under which one would discover similar things: self-maintenance concerns, needs, plans derived from needs etc., etc. In that sense yes, there are functional similarities between the living and the artificial. But there are also the differences and being aware of both is what I am asking for in a proper consideration of the nature of an artificial consciousness. We have no measures for evaluating the importance of the similarities and differences, but we humans are generally very sensitive to the difference between us and things that are claimed to be like us.

RC: But – if you build a 'self' into a system you make the information it receives meaningful, which in turn produces (or is) emotion. Now, it might be a failure of imagination on my part, but I cannot conceive of an emotion that is not 'like' the emotions we have. So in that sense (which is surely the most important sense) an artificial consciousness would be 'like' the consciousness which arises in biological organisms. It might not want the same things as us but it would want the robotty equivalent (metal polish? Damp-Start?) and the wanting bit would be like our wanting.

IA: I fully agree that the artificial emotions would refer to basic effects on the self (threats to the self or aids to the self). So it is like my emotion in a sense. Maybe I have been labouring the defence too much, as 'like' in some people's vocabulary would cut out the Damp-Start and insert falling in love instead. So again it becomes a case of process against content. Basic fears and pleasures in a robot would arise from there being a process that creates content being relevant to the make-up of the robot. Falling in love may be dependent on my biological processes (how unromantic) and hence, in content, different from the emotion in a robot. Similarities and differences again!

refer? How does the token concept – the word 'intelligent', in this case – relate to the fantastically flexible and complex idea that we hold of it? Simply referring it to another 'sign' – the size of a skull – is hopelessly inadequate. Indeed, if Samaritan had not been given arms, the words 'size' and 'skull' would be meaningless. You could provide the machine with all the synonyms, and all the known properties of size and skulls, but all that would equip it to do would be to come up with a complete description of them. It would be like the man in Searle's Chinese Room – capable of handing out perfect answers but without a glimmer of understanding.

This vacuum at the heart of computational theories of consciousness has led to the resurgence of a much older notion: that a brain alone cannot produce the feeling of what anything is like – it needs to have a body, too, and one, furthermore, that is embedded in a particular environment.

There are many varieties of 'embodied' consciousness, but what they all have in common is that they challenge the idea of the brain as an input-output device and see its activity instead as one part of an unbroken, circular process in which sensation merges with perception, which becomes action and – importantly – interaction with the world. This then plays back as sensation. So any representation in the brain is formed (and continuously re-formed) by physical interaction with other physical things. In other words, it can never be wholly abstract.

In this scheme the brain is not qualitatively different from that of any other bit of the body. It is simply the most complex part of a distributed control system. When we reach out into the world with our bodies, our minds reach

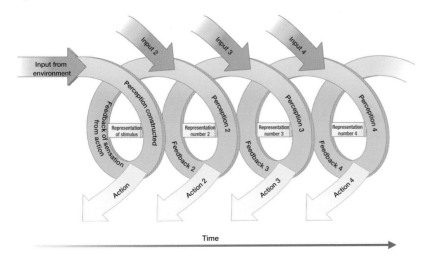

Human cognition is an 'open' system. External stimuli enter it by triggering neural activity, which in turn creates behaviour (actions) that alters the external environment and thus modifies incoming stimuli. The internal 'mental' world is therefore inextricably linked to the external and is never wholly abstract.

out too, and it is the total system – the brain, body and environment – that determines the contents of our consciousness.

Embodiment offers a solution to the grounding problem by showing that what seem at first to be tokens – words and other symbolic representations of things 'out there' – are, at least in part, physical acts. It also helps to explain a number of strange aspects of consciousness. Its 'gappiness', for example, is less of a puzzle once you realize that we do not have to construct a complete representation of our environment at every step, because the environment itself is effectively part of us, almost like an 'add-on' bit of the brain. Generally speaking, things don't change much from moment to moment, so we can afford to attend to (and thus represent) just a few important items, secure in the knowledge that if anything else becomes important it will grab our attention and thus provoke us to represent it and bring it to consciousness. Indeed, we are so secure in this knowledge that we assume we are conscious of far more than we really are (see chapter one).

It also provides one possible explanation for why each individual's experience is private: it can never be shared because it consists of knowing 'how' as well as knowing 'what'. And, although you can help someone else to know how, say, to ride a bike, you cannot actually transfer that knowledge to them because it is inextricable from your body. You can describe what your muscles do as you pedal away, but you can't actually convey the feeling – and until you get a feeling for it you cannot ride a bike, however much you might have been told about it.

If embodiment is really the thing that makes everything else meaningful, it figures that anything we can think about, or describe, must have some physical 'presence' for us. Every word and every thought must be connected to a bodily experience.

The bodily elements are easy enough to grasp when we think in images. Every image implies our physical existence because it is imagined from a distinct point of view. We see a tree in our imagination *as if* we are looking at it from within our body. A dis-located image – the tree from every possible angle, for example – is impossible. But what about, say, a chair? We don't visualize a chair every time we say the word – sentences are not like those dumbed-down television documentaries where every word of the script has to be accompanied by the matching image. Therefore it is easy to think that the word chair is used *instead* of a sensation, that the 'felt' meaning of the object has been transferred into a symbol. But this is not so.

We learn new concepts by linking them to ones we already have. These conglomerations form categories – living things, for example, may be one category; man-made things another. And categories are organized like Russian dolls: 'furniture' for example, may be nested within the larger category of 'man-made things'; and 'chairs' may be nested inside the 'furniture' category. Types of chairs – a throne, say – will in turn be nested within the 'chairs' category and 'the Bishop's throne', within that.

The classic 'objectivist' view of cognition has it that these categories and their hierarchical status are facts about the external world which the mind recognizes as it develops. As each category is as 'real' as any other, they are all the same to the brain. So a child might first learn about their grandmother's rocking chair and then learn to 'nest it' within the larger category of chair, working from the bottom-up. Or in different circumstances they might first learn that there are objects called 'furniture' and then learn to discriminate chairs. If the brain was working as a detached learning machine, it really wouldn't matter which concept came first.

But it does matter. The 'chair' level categories (other examples might be 'tree' as opposed to 'plant' or 'oak tree'; or 'horse' as opposed to 'animal' or 'carthorse') are, in crucial ways, more 'basic' to the brain. They are learned first; enter language before the others; and are identified faster by nearly everyone. They seem to comprise our 'default' picture of the world.[2]

This may be because this is the highest categorical level at which you, and I, and everyone else who uses chairs, find common meaning through our bodies. I can't imagine sitting in 'Grandmother's rocking chair' if my grandmother never had one. Or rather, to do so I would first have to create an imaginary rocking chair, imagine it belonging to my grandmother, then imagine myself sitting in it, which is quite a conceptual effort. And I can't intuitively know what to do with 'furniture' because it could be anything from a bed to a bookcase. But say 'chair' to anyone and they know how their body would interact with it – you put your backside on the seat and bend your knees (normally) with every sort of chair. Each member of the furniture category, by contrast, requires a different sort of motor action: lying down (if it's a bed); opening a door (if it's a cupboard); placing things on it (if it's a table), and so on. Therefore it seems that the perfect example of any category is not the one that best encompasses all the others (as you might think) but the one that best exemplifies the way everything in the category is physically experienced.

The way that we store and retrieve concepts also reveals their links to physical movement. Word knowledge is 'stored' in the language areas of the

Jaak Panksepp
Distinguished Research Professor
Bowling Green State University, Ohio, USA

The Primordial SELF

The 'homuncular' idea of the self – that of an observer within the self – has long been unpopular because traditional views of it have led to troublesome paradoxes such as the 'infinite regress' of selves-within-selves. The SELF system I propose, however, is no ordinary homunculus. Rather it is a neuronal structure which provides the basis for self-representation and primal forms of intentionality that help generate distinct emotional feelings.

There are good reasons to believe that a primitive, goal-directed consciousness consisting of raw emotions can be distinguished from more recent forms of 'cognitive consciousness' such as complex thoughts. In fact it is unlikely that these higher forms of consciousness could exist without the primitive affective forms that evolved much earlier.

To gain a deep understanding of the original sources of consciousness, we must try to imagine the transition in brain evolution that led to the first glimmers of primitive awareness emerging from unconscious neural mechanisms.

These flickers of consciousness were created by the neural mechanisms that first allowed organisms to behave as internally motivated, coherently functioning creatures that could be proactive as opposed to simply reactive. They would therefore have been emotional in quality – the precursors of feelings like fear and desire.

The rudiments of consciousness were probably built upon neural systems that symbolize biological values – the basic motivational and emotional systems of the brain that inform organisms how they are faring in the game of survival.[1]

These systems automatically generate internal states that guide behavioural choices so as to maximize evolutionary fitness. We humans experience such neural functions as distinct affective feelings – emotions. They are mediated by extended, longitudinally coursing neural systems that govern a variety of distinct emotional tendencies. The systems that generate basic emotional actions and feelings (probably two sides of the same coin) are concentrated in primitive midline brainstem areas, adjacent to the ventricles (see picture, right) and extending to distinct ancient cortical zones of the limbic system.[2]

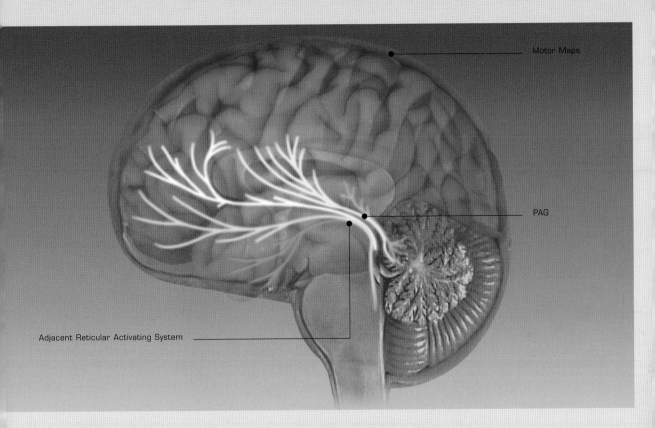

Motor Maps

PAG

Adjacent Reticular Activating System

Wherever such basic emotional and motivational systems converge massively in the brain, we can anticipate that the resulting neural interactions will serve to create a fundamental sense of self. Indeed, this type of neural integration may be the very foundation of the brain–mind entity that has traditionally been conceptualized as the soul.

One of the densest and most ancient convergence areas is in the periaqueductal gray (PAG) region of the midbrain. From this brain area, which is rich in visceral representations, one can evoke a variety of coherent emotional behavioural tendencies with localized electrical and chemical stimulation of the brain. Such coherent 'intentions in action' are aroused with lower levels of stimulation than are needed to evoke similar behaviour sequences elsewhere in the brain. In addition, animals' conscious presence in the world is compromised here with the smallest amounts of brain damage. Finally, this brain region is linked profusely to other brain areas, which allow other brain/mind functions, including arousal of the adjacent reticular activating system, to be coordinated with emotional responses. These properties suggest that the PAG and surrounding brainstem areas are the epicentre for a primordial, viscerally based, form of self-representation in the brain.

The PAG generates internal states which produce emotional behavioural tendencies. It lies close to the RAS, which mediates controls arousal.

The PAG lies just adjacent to an area known as the tectum, which elaborates primitive multimodal integration of vision, hearing and touch, in a brain region metaphorically called the four twins – the four protuberances on the back of the brainstem known as superior and inferior colliculi. This tectum, or 'roof' of the midbrain, elaborates primitive sensory maps of the world and motor maps of the body that lie just above and adjacent to the PAG. Such sensory controls help guide the simple but stable motor representations of the body, yielding rapid orienting responses closely integrated with the emotional tendencies represented in the underlying PAG. No young animal lacking this intriguing part of the brain has ever been found to grow into a mature functioning organism.

These closely integrated areas appear to neuro-symbolically represent the organism as a coherent living creature and may constitute a core SELF for each organism – a Simple Ego-type Life Force, which provides an archetypal homuncular form, a primal soul if you will – upon which innumerable brain complexities were built. This basic SELF-structure may be remarkably similar in all mammalian species and probably other vertebrates.

[1] Antonio R. Damasio, *The Feeling of What Happens: Body and Emotion in the Making of Consciousness* (New York, Harcourt Brace, 1999); Jaak Panksepp, *Affective Neuroscience: The Foundations of Human and Animal Emotion* (New York, Oxford University Press, 1998).
[2] Antonio R. Damasio et al, 'Subcortical and cortical brain activity during the feeling of self-generated emotions', *Nature Neuroscience*, 3 (2000), 1049–56.

brain, but when a person is asked to think of a particular word, it does not just 'pop up' from the word bank. Brain-imaging studies show that the meaning is 'gathered' from widespread brain areas, including those that process sensations and plan movements in response to the object represented by that word.

It may not be immediately obvious, but it is impossible even to think of a word without moving. Language-based thought (and most thought is contained in language) is accompanied by the beginnings of the motor actions required to produce the words aloud. The area of the brain most closely concerned with speech production, Broca's area, is essentially a movement area – it triggers activity in the muscles that allow the lips, tongue and throat muscles to produce sounds. When people read aloud this area produces tiny contractions of those muscles, even if they long ago learned to stop their lips actually moving. The amount of activity is not related so much to the complexity of the words that are being uttered but the amount of movement implied by their meaning. Reading a list of verbs, for example, produces more motor activity than reading a list of passive words.

Furthermore, the movement is not limited to Broca's area. One study found that when people saw words relating to tools – things that they would expect to pick up and use – the part of the brain which would normally plan the body movements required to do this became active as though the tool was right there in front of the person, just begging to be put to use.[3]

This covert 'sensational' knowledge of objects – the direct, physical effect of them on our bodies – endows them with potential meaning, in that it gives them a sort of 'virtual reality'. However, this is only one side of the story. The other side is the physical effect that we can have on them.

Another brain-imaging experiment showed that Broca's area lit up when volunteers made movements such as wiggling their toes and tongues, mimicking hand movements and tapping their fingers. This happened even though the people were not talking about what they were doing, or even consciously thinking about it verbally.[4] Another experiment showed that even thinking about making a move – especially a complex hand movement – activated the Broca's area.[5]

So it is a two-way street. Symbols may be partially abstracted – that is, taken away from the experiences that they represent – but they are never cut off from them entirely. The brain keeps them connected through its elaborate feedback system, by which concepts track back to the sensations and actions associated with them. Conversely, actions and sensations constantly form and update their symbols.

The sort of activity triggered by words is not usually conscious, of course. When you talk about wiggling your toes you don't necessarily feel a wiggle coming on, whatever your brain may be doing. So how does the movement bit of the story help to make a concept conscious?

One (speculative) possibility is that action related to an object – or rather, the brain's intention to act with regard to it – is what brings that object to attention.

When visual information from an object enters the brain it is placed on an assembly line consisting of neural pathways that run forward and down, along the lower edge of the occipital, temporal and frontal lobes. Along the way it is constructed – it is put together visually, recognized, and, depending on how far it travels, is named. At the end of this process it is well-formed enough to be made conscious. As we have seen, though, not everything that travels this route ends up in consciousness – indeed most of it doesn't. Those items that do are the ones that 'grab' attention – and that requires them to be integrated with activity in other areas of the brain, especially the parietal lobes.

If the visual information travelled only along one pathway it is difficult to see how it might do this. But it doesn't – the data is also conveyed along parallel routes, which deal with it in other ways. One of them is the road through the limbic system, where it is assessed for significance by the amygdala. Another is a pathway that carries incoming information up and over the brain, through the parietal cortex and towards the motor cortex. Construction happens along this pathway too – the image is built up from its separate components (form, dimension, motion etc.) to create a whole object. This is not a visual whole, it is a 'know-how' whole rather than a 'know-what' whole. Instead of adding things like memories and names to the construction, the brain modules working upstream on this line produce 'action schemas' in relation to the object: concepts, if you like, about how the body will deal with it. If it is a small object, for example, the schema might involve moving the thumb and forefinger to match the precise dimensions of the object; or arranging the hand to grasp its handle.

These action plans do not usually get carried out because they are actively inhibited by feedback from the prefrontal cortex, which is concerned with using the motor cortex to carry out its much grander 'thought out' (or at least more highly processed) plans. However, as each one flits into momentary being, it produces a potential external physical action – what you might call an intention towards the object.

Now all of this happens unconsciously and quite separately from the path that processes objects for consciousness. Indeed, they are so separate that the

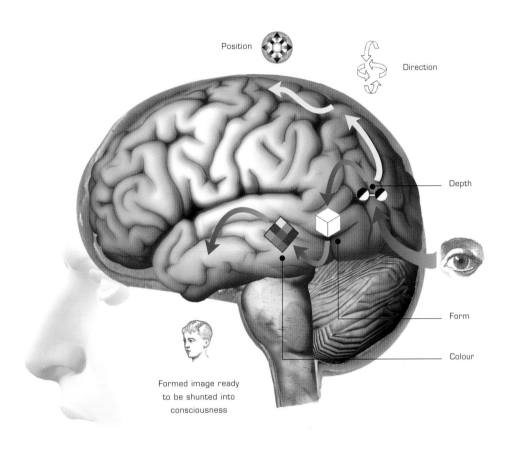

'Where?' and action schema pathway

Position

Direction

Depth

Form

Colour

Formed image ready to be shunted into consciousness

'What?' pathway

Visual information is constructed along parallel pathways. The one that travels through the parietal lobes produces unconsious plans of action with regard to the stimulus.

The Creation of Adam. Detail from
the Sistine Chapel by Michaelangelo,
1508–12.
The dynamic figure of God reaches
out to awaken a languorous Adam.
Do the action-oriented intentions in
our brain nudge us to consciousness
in much the same way? And is it just
a coincidence that God seems to be
emerging from a brain-shaped crucible?

latter route may be damaged to such an extent that a person may be unable to recognize an object consciously at all, yet still be able to handle it with expert proficiency.[6] One patient, for example, when presented with a postbox, was unable to say what it was or even to describe it. But when she was given a letter she popped it through the slit without hesitation.

Although the action schema pathway is unconscious it may help select objects for consciousness. The region of the brain where action schemas are created is also concerned with attention, and it is possible that schemas which are particularly strong nudge nearby attention mechanisms and cause the brain to zoom in on (orient) the perception as it emerges from the lower processing line.[7]

If this is so, it makes sense of the claim by some embodiment theorists that the only things we are conscious of are those which offer opportunities for action.[8] They have to be large and solid enough to interact in some way with our bodies – in other words, to be potentially *useful*. Such 'affordances' provoke in us an intention to act in regard to them and maybe it is this fleeting (and usually inhibited) inner movement which brings them to consciousness. From this it would follow that if an object has no potential for physical interaction we simply do not see it.

It is impossible, of course, to point to examples of things of which we are not conscious. The best we can do in that regard is to bring objects into consciousness – like the Darth Vader image – and then reflect on how they had been previously 'in front of our eyes' yet unseen. But perhaps that is enough to allow us to understand how we might similarly be blind to many aspects of the world, simply because we do not create an intention to act on them.

The only surfaces we see, for example, are those which can be deployed in some way by us – to stand on, move across or place things on. We do not see the surface of a bank of hot air in the sky, though a gull, looking to hitch itself a ride on a rising current, may see it clearly. This is not necessarily just a matter of not having evolved the right sensory equipment – experienced glider pilots can 'read' the sky in a way that others cannot, just as a fisherman sees subtle changes in the sea which escape landlubbers. The only sort of consciousness we have of these 'hidden' things is that derived from our existing, rather vague, experiences of hot air and sea-changes. These 'near-to' concepts may be enough to give us some idea of what the real thing may be like – much as a blind person might get an idea of red by thinking of the rich tone of a bassoon – but it is only an approximation. A glider pilot may learn to see hot air banks by associating the physical experience of being carried in his craft on one. But to be automatically conscious of the real thing you would have to construct an action schema that involved preparing your wings to glide on the surface. And that, alas, is beyond even the most imaginative of us.

Action plans also inform language in a direct way due to the anatomy of the brain. The language articulation area is situated adjacent to those which plan and execute hand movements, and almost certainly evolved out of them. This primordial linkage between hand and mouth is evident in the behaviour of newborn babies. If you stroke the palm of a newborn infant it will open its mouth, a reaction called Babkin's reflex.

One plausible evolutionary story is that the area around the junction of the frontal and temporal lobes – in both hemispheres – was once devoted to making fine hand movements, including (or perhaps particularly) those associated with 'hand-to-mouth' behaviour relating to food-gathering and feeding. At some stage in primate evolution, probably when our ancestors evolved a rudimentary theory of mind (see 'Entering Other Minds', page 292), these movements started to be used 'as if' they were feeding routines – in other words, as gestures. Then, when we stood on two legs, the structure of the vocal tract changed to accommodate the new posture and became capable of producing finely articulated sounds. The 'mouth' part of the mouth/hand gestural system then became, if you like, internalized. The lips, tongue and jaw were used not just to give visual signals but to produce sounds which were 'articulated' – cut up into bits – much as the visual gestures were once articulated in space. These oral 'gestures' proved capable of finer and finer discrimination, and so took over more and more of the 'gesture' area in the left hemisphere. Eventually the area on that side (usually) was given over almost entirely to speech, leaving hand gestures to be processed in the right hemisphere.

But the system never divided entirely – gesture and language remain closely linked. Wholly gestural languages, such as formal signing by the deaf, have the same structure as oral language even when they develop among groups who have never heard the spoken word,[9] and blind people gesture to one another when they converse.[10] When we are lost for a word we commonly 'describe it' with our hands, and gestures are usually executed at precisely the same time as the words they refer to. This suggests they are an intrinsic part of language rather than a subsequent 'add-on'.[11] Indeed, the gestures we make when we are stumped for a word may be less an attempt to convey the concept by alternative means than a way of amplifying the bodily basis of the concept in order simultaneously to amplify its symbolic 'wrapping' – the word.

When we use words, then, we are in effect using gestures which mimic physical actions. And because physical gestures take place in space, language too has a spatial framework. We speak of time, for instance, as 'flitting', 'flowing', 'creeping' – as though it is a physical entity whose progress could be indicated by a movement of the hand. And we relate it to our body: events in time are 'passed' or 'approaching'. The future lies 'in front' and the past 'behind', as though it is something we can reach out and touch. Even ideas of morality such as 'uprightness', 'straightforwardness' and 'crookedness' relate to physical features. Useful ideas are referred to as 'progressive' or 'advanced'; clever thinkers are 'ahead' of 'backward' ones; we get 'stuck' with problems; but 'arrive' at our 'goal' when we overcome them.

Nevertheless, it sometimes seems as though words – and the concepts they relate to – have succeeded in floating free of the physical world. The idea of a chair might provoke some tiny flex of the knee, and the idea of 'uprightness' might induce a stiffening of the spine. But what physical movement could you associate with, say, democracy?

This is where consciousness starts to get personal. Your reaction (re-'action', note) and mine, to the word democracy might be different. But if the word carries any meaning for us at all – that is, if we are 'conscious' of it as more than a few printed squiggles (as we are conscious of Darth Vader rather than blobs) it is because it creates in us an emotional feeling. The root of the word emotion is the Latin *movere* – to move and we still use the word 'moved' to describe a strong mental feeling. In doing so we are being more literal than we might think.

The action from which the idea of a chair is derived, and that which underlies our understanding of a word like democracy, however, are different in that while the first is matched to the physical sensations directly created by the object, the second is indirect, and internal.

Most people in the West associate democracy with 'good'. And 'good' is in turn associated with physical things which are useful to us – that is, things which further our survival and reproduction. Food and sex are perhaps the most obvious of such things. When 'good' things are laid before us our bodies

John Bulwer's *Chirologia, or the Naturall [sic] Language of the Hand* (1664).
Gestures often speak louder than words – and formal signing has a rich grammatical structure that is similar to spoken language.

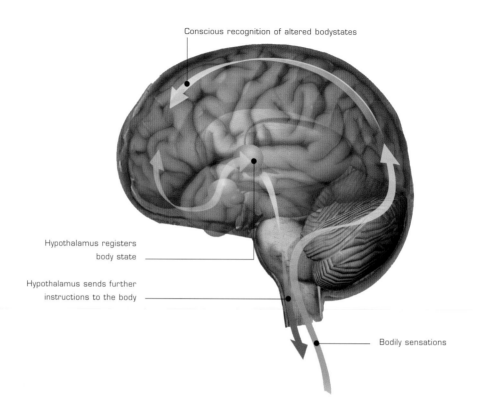

Conscious recognition of altered bodystates

Hypothalamus registers body state

Hypothalamus sends further instructions to the body

Bodily sensations

are automatically propelled towards them – the action schema triggered by them is to reach out and grasp them. We soon learn not to do this in most circumstances but the bodily actions never disappear completely. They become truncated – to a mere twitch, perhaps (like the muscle movements associated with reading) – discernible only by some special skin sensor.

In addition to this, value-laden objects also produce emotional reactions. Emotions are usually thought of as mental events, which we might imagine could be experienced as well by a brain in a vat as by a brain in a body. But in fact the conscious mental effect of emotion is secondary to bodily changes, which in turn are primarily designed to bring about bodily action. The 'feeling' of an emotion is the conscious recognition of a 'bad' or 'good' brain state, not its cause.

Emotional reactions are the result of processing along the parallel neural pathway that goes through the limbic system. A familiar face, for example, creates more activity in these regions than an unfamiliar one, and a lover's face, or one that looks threatening, sets the circuitry zinging with excitement.

As well as producing instant, specific reactions, such as running or reaching, emotional excitement brings about peripheral changes in the body state which prepares the body generally for 'fight, grab or flight' behaviour. These changes – mediated by hormones and neurotransmitters such as adrenalin and cortisol – feed back to the limbic system and amplify activity there, which in turn feeds up to the prefrontal cortex where it is experienced as 'felt' emotions such as fear, joy or sadness.

What is 'good' and what is 'bad' differs from person to person, moment to moment, and culture to culture, but certain values are 'built-in' to the human brain and do not have to be learned. Food, closeness to others of our species and sex, for example, are automatically categorized as 'good'; and physical threat, social rejection and toxic stimuli are 'bad'. Within the broad good/bad categories there are various sub-types, each one 'marked' by a specific kind of neural activity. Certain 'bad' things, for example, produce disgust, which is marked by neural firing in the front of the insula, the deep crevice that divides the frontal lobes of the brain from the temporal lobes. Growls and grimaces provoke fear, while information about tissue damage registers in several areas of the brain, including the cingulate and the somatosensory cortex, which produces pain.

Other good/bad categorizations are learned, usually by association with an intrinsically 'bad' thing. If a certain stimulus is associated with pain, for example, the neutral stimulus becomes 'bad', too. And this sort of associative 'value' learning happens in the body, not just in the brain. For example, just as Pavlov's dogs could be conditioned to salivate at the ring of a bell, so the body's immune system can be conditioned to react to things which would normally have no effect on it.

This discovery was made by the American researcher Robert Ader in 1974. Ader and his colleagues were working on Pavlovian conditioning in rodents, and one of their experiments involved giving the animals a drug called Cyclophosamide, coupled with a saccharin-flavoured drink. Cyclophosamide is an immune suppressant and when the animals were given it their ability to produce antibodies to invading organisms was severely reduced. What Ader then discovered was that a similar response occurred in conditioned animals when they were given sweet water on its own – their immune systems had 'learned' to respond to the water as though it was the drug it had once been associated with.

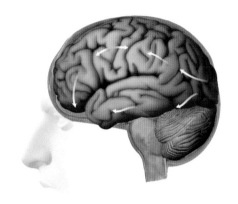

Visual stimuli are processed along parallel routes, one 'constructs' the stimuli as an object while another attaches emotion to it. The upper pathway shown in the diagram is one of the 'construction' routes which run through the cortex. The lower pathway travels through the centre of the brain, fleshing out the perception with emotional salience.

Connections

Many of the pathways linking mind and body are still shrouded in fog, but two routes have been revealed clearly. One lies in the wiring of the nervous system. Some branches of the peripheral nervous system have been shown to extend right into immune system organs and tissues such as the spleen, lymph nodes, thymus and bone marrow. Signals sent from the brain to these areas may stimulate or inhibit them directly. The second main route is via circulating molecules – the messengers which carry information from one part of the body to another. Neurotransmitters, hormones and cytokines (proteins which help defend the body against disease) used to each be associated with just one system – endorphins and neurotransmitters with the nervous system, hormones with the endocrine system and cytokines with the immune system. But now they have been discovered to be part of a single family of messenger cells which mediates between the systems as well as working within them.

The knock-on effect, from one system to another, of molecular changes explains why a condition such as depression – normally thought of as an illness of the 'mind' – may also have profound effects on many other parts of the body. For example, one common bodily change in depression (and dementia) is a drop in the levels of the excitatory neurotransmitter noradrenalin. This manifests as mental sluggishness because noradrenalin stimulates brain cells in the cortex, helping to generate thoughts and perceptions. However, reduced levels of noradrenalin also cuts down activity in the nerves which stimulate the tissues that keep certain immune cells circulating. So instead of moving around the body, seeking out and fighting invaders like bacteria and viruses, the immune cells sit around in the body tissues, allowing infections to flourish.

Anxiety damps down the immune system in a similarly indirect way. When we are bombarded by events that are hard to cope with our brains continually send messages to the adrenal glands telling them to prepare our bodies for fight or flight. The adrenals respond by flooding the body with cortisol. Cortisol is useful during emergencies because it thickens the blood (helping to prevent catastrophic bleeding in the event of injury), tenses the muscles (for fighting or fleeing), and heightens mental alertness. But while all this is happening the everyday business of body maintenance is put on hold. Suspended activity includes the routine tracking down and destruction of foreign or errant cells, including any that won't stop dividing when they should and which may therefore produce cancer. Although anxiety is certainly not the cause of cancer, it may in this way allow a tumour to escape destruction at an early stage.

Positive mental experiences, on the other hand, can stimulate the immune system, helping to keep illness at bay. Laughter, for example, brings about profound changes in many parts of the body – it relaxes the muscles, increases blood flow to the peripheries and stimulates the production of 'feel-good' neurotransmitters which in turn affect other glands. Anger and hostility, on the other hand, reverse these changes.

The bodily changes produced by value-laden stimuli in turn produce further changes in the brain. These changes differ according to whether the information suggests pleasure or advantage (the lover) or peril (the threatening face). Fearful stimuli, for example, produce muscle tension, adrenalin release, and an increase in blood pressure and heart rate; while attractive stimuli stimulate the release of neurotransmitters like dopamine or oxytocin. These internal 'motions' produce activation in the 'intentional' areas of the brain, where actions are prepared. These may in turn 'knock on' to the motor cortex itself, producing either those faint muscular twitches, or – if the activation is strong enough – overt action. When our hapless human captive biffed the Martian's antenna (see chapter three) it was these activations that registered on the scanning monitor.

It is only when the 'good' or 'bad' pattern of brain activation reaches a certain strength, or endures for a long enough time, that it knocks on to the cortical areas which bring it to consciousness. Hence it is possible to be in a state of anger, or even in a state of pain, without knowing it. When a surgeon cuts into an anaesthetized person the knife causes the brain to go into a state which is very similar to that seen in an individual who is feeling pain. The difference is that the cortical areas of the brain are cut off from the underlying areas, so the feeling is not (usually) conscious, at least in the normal 'reportable' way. Similarly the pain-related brain state remains in a person who has taken a narcotic analgesic, or has been hypnotized and told not to feel pain. In these cases some of the cortical areas associated with the conscious experience are cut off from the underlying state, but not all of them. In other words, like any other form of consciousness, felt emotion, or felt pain, is a double-layered, interconnected brain state consisting of a lower level of awareness, usually produced by external stimuli, and a higher-order representation of that state.

At the time there seemed to be no explanation for this because the immune system and the nervous system were thought to be entirely separate. Immunology was based on molecular activity which appeared to occur quite independently – indeed, it could be seen to happen in a test tube! The idea that these apparently automatic chemical processes could be learned seemed impossible.

Since then, however, biologists have discovered numerous bridges that effectively bind the nervous and immune systems into one hugely complex, interactive whole. Thus things that happen at the very 'highest' level of the nervous system – thoughts, beliefs and perceptions – can affect individual molecules in the furthest reaches of the body, and vice versa.

So – to return to the concept of democracy. Its meaning will be learned by association with something that has a more obvious emotional affect. For example, if you think democracy is a good thing you were probably brought up in an environment where it was usually spoken of with approval – people's speech tends to sound 'warmer' when they talk of things that they think are good, and we are exquisitely (and instinctively) sensitive to tone of voice. Like any other concept it has its roots in sensation and is activated by the shadow of an intention to act.

You will not, of course, be consciously aware of that sensation/intention every time you hear or think of the word 'democracy'. And you may have dissected the idea of democracy rationally, and concluded that it became meaningful to you only because your 'thinking through' led you to approve of it. But the chances are that your judgement was primarily emotional and that what you thought was a rational judgement was actually a rationalization. It is rather like the average Westerner's reaction to the idea of dog-meat: 'ugh!' It is rarely based on experience (by the accounts I have heard it tastes rather like lamb) and is usually more to do with a clash between the 'good' associations most of us have of dogs by knowing them as pets, and the thus 'bad' idea of eating them, rather than the frequently proferred rationalization that the practice is cruel.

This is not to say that rational examination of concepts can't alter beliefs, of course. If we were brought up, say, to dislike people of a certain colour we might later re-think our racist concepts and override our knee-jerk reactions. But in doing so we would not render them devoid of emotional content, we would simply develop a different emotional attachment to them – changing 'bad' to 'good'.

Such changes are not that easy to bring about though. One reason that emotion has such an overwhelming effect on us is because there are more upward neuronal pathways from the limbic system, where emotional salience is evaluated, than there are pathways going down from the cortex.[12] Where you have a connection between two brain areas which process information in conflicting ways, they act rather like a seesaw – the one that sends out the strongest signals inhibits the other. With more outward-leading pathways, the limbic system can more easily overcome cortical activity than vice versa. 'Thinking something through' may therefore have little influence on our unconscious response to it. We may 'think' something is good, but 'feel' that it is bad. Only when the conscious thoughts become automatic by repetition over time do they start to alter emotions.

Because concepts remain attached to their physical roots, it is difficult to construct ideas that go against our day-to-day bodily experience. Gravity – though actually very weird – seems quite understandable because we feel its effects on our bodies every moment of every day. If, though, you had been brought up in an orbiting space station, with no contact with earth-bound communities or anyone who had ever lived in the presence of gravity, things might be different. If some on-board philosopher came up with the notion that objects in space had gravitational fields, would you be able to understand what she was talking about? If a scientist then deduced that this was so from the craft's orbit, and explained that the effect of gravity would be to make everyone and everything travel 'naturally' in one direction (and couched his description of the phenomenon in neologies like 'weight', 'fall' and 'down'), would you believe it? Would all the other philosophers argue about whether gravity was 'real', and would the scientists argue about whether it was a 'process' or a 'thing'?

And what sort of internal structuring would you bring to bear on other concepts without that of 'upness' and 'downness'? How would you conceptualize things like 'uprightness', 'high-flying' or 'raising standards'? Would you, perhaps, be limited to 'near-to' concepts like 'straight', 'long-reaching' and 'furthering standards'? If so, without the subtly different concepts implied by the 'up/down' metaphors, would you be conscious of the difference between the 'objects' they represent? Could you, for example, distinguish between a person who was upright – that is, who was both honest, and, perhaps, a bit stiff and unyielding, and one who was just honest? Would you recognize a high-flier (a talent with potential for a fall) if you met one?

One reason why most of us find ideas like relativity and quantum mechanics so difficult to grasp is that they contradict some of the concepts which are already plumbed into our bodies. Our physical interactions with the world give no hint that space-time might be curved, or that matter is both wave and particle – our brains present the world already split into time and space and constructed into solid matter. So however often we may be told the explanations for these things, we find it almost impossible to be conscious of them intuitively – the best we can do is to contrive 'near-to' concepts through metaphors.

That is not to say that we can't make them conscious, given sufficient stimulus. Indeed, maybe the last paragraph is enough of a stimulus for you to become conscious of your intuitive conviction that time and matter are separate? If so, you now have a fighting chance of amending it because when a concept is raised into consciousness it can be altered.

Whatever one might think of psychoanalysis, it has at least made one great contribution to the world – the recognition that you have to access unconscious beliefs if you want to change them. This is the basis of nearly all psychotherapy. However, accessing and then merely rehearsing a concept (repeating a prejudice, say) only etches it deeper in the brain. Accessing it and then thinking about it in tandem with alternative beliefs – creating synchrony between the neural firing patterns which encode the prejudice and the neural patterns which comprise the new idea – can alter it. When the neurons stop firing, and drop back into the unconscious, they will have formed new associations. So if you utter a prejudice and get challenged by someone with an alternative view, your beliefs will never be quite the same again provided you listen. Debate, even argument, is a great way to change minds and, ideally, to bring them into greater harmony.

Concepts pile up in the brain like heap upon heap of treasure – or rubbish. The earlier a concept is formed the more likely it is to remain unconscious and so the less likely it is to be dug up and re-moulded. In dementia it is the most recent concepts that degenerate first, leaving the old, intact ones to surface and manifest themselves as memories or infantile behaviours.

Early ideas – those formed before speech develops and provides the 'hook' for them to be retrieved – may be known only by their effects on behaviour. Seemingly inexplicable phobias, for example, may be due to such concepts. If a child is badly frightened by, say, a cow, then the concept 'cows = dangerous' will be laid down like every other memory and the idea may 'stick', consolidated in the linkages between the brain cells that once fired together to produce the terrifying experience. Because the experience was laid down without word hooks, new concepts cannot easily link up to it. So although a new notion, 'cows are gentle', may eventually hook into some extended 'cow' concept which is consciously available, the original body memory associated with cows cannot be accessed and adapted to fit with the new idea. It may therefore remain encoded for life, triggered by cows, despite the conscious recognition that it is inappropriate.

Some studies suggest that pre-verbal memories are stored in the limbic system rather than in the cortex. Frightening experiences, for example, may lodge in the amygdala – the part of the brain which generates fear.[13] Post-traumatic Stress Disorder may be due to such a non-symbolic concept. Though not normally available to consciousness, it may be triggered by associations, causing the person who holds them to be suddenly overwhelmed by panic as it clicks in and produces the bodily state that accompanied its formation. The experience may include vivid sensory flashbacks, or merely be felt as nameless terror.

The gut reactions we feel towards things which seem to go 'against nature' are similarly derived from unconscious beliefs. For example, most people find the idea of taking organs from donors whose hearts are still beating distasteful, because their warm, breathing bodies are intuitively encoded as 'alive' – whatever the official definition of that word may be. When deeply entrenched concepts such as these are challenged we are disturbed, like the baby whose toy is made to disappear, breaching its instinctive knowledge that such things just can't happen.

As our concepts become more numerous and sophisticated they come to inform everything we experience. The perception of pain, for example, is influenced not just by attention, but also by how bad you think the pain is going to be. In one experiment, students who signed a consent form which suggested they would be subjected to discomfort reported a 'stinging' or 'burning' feeling when their hands were stimulated by a vibrator. Those who had been told the experiment would feel pleasant reported a pleasant 'tingling' when they were given the same stimulus, while those who had been led to expect a neutral sensation described just that.[14]

Even the effect of drugs is altered by expectation: in another experiment volunteers were given coffee before carrying out tests to measure reaction times. Those who thought they had been given caffeinated coffee performed

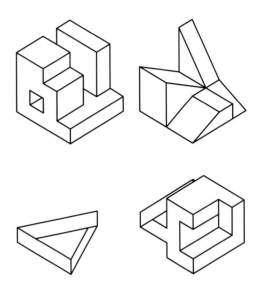

The brain deals in a different way with concepts that have no 'grounding' in the real world, even unconsciously. The top two images above are physically possible – that is they could exist in three-dimensional space. The bottom two are impossible. If the images are shown to subjects very briefly – too quickly for them to work out that some are impossible, then shown to them again shortly after, they will recognize the possible objects as familiar but not the impossible ones. It is as though the brain rejects the impossible information before it is processed to a high enough level to effect subsequent conscious actions.[15]

Seeing it One Way ... or Another

Our concepts of how things are affect the way we see them, and sometimes we see *only* what we expect to see.

When you look at the image (top left) you see one square board partially obscuring another. But what you are looking at could equally be the set-up shown just below (bottom left), from another angle. Most of the time our prejudices about how things are help us to function – we would dither endlessly if we considered every possible interpretation of common-or-garden sights. Sometimes though, they can lead us to make serious errors. In the early twentieth century the American astronomer Percival Lowell noted what seemed to be a number of straight lines on Mars. He became convinced that these were canals, constructed by Martians. Subsequently he recorded a vast network of canals criss-crossing the planet, and gave rise to a myth that lingered for more than fifty years. Lowell was almost certainly sincere in his belief that these

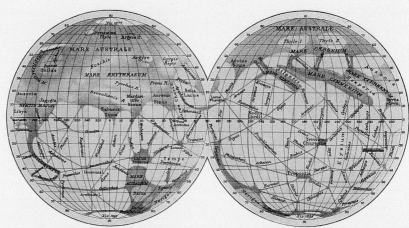

canals were there – and no doubt 'saw' them, just as he reported.

The drawing on page 205 looks pretty meaningless to most people at first sight. But give them a 'concept' and they will interpret it accordingly. Read this sentence:

'Mrs Henderson believed in doing things the old-fashioned way. To scrub the kitchen floor she filled a pail with sudsy water then lowered her huge bulk onto her knees and set about scrubbing it ...'

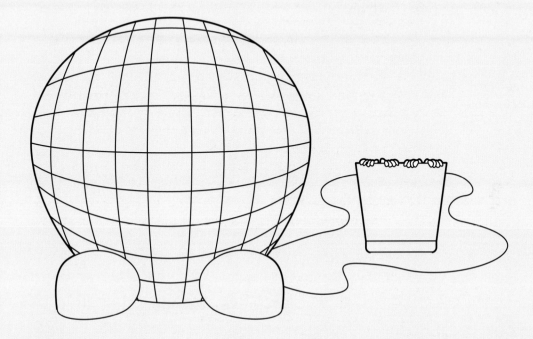

Look back at the drawing – has the subject (like Darth Vader) 'popped out'?

Now read this:

'The first attempt to launch the hot-air balloon was a failure. The balloon rose a few feet, then shifted gently in the breeze and came back to land a few feet to the left of the basket, the ropes trailing between them. The passengers were thrown to the floor of the basket, but after the balloon settled they slowly reached up, grasped the sides of the basket and got to their feet ...'

Does the drawing still show Mrs Henderson, or does it now reveal the gently billowing outlines of a collapsed hot-air balloon?

The Innocent Eye

As we mature, top-down conceptual brain processing largely overwhelms our ability to process incoming information from the bottom-up, and to a large extent we cease to be conscious of the outside world and see only our own concepts. Very young children probably see the world much as it is, but concepts soon start to cloud the view. If you ask a five- or six-year-old child to draw two identical objects, one behind the other, they will almost certainly draw them as being of similar size – they know the objects are the same size, so they fail to see that to their eyes the farthest one actually looks smaller. Once they have learned the concept of perspective, however, their drawing becomes more accurate. This is not because they see them more clearly, but because they are representing a more sophisticated concept.

People with autism do not have the ability to form concepts and as a result their view of the world may in some ways be clearer. The horse drawings done by the five-year-old autistic savant Nadia (above left) are phenomenally lifelike. This is probably because she was not labouring under the weight of preconceptions about how horses look. Normal four-year-olds, by contrast, already have certain concepts about horses – that they have four legs, for example. So they dutifully reproduce the legs (above right), even though what they have actually seen of horses is more likely to have resembled the blur of legs captured by Nadia.

Artistic genius may therefore be a matter of somehow bypassing concepts and seeing things through the 'innocent' eye of someone like Nadia.

faster and more accurately than those who thought they had been given decaffeinated, whether or not the drink actually contained the stimulant.[16]

If a concept is constantly reinforced it comes to have a greater and greater effect. If the first time we have an injection it hurts, we are more likely to feel pain the second time, which in turn strengthens the likelihood of our feeling it the third time. Eventually the expectation of pain will be so strong that even if the needle enters our skin without touching a nerve we will flinch. If, however, the first experience of an injection happens not to be painful, we will be less likely to feel the pain the second time.

A certain degree of prejudice is useful because it encourages us to avoid potentially painful situations. But if the prejudicial concept is laid down too firmly we become blind to the possibility of change, our fears become self-fulfilling, and we lose the ability to react appropriately to novel events. One reason children are in some ways more open-minded and adaptable is because their paucity of learned concepts gives them a relatively greater 'bottom-up' approach to things. Thus new information has fewer prejudices to overcome in order to seed new ideas.

And so over the years the flow of external data, and the sensation and actions triggered by them, feed into the ordering framework of our brains and create an ever more elaborate, and ever more idiosyncratic internal conceptual universe. It forms the likes and dislikes, habits of thought, dispositions, beliefs and memories that in time we come to think of as our 'selves'.

The self, however, is not just any old bundle of notions. At its base lie built-in concepts that give us a sense of ownership of experience – without which it is arguable that it is not experience at all. And it gives us the feeling of agency – that we are acting, intentional beings. In other words, it is the self – the subject – that gives us subject*ivity* and which locks us into our own private experiential universe.

The next chapter pulls apart the bundle of concepts that comprise the self, to see how the trick is done.

The Conscious Self

'You enter the brain through the eye, march up the optic nerve, round and round the cortex looking behind every neuron, and then, before you know it, you emerge into daylight on the spike of a motor nerve impulse, scratching your head and wondering where the self is.'

Daniel Dennett, *Elbow Room – The Varieties of Free Will Worth Wanting*

What would consciousness be without a 'self' to experience it? Can you imagine feeling pain that was not 'your' pain? Thinking a thought that was not your 'own', or seeing something that was not 'your' view of it?

It might be that you experience this 'selfless' state for large parts of your waking life, submerged in 'pure' qualia. But if you do you can't say what it is like because, by definition, 'you' aren't there to report back. Try to catch yourself just 'being' rather than 'having' an experience and you will fail, because the instant you examine the contents of your consciousness you invoke a shadowy presence that inserts itself between the experience and the thing that is being experienced. Red ceases to be just 'red' and becomes red-out-there, pushed away by the unconscious acknowledgement that 'I, in here, am seeing it'. It's the fridge light problem again.

When we talk about normal experience, then, we are talking about self-consciousness. That is, not consciousness *of* self, but consciousness *with* self. Thoughts, feelings and perceptions are things that happen to, or are done by, this self and may have no existence without it. Conversely, it is difficult to imagine what would be left of the self if the stream of experience stopped flowing through it – a self without an inner life is not our idea of a self at all. Yet self and experience are not one and the same. Every night, when we enter the quietest stage of sleep, experience is reduced to little or (perhaps) nothing. Yet our self pops up again in the morning, undiminished. So even if it depends on the flow of experience for its moment by moment existence, it must also have some durable form – enough, anyway, for it to be reborn each morning.

Anatomy of the Self

1) Orbito-frontal cortex.
This area inhibits inappropriate actions, freeing us from the tyranny of our urges and allowing us to defer immediate reward in favour of long-term advantage.

2) Dorsolateral prefrontal cortex.
Things are held 'in mind' here, and manipulated to form plans and concepts. This area also seems to choose to do one thing rather than another.

3) Ventromedial cortex.
This is where emotions are experienced and meaning bestowed on our perceptions.

4) Anterior cingulate cortex.
This helps focus attention and 'tune in' to our own thoughts.

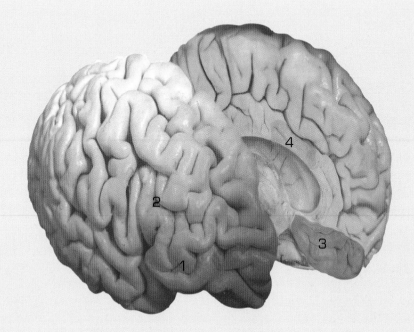

Consciousness-with-self is created, in part, by structural aspects of the brain, which determine the way that neural activity patterns are formed.

Our point of view, the sense of ownership and agency, unity and continuity, are created by systems which are distributed throughout the brain. However, a single area – the prefrontal cortex (PFC) – is responsible for binding these concepts to the thoughts, actions and perceptions that comprise our stream of consciousness. During dreaming the PFC is deactivated, so the experience is weirdly distorted.

Dali from the Back Painting Gala from the Back, Salvador Dali, (1972–3). The observing 'I' is always outside the frame ...

So what is this self? Clearly there are two sides to it: the permanent, objective self that other people recognize and that we ourselves think of as being always there – the 'me' that continues to exist through the deepest, longest sleep. And there is also the active, experiencing self – the 'I' that thinks, feels and acts. Bound together they seem to make a satisfyingly solid, intransient object, so real as to survive any doubt. Yet look at it more closely and the self becomes curiously nebulous.

Let's start with the 'me' – the visible, public individual with an objective history, a character, a body, a role in the world and a set of characteristic behaviours. This self is open to public scrutiny, in fact other people may be better able to give an accurate account of it than the person who inhabits it, who may be entirely deluded about how they appear from the outside.

If you were asked to describe the 'components' that make up this self you would probably include your body, your 'personality' – that is the way you behave – your thoughts, feelings, perceptions and beliefs, and your personal history. You might also include your place in society: 'lawyer' or 'mother' or 'British citizen'.

It is impossible to examine the 'I' because as soon as you try, another shadowy self springs up that is observing the 'I' observing the 'I' …

Like a many-stranded piece of rope, together these components make up a recognizable and resilient whole. But if you tease the components apart each one can be seen to be pretty frail.

Even the most seemingly stable and circumscribed of them, your body, is in a constant state of flux. Every molecule in it is different now from a few years ago and the form 'you' took as a three-year-old is probably not even recognizable as the form you inhabit today. Yet you do not (I presume) think your old self disappeared with the dead cells and a new self came into being with the replacements. You could probably imagine having a whole-body transplant while retaining your essential self.

So does your self reside in your behaviour? Or perhaps in your experience – the things you think, feel and see?

Again there is the problem of transience. If behaviour was the measure of self-identity you would only be 'yourself' so long as you behaved consistently, which none of us do. And what if you suffered an injury – a stroke, say, or underwent some traumatic experience that altered your behaviour beyond recognition? You may say something like 'I'm just not myself nowadays' but if pressed for a literal description you would more likely say: 'I am still here – but changed.'

A similar question hovers over your perceptions, thoughts and feelings. They change several times a second, so how can they constitute something which lasts a lifetime? Even if you take the sum of your experience, your personal history, you will find it is not written in stone. Memories change. The story is constantly being edited and elaborated. And if you relied on your autobiography to identify you what would happen to your self if you suffered retrospective amnesia? Would 'you' disappear? Would your self just be a public memory, as it will be when you are dead? And if you see your self as a thread in the fabric of society, would it disappear if you were cast up on a desert island?

A razor's edge looks sharply defined to the naked eye, but under a microscope it becomes fuzzy.

None of this, you may argue, matters. Because it seems you could lose all the characteristics that identify you outwardly and still exist – diminished perhaps, and changed, but still, essentially, your self. Strip away the 'public' aspects of self, erase the familiar 'contents' of your mind and still there is the sense of being an 'I' – the observer, rather than that which is observed – a subjective 'ground' of consciousness on which all the rest is built.

This essential 'I' is so fundamental that it is impossible to imagine it away. Does it, though, have any more claim to be 'real' than the transient, ever-shifting components that could conceivably be erased by a cerebral accident or catastrophic change in circumstances? I think not. Rather it is a set of concepts – intuitive, unconscious beliefs and ways of interpreting information that are programmed into our brains, partly by our genes and partly by our environment.

The first of these concepts is that of boundedness – that there is a place within which your consciousness exists and a place where it doesn't. With that comes ownership of experience – the knowledge that this view, this thought, this pain is yours and not someone else's. Then there is agency. When you pick up a pencil it is you who picks it up, not the person next to you, or even the hand at the end of your arm. Finally there is the conviction of unity, both in the moment (there is only one of me) and over time (the 'me' I am now is the 'me' I will be tomorrow).

These assumptions are endowed with the certainty that only intuitive knowledge carries. But this does not necessarily mean they are indubitable. Like our unconscious concepts of the physical world (the intuition, for example, that physical objects cannot disappear) they have evolved not to give insight into

Blow Up

Antonioni's film *Blow Up* explored the uncertainty brought about by changing scale. A photographer thinks he has accidentally snapped a sequence of events in which a person is murdered.

At normal size the photographs show only vague hints – but when blown up one frame seems to clearly show a man's hand in the bushes, holding a gun. However, when the picture is blown up still further, instead of clarifying the image it becomes less distinct.

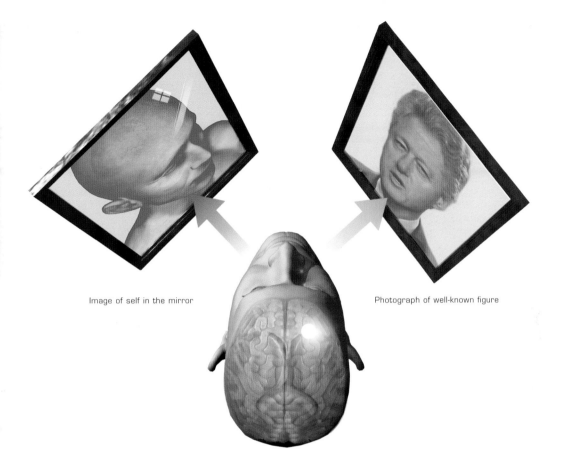

Image of self in the mirror

Photograph of well-known figure

essential truth but to allow us to function in the material universe. If they did not exist we would have to invent them – which is, in a way, what we do.

A thing must have a boundary in order for us to name it, categorize it and deal with it. Even the universe exists in our minds as a concept only by virtue of the fact that we have an opposing concept – however vague – of 'no-thing', from which it can be distinguished.

No-thing is, by definition, not a thing at all. But in order to have a concept of it we have to *make* it a thing, which means giving it a boundary. Then of course, we have to create a background 'thing' to distinguish the *no*-thing ... and so on. Once we start creating bounded 'things' in our heads we have to create more bounded things for them to stand out from – we can't just 'do' boundless infinity. Try it, and see how far you get.

Even the most apparently immutable boundaries are created by us for convenience, rather than fixed in objective reality. Rocks and cups – being within the scale of time and space which affect us – are distinguished as

Comparing one's own face with another triggers activity in the prefrontal cortex. Parts of this region seem to specialize in 'self-related' cognition.[1]

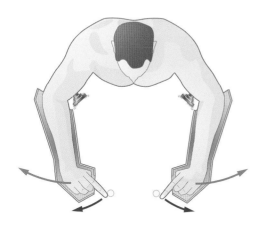

discrete objects. But if we were the size of an atom we would see the rock's atoms rather as we see the Milky Way, it would not be at all clear where it begins or ends. Just as our naked eyes see the universe extending into boundless infinity, an atom-sized observer would see the surface atoms of the rock mingling with the atoms beyond it in an indeterminate blur.

You can get an idea of the fuzziness of boundaries by looking at what seems to us to have the very sharpest of edges – a razor, for example – through an electron microscope. At that scale what seems normally to be clear-cut is revealed to be fuzzy and changeable, the atoms of metal mingling with atmospheric dust and falling away, like crumbs from a cake, at the slightest movement. And at quantum level matter itself seems to lose its material structure and become indistinguishable from energy. So, although a rock may seem clearly defined, if our spatial scale was altered it would have no more of a boundary than a ripple in a stream. And who can say with precision where one ripple begins and ends?

Internally generated signals from muscles can fool us into feeling that our body (or parts of it) is in a different location to where it actually is, and this illusion may then influence our perception of things outside us. In one experiment, small target lights were attached to the index fingers of subjects sitting in a darkened room. The subjects' arms were strapped down so they could not move, while their biceps were vibrated to create the same internal sensation that would normally accompany arm movement. The subjects reported feeling that their arms were moving outwards – and they also reported seeing an increase in the distance between the target lights. In fact their arms stayed still, along with the lights.

The boundaries that contain our private selves are similarly drawn in the sand of our perceptions rather than in some 'actual' categorical universe. Most of the time the 'I' is experienced merely as the background against which we can distinguish the 'things' that are the objects of our consciousness. We are not normally conscious of it, but when we examine it – in *order* to examine it – we experience it as bounded, and, furthermore, bounded in space. It is often felt to be inside the head, or even more precisely, just behind our eyes. Yet again, when we come to examine it more closely, we find the line that distinguishes 'I' from 'not-I' is very blurred indeed.

What we experience as the physical boundary of our self is fluid, and may even incorporate external material things. Pick up a pencil now and run the end of it over a rough surface. Where do you feel the texture? Not where the pencil meets your flesh, but at the end of the pencil, correct? The boundary of your sensory consciousness has pushed out to the place where it is needed. Now switch your attention to the feeling of the pencil itself. What happens? Suddenly you are back within your skin. Similarly, a driver negotiating a fast bend with perfect precision may feel that his car is an extension of himself rather than an object he must manipulate.

Our sense of physical boundedness, as we have seen, is created by neural body maps – representations of our bodies – rather than by any 'actual' interface between skin and air. Amputees suffer from phantom limbs because the body map in their brains keeps telling them their boundary is where it used to be and not where it is now, and people born without limbs may complain of phantoms even though they have never had the parts that they experience.[2]

Our body maps are 'built-in' rather than learned concepts, yet they are firmly grounded in the external world and remain intact only so long as they receive appropriate sensory feedback from physical interaction between the body and the environment. The maps sometimes get 'stuck' in a configuration that is incongruent with the real body – as with phantom limbs – but normally they adapt to match the changes in the physical body so well that we are unaware of their illusory nature. They move as the body moves, grow as it grows, and age as the flesh ages. Yet the boundaries of our body maps are not drawn rigidly around the surface of our skin – rather they reflect a more fluid idea of where the body begins and ends. An experiment with monkeys found, for example, that their body maps can, when it is useful, incorporate tools.

Self-portraits are one of the most common subjects of children's drawings. Producing these external representations of themselves may help children to recognise their own boundaries. It is notable that the extremities in children's self-portraits are sometimes forgotten (Gloria) and feet or shoes are typically less detailed than hands, which are used more to interact with the world (Liam).

When does a Self have Rights?

A human 'self' has rights accorded to it in nearly all societies, and in the developed world these are often enshrined in law. But what counts as a 'self'? Just as the boundary between one's 'self' and 'others' is blurred, so is the demarcation between individuals with selves and those without. This is seen most clearly in debates about the line between a human body – an 'itself', and a person – a 'him/herself'. Is a brain-dead but breathing body an 'it' or a 'him/her'? What about an 18-week foetus? The categorical distinctions differ from time to time and culture to culture.

The only sort of consciousness we can describe, or even imagine, involves a sense of self. However, we probably spend a large amount of time experiencing basic consciousness – the wordless, reflectionless absorption in qualia. The brain systems which generate this state in people – the emotional areas, first- and second-order body maps and their links to sensory brain areas – are shared by all mammals and some invertebrates, and it seems likely therefore that these animals have core consciousness too.

But what about self-consciousness? Do they know that their experiences are theirs and that their actions are done by 'them'? Do they understand that others may have quite different experiences and ideas? And have they any concept of themselves in time, or is it true that 'a dog may be scared that its master will beat it, but not that he might beat it tomorrow'?

Issues like cloning, abortion, organ transplantation, the ability to keep severely handicapped or brain-damaged people alive by artificial means, and stem-cell therapy (which involves 'harvesting' foetal cells for use in others) present us with a pressing need to determine the essential qualities that make it worse for us to kill something that possesses a self than to kill any other form of life. According to philosopher Peter Singer, of Princeton University, the best candidate is self-consciousness:

'[it] can't be ... simply the fact that the human is a member of the species *Homo sapiens*. So if it's not that, it looks like it will have to be some specific mental capacities that normal humans have and that plants and at least some animals don't have. I think the ones that most plausibly relate to the wrongness of killing are capacities that make it possible for the being to live its life from the inside, not just moment by moment but over a period of time. I see these as significant for the wrongness of killing. I reject the idea that they are some sort of determinant of the worth of a being. Even if it's not self-aware, it's still wrong to make it suffer.'

The consequences of continuing to refuse to link a person's (or an animal's) level of consciousness to their right to life could be disastrous, says Singer:

'The traditional ethic of the sanctity of life is being eroded on all sides by practices related to medical technology ... In future we may end up paying lip service to the ethic. Eventually people could simply abandon it but they won't have anything to put in its place. The result could be a complete confusion about what might make killing wrong in any circumstances.'

'Adopting a principle [like self-conscious creatures must not be killed] is more likely to be successful in preventing things like the Holocaust than sticking to an ethic that really only makes sense within the context of a Judaeo-Christian world view.'

Singer, whose views include the need for a legal framework to protect animals from human exploitation, was greeted on his arrival in the US, from Australia, by protesters carrying banners reading 'Nazi'.

Quotes from an interview in *New Scientist* (8 January 2000).

Certain cells in the brain are specialized to react to objects in near space – that is, within the animal's natural reach. However, when these cells were monitored while a monkey reached for an object with a rake, the cells fired in response to the object at the end of the rake. This suggests that the brain 'recognized' the rake, temporarily, as an extension of the animal's body.[3] Similarly a driver's conceptual body might expand into his machine when they are 'at one' with their vehicle.

It seems, then, that the boundary we draw to define 'self' from 'non-self' in physical terms is permeable and fluid – dependent on a brain system which can be shown up in certain situations as a mere illusion-maker.

The boundary we draw around our non-physical conceptual self is even more plastic. Sometimes we feel our mental realm is huge, solid and impervious. At other times we feel shrunken and transparent, as though – to quote a famously unstable ego – 'you could dissolve, like a Disprin, in a glass of water.'[4]

The social context in which we develop has a profound effect on where we draw the boundary of our ego-self. The modern Western world is highly individuated and the selves within it generally regard themselves as discrete 'atoms' of consciousness, constantly interacting with one another, but essentially separate. In some cultures, however, the self, including its boundaries, is primarily defined in terms of its relationship to others. Some Polynesian islanders, for example, speak of themselves almost exclusively in terms of social interactions. Asked, for example, to describe an emotion like sadness, the response will be to describe a sad social situation – like a neighbour leaving the island – rather than an inner feeling.[5]

Even those of us within an 'atomist' society experience the boundaries of our selves as flexible. One of the heady delights of falling in love is the feeling of merging with another person, allowing our boundary to adhere to theirs and bleed into it. When we join with others to common purpose – singing in a choir or cheering on our team in a sporting event – our boundaries become permeable. Like ants in a colony or bees in a hive, our individual intentions become subsumed by that of the group.

Traditional, close-knit societies which give high importance to kinship and family encourage this extension of self and the downgrading of individual intention. It has its advantages, especially among groups which need to cooperate closely and 'stick together' for support in a hostile world. But it can be suffocating for those who have glimpsed a more individualistic lifestyle.

The social controls which prevent individuals from breaking away from the group vary. In some cultures they are rigidly enforced by laws like those

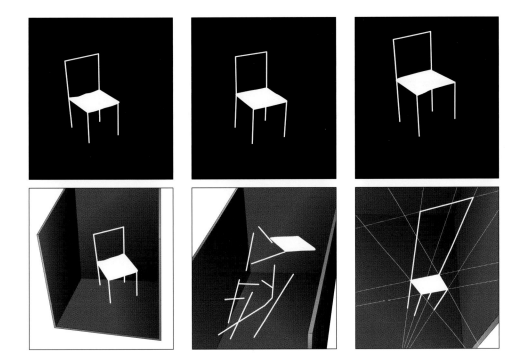

prohibiting marriage with outsiders. Other societies rely on less formalized ways of ensuring cohesion, like disapproval of those who depart from shared customs and ridiculing of those who 'get above themselves'. When times are bad – during war, for example – these pressures are stepped up. Most people are very vulnerable to them – religious cults which brainwash their members into a state of unquestioning obedience are only the most extreme examples.

The boundary of self is not, then, firm and stable, but shifting and permeable and drawn at least partly by social and environmental contingencies. Nevertheless, it is essential that we think it is firm and unyielding, because only then can we think of ourselves as located within it. And only by being located can we have a point of view which is ours and ours alone – a unique, private and owned little slice of the conscious universe.

'Owned' experience is our window on the outside world, but one that only ever accords a limited view. For example, we see objects literally from the point from which we view them. Even if we know that the ball in front of us is spherical we can't be sure that the hidden hemisphere exists unless we turn it around and have a look. Consciousness of abstract things like ideas or facts, is

The external world is always seen from a particular point of view. The three 'chairs' in the top row look similar when seen from one perspective. However, only one of them (top left) is a real chair and therefore remains recognizable as such (bottom left) when you shift your point of view. The others (bottom centre and right), seen from the new perspective, turn out to be clever illusions created by wires and mirrors.

Body Swap

Imagine you were told that – by some weird futuristic technique – the content of your mind was going to be swapped with that of another. Your body (call it body A) would then be the vehicle for all the thoughts, memories and experiences currently taking place in mind B, while mind B's current body (body B) would contain all your experience (mind A).

Now imagine you were informed that, once this operation had been carried out, one of the bodies would be subject to torture. It is up to you to decide which of the A/B combinations should suffer the pain.

If you have a robust sense of self-preservation you will opt for the A body, containing the B mind, because 'you' will have vacated it and thus not experience the torture.

And yet, can you really 'amputate' your self from your body? Consider some variations on the mind-transplant theme. Say that, instead of having your mind swapped with B's, you are informed that your mind will be treated in such a way as to cause total amnesia for all your personal memories, right down to your name and identity. Which of the two would you now choose to have the torture? The future person with your body, or 'B'?

Let's assume you opt for B. After all, A is still your body and your brain – albeit emptied of its contents. But now ask yourself who would you choose in the following scenarios:

1) B is unaffected but your mind is to be made amnesic and changed so that it thinks and behaves in a different way.
2) As before, but the changes are such that your mind is now filled with false memories relating to some fictional other life.
3) Similar, but the memories are designed to be identical to B's real memories
4) The same as the last, except that the method used is to transfer them. from B's mind while leaving B unaltered.

Now it follows that, having assumed that some sort of 'self' would survive the amnesia operation, it should still be inhabiting A. But now imagine a further variation:

Everything is the same as (4) except that, after the changes have been made in your mind, B is now subjected to an operation in which all the thoughts and memories currently being experienced by you are replicated in him.

This, of course, is the same situation as we started with. So if you thought the

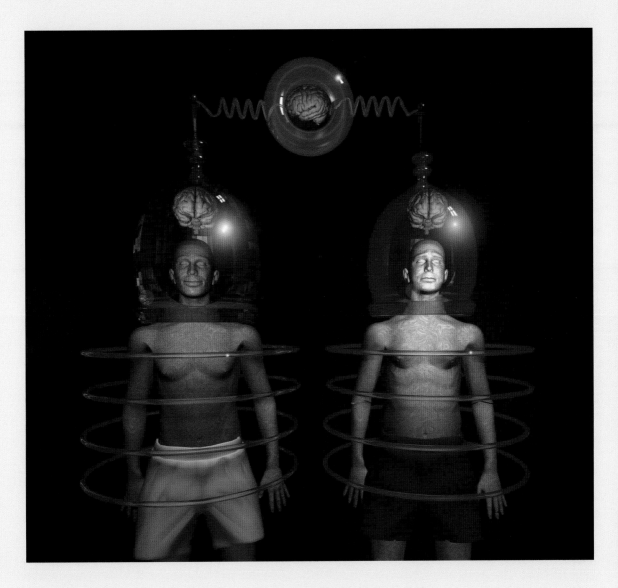

'A' body should be tortured the first time around it should still be the 'A' body now. Yet the 'A' body – and mind – is the same as it was in (4), when you were concerned to protect it. If it contained your 'self' then, it must still contain it. And if there could be only one self it cannot be in 'B' s body at the same time.

This is a simplified version of a thought experiment first presented by philosopher Bernard Williams.

Stuck in Space

The robot rover that NASA sent to Mars was equipped in such a way that it could plausibly be said to be 'aware'. That is, it had sensors which could take in information from the environment and use it for action. However, it was almost certainly not conscious.

Its system was perfectly adequate for its needs – until it hit a particular problem. To be specific, it got stuck behind a rock. There was no obvious reason why the rover could not get out. Information about its situation was coming in clearly, and was linked to mechanisms which would have allowed it to move appropriately. Yet it didn't. Instead it remained stuck. The reason for this was not incompetence but lack of that second layer of awareness. It may have known there was a 'stuck situation' going on, but it did not know it was stuck because it didn't know it was an 'it' at all. And without knowing that, it had no reason to do anything about it.

less clearly harnessed to a viewpoint, but our language reflects the intuitive sense that we regard them in much the same manner as we regard material objects. We 'see' one side or another of an argument, for example. And even if we struggle to see all sides, we cannot see them all at the same time – we have to move around the issue, mentally, 'looking' at it first from one 'point of view' and then another. Our world – including our conceptual world – is always 'out there', if not literally in space, then metaphorically so.

A viewpoint is necessary for us because if we did not have one we could not act. You can only go 'forward' if you see some things as 'in front' of you and others as 'behind' you. And you can only make a decision to do something if you see the situation as one 'way' or another. Without a point of view you would be frozen.

Sensations and actions are essentially the same (see chapter six). Seeing and hearing don't 'just happen' to us, we have to 'do' them, 'reaching out' with our minds into the environment and activating the concepts that allow them to be made conscious. These internal actions translate into observed behaviour when they affect our bodies sufficiently to be externally apparent.

Some of these actions seem to be 'done' by us more than others: thinking rather than perceiving; listening rather than hearing; moving as opposed to being moved by emotion. We feel we cause them by our own volition, and it is this sensation of being a determined 'doer' that makes us feel as though we are in charge of our own minds. This sense of agency is perhaps the single most convincing evidence for the 'I'.

Libet's experiments (see page 84) show that this sense of agency is misleading, at least at the level of simple motor actions. Yet it is almost impossible to wish away the feeling of having choice in what you do, even if you believe it is an illusion. You can't (as John Searle points out) just go into a restaurant and tell the waiter you will have what you are going to have. And even if you did, that in itself would feel like an act of will. It seems there is no way out of feeling as though you are in charge.

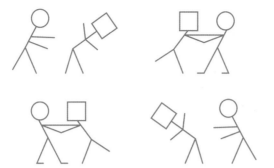

Even if the objects are obviously inanimate, our instinct to read intention into movement is irresistible. It is very clear what these stick men are doing ...

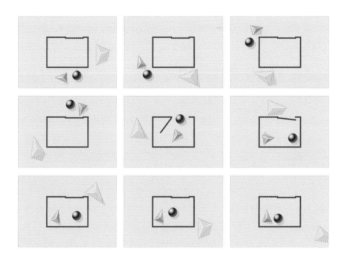

Here, it seems clear that the yellow arrow is 'chasing' the smaller objects, and that they 'dodge' into the box to escape capture. The Belgian psychologist Albert Michotte (1881–1965) showed that even simple coloured balls, if moved in a way that reminds us of human movement, are automatically regarded as having intentions.

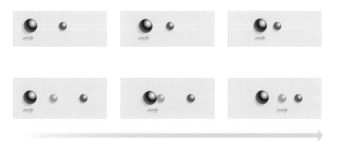

When a red ball and a blue ball roll across our field of vision, one after the other, most people say that one is leading, or chasing, the other, as though in a game of tag. And if the balls are of different sizes the one that is seen to be doing the causing – that is the leading, or the chasing ball – is always the biggest. Causal effectiveness = big = strong = power. No wonder we claim it for ourselves.

Animals are assumed – correctly – to have intentions, but generally we recognize that these intentions are not as elaborate as those that can be created by self-aware humans. The law, for example, does not hold an animal responsible for its actions – if a dog bites someone it is the owner who is penalized. (Executing the dog is not meant to be punishment but prevention.) This was not always the case, however. In the Middle Ages, courts in many countries put animals on trial with all the pomp and ceremony accorded to human trials. If found guilty, the animals were punished. Here an errant pig that has been convicted of stealing someone's dinner is being hung for the offence.

If free will is an illusion, and each of our actions is determined by unconscious cognitive processes in response to external stimuli, why should our brains delude us into thinking it is otherwise? Recall that Libet's experiments found that a stimulus (instruction to move a finger) was followed by unconscious initiation of the act and then by the conscious 'decision' to do it. Given that the action is already underway, why do we experience our consciousness of its beginning as a decision, instead of just the knowledge of what our bodies are about to do? If we are passengers in this machine, why can't we just sit back and enjoy the view instead of wrestling with what is actually a disconnected steering wheel?

One possibility is that the sense of agency is an integral part of the self, and thus arises automatically when we become self-conscious. Certainly our sense of agency helps to build our concept of self because it binds us, as 'actors', to our 'acts' in such a way that we become responsible for them. And that in turn allows us to build a more satisfying narrative around both ourselves and others. The main thread of any story is the chain of events which appear to be set in motion by a protagonist. Such 'caused' acts are meaningful in a way that accidental events are not, because they seem to be – potentially at least – within our control. When something happens 'for no reason' we assure one another that 'there is no point in thinking about it', whereas the putative motives behind human actions are endlessly debated.

Meaningful actions and conscious deliberation are so closely linked in our minds that when something happens which affects us we instinctively assume some sentient being must be responsible, and when there clearly isn't one we endow the non-sentient cause with a sort of honorary 'selfdom'. Thus earthquakes and floods are spoken of as 'Acts of God' and hurricanes and volcanoes are given names.

Along with the illusion of control, our sense of agency brings the burden of individual responsibility. Though this may sometimes weigh heavily on us

Chris Frith FRS
Professor of Neuropsychology
Wellcome Department of Cognitive Neurology, London

Ownership and Agency

One of the most important aspects of my consciousness is the distinction between me (the self) and the outside world. I am aware of myself moving through the world and acting upon it. I have a sense of ownership; it is me who is moving and having these experiences. I also have a sense of agency; it is me who is deciding what to do and causing my actions to occur. We are so used to these experiences of ourselves that we take them for granted. How could I not be thinking my own thoughts and causing my own actions?

Studies of neurological and psychiatric patients show how fragile this sense of ownership and agency can be. Shortly after damage to the right side of the brain, usually caused by a stroke leading to partial paralysis, patients often have strange alterations in their sense of ownership and agency. Some will deny ownership of their paralyzed arm and extreme cases claim that the arm in question must belong to the doctor who now has three arms.

Other patients will claim to have moved their paralyzed arm when no such movement has occurred. In contrast, damage to the middle of the brain at the front (anterior cingulate cortex) can lead to the patient having an anarchic hand. Rather than being paralyzed this hand has a will of its own, carrying out actions which the patient does not intend. Sometimes the anarchic hand acts directly against the will of the patient, undoing buttons as fast as the 'good' hand does them up. However, these problems of ownership and agency are restricted. They usually apply to the arm on the opposite side of the body to the brain damage. For other limbs and for thoughts the patient's experience of ownership and agency are completely normal.

The experience is much more general for patients with schizophrenia. They may have the experience, referred to as a delusion of control, in which they feel as if their actions are being made for them by some alien force. 'The force moved my lips. I began to speak. The words were made for me.' Their thoughts as well as their actions can seem to be controlled by these external forces (thought insertion). 'Thoughts are put into my mind like "Kill God." It's just like my mind working, but it isn't. They come from this chap, Chris. They're his thoughts.'

What these patients are trying to describe seems to be a loss of their sense of agency, not a loss of their sense of ownership. The patient knows that it is he who is performing the acts and having the thoughts, but he no longer experiences himself as the agent of these acts and thoughts. Such experiences are very distressing since they strike at the heart of one's freedom to act and be oneself.

So where do our senses of ownership and agency come from? How can they be so dramatically disrupted? Like all our experiences our sense of ownership and agency are created by our brain. Our experience of ourselves seems quite different from our experience of the outside world. We seem to know directly about our own body while objects in the outside world can only be experienced indirectly. Yet this distinction is largely an illusion. The experience I have of seeing my own arm is created by activity in the nerves at the back of my eyes and the associated visual regions of the brain. But there is nothing to distinguish this neural activity from the neural activity that occurs when I am seeing someone else's arm or seeing the branch of a tree. Likewise when I touch something, the activity in the touch receptors in the tip of my finger tells me indiscriminately about my finger and about the surface that I am touching.

However, there is one critical difference between sensations relating to myself and sensations relating to the world outside. This difference does not lie in the sensations themselves. It lies in my ability to predict the sensations that relate to my actions. When I move through the world there will be changes in what I see and feel, but I can anticipate exactly what these changes are going to be. When I deliberately move my arm, my brain can anticipate what I am going to see and feel because the commands to the muscles that make my arm move also come from my brain. If someone else moves my arm, then I cannot anticipate precisely what I am going to see and feel. This is why we cannot tickle ourselves. If I stroke the palm of my left hand with my right forefinger then the sensations I feel are not very intense because I can anticipate them. When the expected occurs it is never very exciting. If someone else strokes my palm then the tickling sensations feel much more intense because I cannot anticipate them.

But this prediction system can be fooled. If I intend to move my arm and then it is moved by someone else at just the right moment then I am likely to believe that I have made the movement myself. If I stroke the palm of my hand with a special device that creates a delay between the movements I make with my right hand and the stimulation of my left palm then the tickling sensations are more intense even though I am creating them myself.

We do not know exactly how the brain makes these predictions about our own movements, but the mechanism must depend upon signals from the areas at the front of the brain that generate movements reaching those areas at the back of the brain which process sensations. Brain-imaging studies show that when we tickle ourselves there is far less activity in the brain area concerned with processing touch than when the same stimulus is applied by someone else. The brain always responds less to stimuli that are expected, but in this case the expectation is based on intended actions rather than past experience. There is some evidence that the cerebellum, the miniature brain at the back, has the special function of predicting the sensory consequences of actions, but, as yet, we don't know precisely how this is done.

If something went wrong with the brain mechanism that predicts the sensory consequences of our own actions then we would have an abnormal experience of agency. We would not be able to predict the consequences of our own actions. This would make us feel as if we were no longer in control of ourselves. When I moved my arm it would feel as if someone else was moving it. This is what we think is happening in some people suffering from schizophrenia. When they say that their actions are being controlled by alien forces, they are accurately describing what their movements feel like. We have found that these patients do not feel any difference between tickling themselves and being tickled by someone else. From these clues we hope eventually to discover what has gone wrong in the brain to cause these very distressing experiences.

personally, for society as a whole it is hugely beneficial. Our entire morality and judicial system is dependent on everyone accepting that they are agents of their own misdeeds, and those who don't acknowledge this are – by legal definition – insane. We may not consciously control our own actions, but the cognitive mechanisms that create the illusion that we do keep society functioning.

The brain process underlying the sense of agency seems to be an extension of the process that gives rise to ownership of consciousness. Ownership and agency of action usually go together. As I type this I know both that it is my fingers that are doing the moving, *and* I feel that I am making them do it. In some circumstances, though, ownership and agency become separated. The most obvious is in a situation like a crowded train, when someone pushes you from behind and you lurch forward onto someone else's toe. You intuitively 'own' the action (demonstrating it, if you are English, by saying 'sorry') but you do not feel yourself to be the cause of it. And when your body carries out a reflex action – recoiling from a flame, for example – you know the action is 'yours' but you do not feel you 'did' it.

People can also be duped into assuming agency even when the cause of their actions resides outside their brains. When we are pushed and step on someone's toe, we don't feel responsible for it, but when the brain itself is 'pushed' into bringing about a body movement, we do. Applying Transcranial Magnetic Stimulation (TMS) to one side of the motor area of the brain makes motor cells fire which automatically produce limb movements. They are no more voluntary than the jerk of a knee when it is tapped with a hammer, but an experiment in which people were subjected to TMS on one side and also invited to make spontaneous limb movements, found that the subjects felt they were causing the 'knee jerk' movements brought about by the TMS just as much as the spontaneous ones.[6]

The American neuroscientist V. S. Ramachandran and his colleagues have devised an intriguing experiment which demonstrates that people can even be tricked into feeling they are causing others' actions. A naive subject looks at his own reflection in a half-silvered mirror, in such a way that the reflection is cut off just above his mouth. A dummy head is then placed behind the glass and lined up precisely to 'complete' the image of a full face. The lights are then switched off, and the upper (dummy) half of the face is illuminated with a narrow-beam spotlight, while the mouth of the subject is picked out by another light. If the subject now sticks out his tongue, or bares his teeth while looking at the mirror, he gets the distinct impression that he is in direct control of the dummy's movements. The illusion also fools the subject into

The Phantom Nose

Body maps can be tricked into bizarre misrepresentations. Neuroscientist V. S. Ramachandran and his colleagues at the Brain and Perception Laboratory in La Jolla, California, devised an ingenious experiment which they call the 'Phantom Nose'.

The subject sits in a chair, blindfolded, with an accomplice sitting at his right side, facing the same direction. The experimenter then stands near the subject and, with his left hand, takes hold of the subject's left index finger and uses it to repeatedly and randomly tap and stroke the nose of the accomplice, while at the same time he taps and strokes the subject's nose in precisely the same way, and in perfect synchrony. After a few seconds some subjects developed the uncanny illusion that their nose had either been dislocated, or stretched out several feet to the side. The more random the tapping and stroking, the stronger the illusion. If a drop of icy water was applied to the subject's nose while the illusion is happening, some felt it in the new location.[1]

This type of effect seems to come about when the brain mismatches internal feedback between its motor regions and its 'body maps'. In the experiment above, the motor region of the brain initially indicates that it is stroking a nose, and, indeed, this information maps perfectly on to the sensory input coming from the nose. However, the brain also registers that the stroking is being done in a place where the nose is not usually found. It has two ways to interpret this: either some other person is stroking their nose while forcing their finger to stroke someone else's nose in perfect synchrony – or their nose has been displaced. The primitive brain regions which are called upon to decide which of these is correct are not disposed to experience wandering body parts, but they are even less disposed to imagine the things that go on in experimental psychology laboratories. The body map therefore adapts to accommodate the distant nose.

[1] V. S. Ramachandran and Sandra Blakeslee, *Phantoms in the Brain* (London, Fourth Estate, 1998), 59.

Jeffrey Gray
Emeritus Professor of Psychology
Institute of Psychiatry, London

Predicting the Present

One feature of conscious experience which poses particular difficulties for biological accounts is that it occurs very late in the chain of events between stimulus and response – so late, indeed, that under most circumstances (and particularly those fast-moving circumstances that are vital for biological survival) the response has occurred before the responding subject is consciously aware of the stimulus that provoked it.

In modern times, when people do not often have to escape from attacking lions or leopards, the most dramatic examples of this lateness of conscious experience come from competitive sports. In championship tennis, for example, the serve is returned before the player returning it has had time consciously to see the oncoming ball pass the net.[1]

To those, like me, who are committed to a monist account of consciousness, and moreover an account consistent with Darwinian evolution, the lateness of conscious experience poses a problem. If conscious experience follows the behaviour that it accompanies, then how can it contribute to survival and so be subject to Darwinian selection?

In an attempt to answer this conundrum and to account mechanistically for the lateness of conscious experience, I propose that conscious experiences consist in the outputs of a comparator – a system which compares an event to a prediction of that event and determines the extent to which they match.

The human comparator does three things:

(1) computes a prediction of the contents of the entire perceptual world (visual, auditory, gustatory, olfactory, somatosensory etc.);

(2) compares this prediction to the description of the perceptual world that arises from the activity of thalamocortical sensory systems;

(3) produces an output listing the points of discrepancy between the predicted and actual descriptions.

What we experience, then, is only what has already been, as it were, ticked off (on a first, unconscious pass around perceptual systems) for its value on a scale of expected/unexpected and is in consequence selected for further, conscious processing. It is thus only at a second pass around perceptual systems that some events that have gone round once enter consciousness. The time scale of the comparator system is about right for this process. It usually takes between 100 and 200 milliseconds for stimuli to give rise to conscious experiences. This is consistent with the time it takes for neural signals to transit around the relevant limbic-cortical circuits.

With regard to the survival value of consciousness, I believe the role of the comparator in selecting stimuli for conscious processing is to serve as a late error detector, permitting correction of the error in time for the next occasion on which that behavioural routine might be required (e.g. the tennis player reflecting on what just caused him to miss a shot). This function is particularly clear in the case of anxiety, in which the stimuli selected for conscious processing are those that pose a threat.

The comparator model accounts for many of the features of subjective experience (e.g. that this consists of largely and perhaps entirely perceptual phenomena, that it is closely linked to the outcomes of motor programmes, but that the motor programmes themselves do not enter conscious awareness, etc.). The model is also open to experimental test. It predicts, for example, hippocampal activity associated with novelty detection, a prediction that recent neuroimaging studies tend to confirm.

I admit, though, that it throws no light at all upon the 'hard problem' of consciousness, that is: why such activities of the brain as predicting, comparing, noting mismatch, late error detection and the like should be accompanied by any conscious experiences at all rather than none. For an understanding of the hard problem I think we are all still waiting for a new type of theory, and one that will probably require a new Einstein for its production.

[1] John McCrone, *Going Inside: A Tour Round a Single Moment of Consciousness* (London, Faber and Faber, 1999).

owning sensations. When Ramachandran pinched the dummy's face the subject's skin showed a marked increase in conductance response – a sign of pain.

A similar illusion can be created by getting one person (A) to stand behind another (B) with A's arms extended under B's so that from the front (and from B's perspective) A's arms seem to be attached to B's shoulders. In one experiment, subject A was fitted with an earpiece through which they were told to carry out various movements – hand clapping, gesturing and so on. B was asked if they felt that they had any control over the arms and most of the subjects replied that they didn't. However, in a second experiment, both A and B were fitted with earpieces conveying the instructions while, again, A carried out various movements. This time B – in nearly all cases – reported feeling a strong sense that they themselves were moving the arms.

What seems to happen here is that hearing the instructions causes B's brain to create a 'plan' to move his own arms, which is then suppressed. The motor feedback that would normally follow such a plan is therefore missing (though it is likely that B may have unconsciously flexed the appropriate muscles in response to hearing the instructions), but what B's brain does receive is the visual feedback from A's limbs. Given that they are moving in just the right way, and that they are in the position where his own would normally be, this feedback alone is 'close enough' to his plan to be mapped on to it, thus creating a sense of both ownership of the movement, and agency.

Ownership of action, then, seems to come about from the matching of motor activity – the instructions sent to the muscles from the motor cortex – with sensory feedback (observation and body awareness created by movement and balance sensors in joints and muscles). It does not involve movement plans or intentions, hence you can own an action you did not intend to make. The sense of agency, on the other hand, seems to occur when a plan of action is matched to sensory feedback.

This gives us a clue as to the origin of the sense of agency. Conscious plans and intentions (as opposed to unconscious 'action schemas') are generated in the prefrontal lobes. Specifically they involve activity in an area called the dorsolateral prefrontal cortex (DPFC), the site of 'working memory'. This area takes information from many different places in the brain – sensory and conceptual – and 'juggles' it to come up with ideas for action. It is the part that the Martian investigators in chapter three would have seen illuminated in the brain of their victim when he was trying to work out what he should do.

The prefrontal cortex is the most recent part of the human brain to evolve

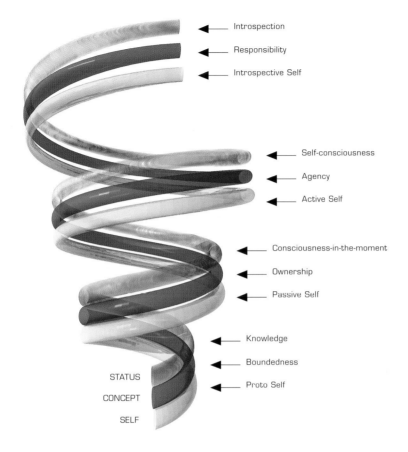

Introspection

Responsibility

Introspective Self

Self-consciousness

Agency

Active Self

Consciousness-in-the-moment

Ownership

Passive Self

Knowledge

Boundedness

STATUS

Proto Self

CONCEPT

SELF

and the last one to come 'on-line' during development. The connections between it and the motor areas arose in early mammals and its original purpose was probably to allow prediction of the effect of a movement, and a quick way to adjust movements that were about to be executed, in the light of new information.

The development of self produces concepts – of boundedness, ownership of experience, agency and responsibility – which are associated with increasingly complex states of consciousness.

If the evolutionary 'just-so' story of chapter three is correct, this 'mapping' system was the precursor to self-consciousness. The mapping of movement effects (feedback from the body) to the motor patterns that created the movements – the 'ownership system' – would provide the initial 'awareness of awareness' that produced pure qualia. But the mapping of predicted movements would bring the 'I' into being, because it would effectively produce the (unconscious) thought: 'that is where "I" will be in a moment.' The thought incorporates the conceptual self necessary for self-consciousness.

It is unlikely, though, that self-consciousness sprung into existence complete with a fully-fledged sense of agency. Rather the effect of mapping a predicted movement on to current motor instructions would originally have produced simply an awareness of what one's body was about to do. The thought would not be 'I am about to do this' but 'I am about to experience this.'

As the conceptualizing abilities of the first conscious beings grew, however, they began to spin stories to explain the world around them. Instead of just accepting that stuff happens they started to note consistent links between events, such as one event always following another. This eventually led to what was perhaps man's first big idea: cause and effect.

The notion of cause and effect – generally, not just in relation to our actions – is a theory, no more. We hold it dear because it explains the way the world seems to be: the sun comes out, the earth gets warm, rain falls down, the grass grows. Of course, we may deduce why things happen in a particular order, but most of the time our theory of cause and effect is derived simply from observation: A happens, then B happens. Every time. So A causes B. QED.

Except that it is not QED. We can never prove that A causes B just by observing that one follows the other, however often we see it happen. To assume a causal relationship is to go beyond the evidence. There could be a third factor – C – which is the hidden cause of both A and B. For example, a cuckoo may pop out of a door in a cuckoo clock when the hands of the clock reach twelve. But it may not be the movement of the hands that propels the bird – the same spring that pushes the hands may also operate the door mechanism, and if the end of the spring attached to the hand becomes detached, the cuckoo might sing out his noon-day song while the hands indicate it is not even time for breakfast.

Most of the time we do not bear this in mind. If A seems to cause B, that is good enough for us – especially in regard to the things that happen frequently and seem 'obviously' to be linked in this linear way. This cavalier application of our theory of cause and effect produces a commonsense view of the world which is very practical. We don't have to spend time deducing what is happening when B follows A – we just assume a straightforward causal connection and act accordingly. Occasionally this leads us to make serious errors – as when we mistakenly attribute the wrong cause to a disease, for example. But most of the time the theory works just fine, and every time it is successfully applied to a particular sequence of events it becomes more firmly established in our minds as 'proven'.

With regard to our own actions our theory of cause and effect works very well indeed. Every time a thought like 'I shall get up now' is followed by an appropriate action (e.g. getting up) the apparent causal link between the two seems to be confirmed. And it happens day in, day out, time and time again; thought-then-action, as consistent as night follows day. Even when the thought 'I shall get up now' is followed by snuggling deeper beneath the covers we can usually discern another thought surfacing in the gap: ('only after I've had another ten minutes in bed'). It is hardly surprising that we conclude that the thoughts cause the actions.

Yet the thought-then-action cycle is explicable in another way: we have the thought AND we perform the action due to a single cause: unconscious brain processes which determine our behaviour. Thus (thought) A and (action) B are both caused by (unconscious brain process) C. The thought always comes first, not because it is causal, but because the cognitive mechanisms that give rise to consciousness of what is about to happen are just that little bit faster than those which bring about the overt action. Furthermore, the thought as it first arises is not 'I shall do X', but 'X is about to happen'. Only on reflection – when we invoke the concept of agency in the process of becoming self-conscious, do we exercise the 'top-down' (unconscious) assumption that the thought is the cause of the action, and thus misinterpret it.

The misinterpretation is made easier by the fact that language does not clearly distinguish between doing and experiencing actions. If we tread on someone's toe, for example, we say 'I stood on your toe', whether we were pushed onto it or did it deliberately. Even reflex actions – in which there is no pre-awareness of any kind – are often described in this way: 'I pulled my hand away from the flame', rather than 'my hand recoiled from the flame'. Language is not just a vehicle for thought – to a large extent it *is* thought. So if we speak about actions that we are not aware of at all until afterwards as though we 'did' them, it is hardly surprising that we think of actions we are pre-aware of in this way.

Our interpretation of the awareness of an action-to-come is largely dependent on the assumptions we make about whether it is one that we assume we have control over or not. Think of the moment just before a sneeze. The thought that accompanies it is 'I am going to sneeze'. This could be either a prediction, *or* an announcement of your decision to expel mucus vapour at great speed from your nose. In most cases you are likely to interpret it as a simple prediction, because sneezing is generally put in the category of 'things that happen to us' rather than 'things that we do'. Now think of the moment just before you go to the fridge for the third chocolate fudge brownie of the morning. The thought that occurs is structured in just the same way as the one that preceded the sneeze: 'I am going to sneeze/get a brownie'. Yet it is interpreted as a decision.

But is there such a categorical difference between sneezing and raiding the fridge that one is necessarily something we do not decide to do, while the other necessarily is? Go back to that moment before the sneeze. Hold it there – with your face screwed up and your breath on hold and that tickle at the back of your nostril ... do you really feel you have no choice at all about what happens next? Imagine you are in a crowded auditorium and the action on stage is at its most tense – would the sneeze still happen? I doubt it. I was a television newsreader for five years, during which I spent about 900 hours, cumulatively, live on air. Never once did I sneeze despite often feeling like it. Conversely, I find myself eating chocolate-chip cookies when I have absolutely no conscious intention of doing so at all.

So what was suppressing the sneeze if it wasn't my conscious volition? I believe it was the inhibitory stimuli provided by the on-air environment. 'Top-down' brain processes informed me that sneezing was just not acceptable in this situation, and their conscious presence in my mind felt like a decision, though it was actually only my awareness of what my brain was directing my body to do (or, to be more accurate, not to do). The reason I sometimes eat cookies without apparently 'deciding' to is that sometimes top-down inhibitory influences ('three chocolate-chip cookies in quick succession will make you FAT') are swamped by more compelling unconscious urges – hunger, chocolate craving or the simple impulse to grab food. So long as I am unaware of these competing stimuli I do not suffer the conscious dilemma (shall I resist or give in?), nor do I feel that I took a decisive part in the action. If I do experience the dilemma it is because I am attending to the battle between my competing dispositions, and my consciousness of which wins out makes it feel as though my action was deliberate.

'Willed' and 'non-willed' actions are therefore not two discrete categories. There are, of course, movements which never feel under our control because they are clearly determined by outside forces – falling, for example, under the force of gravity. And reflex actions do not feel controlled because they bypass the brain. Of those actions which are effected by the motor cortex, however, the difference between 'voluntary' and 'non-voluntary' lies not in the type of act itself but in how we experience and interpret them. Voluntary actions require both that we are aware of the brain processes that bring it about and that we

register this awareness as a decision. Non-voluntary actions are those which are not accompanied by pre-awareness, or if they are, the processes are not interpreted as decisions. Hence walking, say, can be 'willed' when we attend to the movement of each leg, or 'automatic' when we are attending to something else. Sneezing can 'just happen', or it can be something we do.

Our idea of which actions we are 'free' to do and what 'just happens' to us is created by social factors which are present almost from birth. In societies where individuality is celebrated more actions are regarded as free than in those where the individual is expected to subjugate their 'will' to group considerations. In 'atomist' cultures, which reward individual initiative, babies are encouraged to start developing a sense of agency as an integral part of their selves as soon as they start to make movements. 'What a big noise you are making', coos the mother, as baby bashes away with a rattle, 'clever *you*!'. By continually inviting children to be both aware of their actions and to interpret that awareness as a 'decision' fosters the sense of self-responsibility that is essential in a society that requires its individuals to be self-policing. The requirement is greatest in societies which are largely free from external constraints. If you live in a country where you have to work continuously

The Innocent Eye Test by Mark Tansey, (1981) commemorates an experiment in which a cow was brought face-to-face with a painting of her kin to see what reaction she would have. Disappointingly for the researchers, the cow seemed singularly unmoved by the images. To her they were probably just meaningless shapes because she did not have the interpretive mechanisms required to translate canvas and oil to the idea of a living, three-dimensional animal. Her eye and brain were 'innocent'.

simply to survive in the face of natural obstacles like an appalling climate, even if you could make decisions, you couldn't exercise them because any departure from the prescribed course would be perilous. So your policing is done by the environment, or by tribal pressure – there is no need to internalize it.

It therefore seems likely that our sense of agency is a modern phenomenon – a socially constructed concept arising from a misinterpretation of a brain process which is essentially a feedback mechanism designed to ensure that the instructions our brains send to our bodies matches the motor plans contrived in response to sensory stimuli. Very young infants and most animals almost certainly do not have it. They are merely 'aware' of what they are doing, in the way that they are aware of what other objects 'do'. Early hominids probably did not have it: all their actions would have been experienced in the way we experience our automatic activities: walking, chewing, talking – just done, not decided upon. It is only now that we are equipped with language capable of building abstract concepts, and here, in places where we are encouraged to develop our own behavioural constraints, that the illusion of agency flourishes.

Just as we extend our selves beyond the body, we extend our selves, too, in time. This is what gives us the conviction that today's 'me' is the 'me' that was 'there' in the past, is here now and will be 'there' in the future.

There is no obvious reason why we should feel that we exist continuously. The contents of our consciousness, thoughts, feelings, perceptions and so on, shift constantly as the underlying neural firing patterns change. We never have the same blip of experience twice over, every brain state exists for a split second then disappears for ever. It follows (unless you believe in the immortal soul) that the experiencer of each of these sequential 'blips' of consciousness is brought into being with it, and dies when it fades. Yet the brain unifies this ever-changing self into one.

The trick is done, like so many others, by memory. Each brain state is informed by every one that went before it. If neurons A, B and C (multiply this a billion-odd times) fired together a millisecond ago it is likely they will fire again now, even if D, E and F, which also fired together a moment ago, are now quiet while G, H and I fire up instead. And J, K and L, neurons that fired together millions of times in the last year, are likely to fire up as well, just because they are in the habit of firing. These repetitive patterns of neural activity produce a partial replay of past moments of consciousness – slivers of memory – in each succeeding brain state, which bind with the information produced by the new patterns and therefore invest it with familiarity.

Dr Susan J. Blackmore
Senior Lecturer in Psychology
University of the West of England, Bristol

Meme Machines and Consciousness

What would it take for an artificial system to have something like human consciousness? Central to human consciousness is subjectivity and the notion of an experiencing self. I suggest that the self is more like a story or myth than a persisting entity that has free will and consciousness. Memes are information passed from one person to another by imitation, and I propose that the idea of a persisting self is a memeplex; a group of memes that propagate together. This selfplex is the origin of ordinary human consciousness. Therefore, only systems capable of imitation (and hence of sustaining memetic evolution) can have this kind of consciousness.

The concept of the meme derives from Richard Dawkins' 1976 book, *The Selfish Gene*,[1] in which he explained the power of universal Darwinism. This is the idea that whenever you have information that is copied with variation and selection you must get evolution. He called the information that is copied the 'replicator'. Genes are one example of a replicator and it is their competition that drives the evolution of biological design. But Dawkins argued that there are other replicators on this planet and that evolution therefore occurs at many different levels. One of the driving forces of social and cultural evolution is what Dawkins called memes.

Whenever information is copied from person to person by imitation, the copies may vary and not all of them get passed on again. So a new evolutionary process occurs. He called the information that is copied the meme. As examples he suggested 'tunes, ideas, catch-phrases, clothes, fashions, ways of making pots or of building arches.'[2]

Everything you have learned by copying it from someone else is a meme; every word in your language, every catch-phrase or saying. Every story you have ever heard, and every song you know, is a meme. The fact that you drive on the left (or perhaps the right), that you drink lager, think sun-dried tomatoes are passé, and wear jeans and a T-shirt to work are memes. The style of your house and your bicycle, the design of the roads in your city and the colour of the buses – all these are memes. Our culture is swept increasingly often by new memes, as communications and copying facilities improve. Email icons such as ;-), air kisses, pierced tongues, robo-pups, high-five salutations and fusion cuisine have all passed, like infections, around the planet.

It is tempting to say that the meme is information copied from one person to another. This is not misleading as long as we accept that this means only that something has been copied – whether it is a bodily movement, an utterance, a design, or a scientific theory. Whatever it is that is copied – that is the meme.

Since memes are replicators, memetic evolution proceeds not in the interest of the genes, nor in the interest of the individual who carries the memes, but in the interest of the memes themselves, so their survival is not necessarily advantageous to the host. Related memes tend to form mutually supportive meme-complexes such as religions, political ideologies, scientific theories, and New Age dogmas. Some of these may be hugely beneficial to human society, but others are pernicious because they infect people and demand their resources in spite of being false.

The most powerful and insidious of all the memeplexes is, I shall argue, our very own 'self'. It is perhaps hard to think of yourself as a memeplex, but if you look inside a brain you do not see a central place where a self might live, and from where it might direct operations. You just see a lump of porridge-like stuff or, with magnification, millions of neurons connected in billions of ways to each other. Indeed the more you understand about what is going on in the brain, the less need there seems to be for a central experiencing self. Certainly there is a human body and brain that can see, imagine, and think, and these processes may entail hierarchies, control mechanisms, and a body image. However, there is not, in addition, a central, persisting conscious self that receives the impressions or makes the decisions.

The implications for consciousness are this. The whole problem of consciousness stems from making a distinction between the world that is perceived and the self who is perceiving it, but if this self is just a myth, then this distinction must be false.

If the self is a myth, then why are selves constructed at all? The answer, I suggest, is that the memes do it. The twin capabilies of imitation and language – unique to humans – allow all kinds of memes to flourish. So the self becomes a word to which can be attached desires, intentions, loves and hates, ambitions and fears. 'I' love the Simpsons. 'I' am going to be a famous artist. 'I' believe in freedom of speech.

Each of us comes across countless ideas every day but most are forgotten. However, any that become 'my' belief are protected. I will fight for my beliefs; I will argue for them with others and so pass them on. The same is true of my plans for the future. Once I have got it into my head that I want to go to Bali for my holiday I will collect brochures, read books, and buy pictures of Bali. These memes spread better because they are part of 'my' plans. The self becomes an idea to which are attached all sorts of verbal labels – nice, nasty, reliable, punctual, disobedient, friendly or sexy. Note that there is, of course, a body that behaves in certain ways and looks a certain way, but this is not how we talk about ourselves or each other. We speak about our 'self' as being the one who is nice or nasty. We don't just mean the body – we mean the inner 'me' who has this personality and is responsible for 'my' actions. As language and society become more and more complex we can say more and more things about this self, and it can desire more and more possessions and achievements.

In this way all kinds of memes succeed better because they become part of a self, and so the selfplex grows – and grows. This is how we come to acquire a story about a little self inside that has desires and plans, that has free will and the power to make decisions, and that has consciousness. Ordinary human consciousness is thus constructed by the memes, using the human meme machine. Our consciousness is the way it is because of the success of the memes that make up the selfplex.

Susan Blackmore is author of *The Meme Machine* (Oxford, Oxford University Press, 1999).

1 Richard Dawkins, *The Selfish Gene* (Oxford, Oxford University Press (1976). New edition with additional material (1989).
2 Ibid.

The neurological integration required to produce the sense of unity becomes habitual mainly due to the hippocampus repeatedly triggering similar neural firing patterns. This consistency is helped by input from other people. Being recognized, consistently, as a single person shores up our own sense of ourselves, and the stories that others tell about us helps mould the shape of the personality that emerges: 'You're always so decisive/cheerful/calm in a crisis!' Remarks like this often become self-fulfilling – we may come away from a crisis thinking that we dithered and whined and panicked, but if enough people tell us we behaved marvelously, chances are we will re-write our memory to fit the story.

By identifying with the self who has inhabited our body until now we build a story which features us as the central protagonist and helps us to know – by reference to the past actions of our body-inhabitant – what sort of person we are. This ongoing autobiography gives shape and meaning to our lives. By extending backward in time we count our achievements, and by extending forward we create goals which motivate us in the here and now. It also keeps society together – where would we be if the signatories to a contract later denied they were bound by it because it was not 'them' who signed it? Most importantly, it shores up our sense of responsibility: we feel guilty about what we have done wrong in the past because we believe 'we' did it and not someone else. And it makes us careful of what we do today because 'we' will suffer the consequences tomorrow. A stronger mechanism for personal survival and social cohesion is hard to imagine.

Some people have a much stronger – and longer – sense of self-continuity than others. There are those who seem to live for the moment, caring little about what happens to them in the future and taking little responsibility for the things they did in the past. Conversely, some suffer agonies of guilt about misdeeds which others (including those who suffered from them) may have long forgotten. Many people even have an idea of self that goes beyond their material existence, manifested in a belief in some personal, identifiable 'life after death', or just the desire to leave something to be remembered by – a master-work, monument or reputation.

Not all past and future 'I's are within the fold, though. The time boundary of self does not necessarily go back to the womb or forward to (let alone beyond) the grave. Intellectually we may think it does, but our emotions tell a different story. Think back (if you can bear to) to the last time you did something that embarrassed you. If it was within the last few days, or weeks, chances are that the thought will bring the feeling back – it is almost as though you are doing it again. Now think of something similar that happened much further back – 10 or 15 years ago. The feeling is not so strong, is it? Even if your memory is clear and the event may have been just as embarrassing at the time it becomes harder to 'own' it. The passage of time has made it seem as if it happened – almost – to someone else. Similarly, the further something is in the future, the less it concerns us. The prospect of a painful visit to the dentist tomorrow is probably more upsetting than the thought of your own death. We all know, intellectually, that we are going to die. But it is only when the prospect becomes imminent that the message really comes home. Until then most of us feel that it will happen to someone else. If we really felt we 'owned' the person who may suffer a painful end in 20 or 50 years' time, we would spend the rest of our lives in a lather of terror, but most of us don't – a certain degree of disunity in time is merciful, and essential, for normal mental health.

These then, are the basic requirements for a sense of self: first, a boundary in space – an elastic one which may incorporate things and people beyond our body, but one that is firm enough to provide a point of view and thus 'ownership' of our individual slice of consciousness. Second, a sense of agency, such that our acts seem to be signatures of some entity distinct from mere physical processes, and finally a sense of unity and continuity that allows us to create an autobiography.

Over and above these most of us elaborate these basics, adding the habits of behaviour we think of as our personality: our social position, our hopes, dreams and beliefs.

All of this is produced by shifting, sparking, fizzing, discontinuous neural firing patterns in our brains. Those that encode the sense of self are among the most robust, but like all brain circuitry they do occasionally break down. There are certain conditions – some of them drug-induced or achieved through techniques like hypnosis or meditation, others due to brain damage or disorder – that eradicate any or all of the founding blocks of self. Some of these alterations produce the highest, most blissful and meaningful experiences we can know. But others produce terrifying alterations in consciousness.

In the next chapter we look at what happens when the normal structure of the self fragments.

Fractured Consciousness

'Though this be madness, there is method in't.'

William Shakespeare, *Hamlet*

If brains construct selves, what is to stop them making more than one each? Or scrapping an old one and making a new model? What if some bit of the self system fails to work or gets erased? Or if its conceptual boundary is lost, or extends, like some over-inflated balloon, to incorporate bits of the world that really have nothing to do with it?

In fact there is nothing to stop these things happening, and they do – all the time. Changes in the sense of self bring alterations in consciousness which vary from mild, transient disturbances to outright psychosis. We all experience them – indeed, one of the most dramatically bizarre altered states occurs in every one of us two or three times in every 24-hour cycle. It is called dreaming.

During dreams the normal sense of self is taken off-line and the result is a crazy distortion of experience. The main thing that distinguishes our mental state during dreams from that of, say, a schizophrenic in the throes of hallucination, is that dream 'madness' is experienced privately. We can't act it out because we are paralysed and when the paralysis disappears, so does the insanity.

Dreaming feels like a very vivid form of imagination, but there are two major differences. When you imagine something it seems that your brain generates a concept which is usually only lightly informed by sensory content. We may think we see a clear image, but if you test that intuition by trying to 'read it off' the scene, as you can an ordinary perception, you realize it is actually very faint and bitty. Dream images, by contrast, are as concrete (though not as stable) as those we see when we are wide awake and looking out.

The second difference between dreaming and daydreaming is that the former is not constrained by the full complement of unconscious assumptions and prejudices that mould waking consciousness. It is this that gives it its weird quality.

When you daydream you can (to some extent) cut off incoming sensory information and generate a virtual reality similar to a dreamscape. But however involved you may get in your inner world, some part of you remains aware that you are only fantasizing. If you create a vision of a flying pig you know it only exists in your mind's eye. Dreaming, by contrast, is more like a hallucination – the unconscious 'reality check' that keeps you tenuously connected to the outside world when you daydream is turned off. The pig, it seems, is really flying.

In some ways dreaming is even more detached from reality than hallucination. When an otherwise normal person hallucinates – sees a ghost, say – they tend to get scared or feel baffled because their unconscious concepts about the way the physical world works are still operating. The fear or confusion results from the clash between what their senses tell them is happening and what those concepts dictate should be happening. In a dreaming state this dissonance does not occur because some of the underlying assumptions about the way things 'really are' are not operating. We happily accept that pigs fly because we have temporarily forgotten that the laws of nature forbid it.

But it is not just our beliefs about the outside world that are suspended in dreams. Part of their weird quality comes from the loss of the normal sense of self. When you daydream both your public and your 'inner' self is intact and your fantasies are constrained by them. You may try out being a fighter pilot or a Nobel prizewinner in your head but you know you are just pretending. In dreams, by contrast, you may be anything: a fish; a drowning goat; the Queen of Hearts; Napoleon, or an infant ... you *are* it. Even when you remain basically yourself in a dream you are usually unable to summon the personal memories that maintain the 'public' elements of that self: where you live, what you did during the day, who your family is and so on. You may also experience an alteration in the sense of ownership and agency: it is quite common, for example, for dreamers to report that they experienced or did something in a dream which was also experienced or done by someone else. You can be both here and there in a dream; this person, and also that one. And continuity goes by the board: one moment you might be you, conducting an orchestra, the next you are a violinist, or even a violin. In dreaming, the self-concept ceases to be a solid, ever-informing presence and becomes fragmented and protean.

The mad meanderings of dream consciousness are created by feedback from memory and conceptual storage areas which mingles with newly memorized experiences – all of it heavily imbued with the emotion that accompanied them. But while that may explain why the brain produces such curious subject-matter, it does not explain why we ourselves are so altered in dreams – disunited and disoriented, bereft of insight and uncritically accepting of the craziest events. The shortest sequence of typical dream consciousness would send us hot-foot to the psychiatrist if it occurred in waking life. Yet when your dream self sees your mother turn into a porcupine and order a pizza you are more likely to bewail the lack of pepperoni than call for an ambulance to take you to the emergency room. It is not just your dream world that is topsy-turvy, your own responses are screwy, too.

The reason for this is that in dreaming, although the overall level of activity in the brain may be as high as during waking, the patterns of activity are different in that some of the neural pathways between brain areas are blocked off entirely, while others are reduced to one-way traffic. Because of this, certain areas of the brain (the bits that know pigs can't fly, for example) are cut off and cannot be brought to bear on the experience.

Neural activity blockage also brings about sleep paralysis – the mechanism that prevents us from acting out our dreams in the real world. It is caused by a change in the spinal motor cells – the nerves that carry signals from the motor cortex in the brain to the muscles. The membranes of these cells becomes resistant to excitation due to a rise in their electrical potential, and this blocks 'messages out'.[1] Occasional bursts of motor activity (observable as twitches) get through this blockade, but only one motor circuit escapes it altogether, and that is the one that causes eye movements. Hence the Rapid Eye Movements (REM) which signify vivid dreaming.

The motor blockade has very little effect on consciousness, though. In the dream state the feel of our movements is quite normal, even if the movements themselves are miraculous, like flying. This is because the motor cortex, in all states of consciousness, sends commands both to the body and – like a carbon copy – to the sensory cortices which will be affected by the movement. This sets up a pattern of activity which is effectively a prediction of what those effects will be. Then, when they happen for real (when moving an arm, for example, produces feedback from the joints and muscles involved in the action) they are mapped on to that prediction – ticked off like a confirmation report: 'plan executed – result correct'.

When you imagine moving your arm while you are awake this 'carbon copy' effect produces a faint impression of how the real movement would feel. However, you are also receiving information about the actual position of your (unmoved) arm, and this partly inhibits the sensory effect of the prediction.

When you are dreaming however, information about your body's actual state is missing. The planning part of the motor cortex is cut off (by sleep paralysis) from the part of it which executes the plans, but the carbon copy still gets sent to the sensory cortex. In the absence of conflicting information from the real world, this prediction is strong enough to produce almost precisely the same sensation as real movement.[2] So your conceptual body floats free of the real thing.

Similarly, sensory images seem real because re-entrant pathways between primary sensory areas and the association areas, where the different sensual elements of a perception – sight and touch, for example – are merged, are active in REM sleep. This allows us to form perfect, multi-sensory images of the things we encounter, so our consciousness of, say, a dream apple is as clear as our consciousness of a real one would be when we are awake. However, the more abstract a perception the more likely it is to be distorted in dreams, because as you go forward in the cortex – from the sensory areas to those that deal with concepts – the more blocked pathways there are. The apple, therefore, may be quite clear to look at, but might not be clearly *conceived* of as an apple – one moment it may be a fruit, the next moment it may be a globe or a tennis ball. And these weird transformations take place without producing the 'mismatch' with conflicting concepts which would normally spark astonishment or disbelief.

One of the areas where neural activity is altered in dreaming is that which identifies other people. A curious feature of dreams is how people we know often pop up in unrecognizable (maybe not even human) guises, and may do totally uncharacteristic things, yet we still 'just know' who they are. One study found that subjects recognized more dream characters in the 'I just know it was him' way, than by facial or behaviour recognition.[3]

Recognizing people in this way gives the impression that each person has some 'essence' which is separate from their appearance or behaviour. A more mundane explanation is that the emotional memory of a person may be accessed during dreaming, but – due to inhibition of the pathways that link the emotional brain to memory and face recognition areas – it is not connected in the dreamer's mind to the other person's more obvious characteristics. And as emotion, alone, is almost impossible to articulate, we are left with the mysterious feeling of 'just knowing'.

Dreaming is an extraordinary business, and we spend huge chunks of our life doing it. Yet apart, perhaps, from indulging in dubious dream analysis we don't generally make much use of it. It is a shame, because dreams offer, potentially, the biggest, cheapest and safest thrills you could hope for. Watching a movie is a poor substitute for a full, 'sensurround' dream spectacular, and the most exciting theme park ride is tame compared to, say, the bliss of flying unaided over beautiful countryside, as one can do in dreams. The only trips that compare to the best that dreaming can provide are those granted by hallucinogenic drugs, and those, unfortunately, tend to be accompanied by undesirable side-effects – one of which, at the moment, can be the acquisition of a criminal record.

The reason we don't make much of our dreams is two-fold: ordinary dreams do not lay down strong memories, so they are quickly forgotten. And our enjoyment of them while they are happening is limited because we cannot control them nor appreciate just how amazing they are.

Dreams do not have to be like this, though. There is a state of consciousness which combines the perceptual contents of dreaming with normal waking alertness, self-awareness, reflection, intentionality, motivation and memory.

This state is known as lucid dreaming, and it happens when the parts of the brain which are normally 'off-line' during dreaming click back in, bringing the dreamer back to self-consciousness while allowing the hallucination to continue. The emergence of self-consciousness allows a lucid dreamer to alter their dream as it goes along, directing events, summoning up companions, trying out various scenarios. It is virtual reality with the advantage of complete control.

When a dream turns lucid it feels exactly like waking up, except that instead of waking in your bed you wake into whatever scene was being enacted in the dream. The usual trigger is a thought along the lines of 'this is just crazy – I can't really be tobogganing down the side of the Empire State building – it must be a dream!' The thought seems to break the spell of the dream, releasing you into full consciousness, yet the hallucination continues as vividly as before. Now, however, you have a choice about how it unfolds. If you are an experienced lucid dreamer you can either allow the dream to meander on while you enjoy the ride, or you can direct it,

Sherrington

'The brain is waking and with it the mind returns. It is as if the Milky Way entered upon some cosmic dance. Swiftly the head-mass becomes an enchanted loom where millions of slashing shuttles wave a dissolving pattern, always a meaningful pattern though never an abiding one; a shifting harmony of sub-patterns.'

Charles Sherrington, 1940

merely by thinking of what you would like to happen next. If you fancy a stroll on a tropical beach you can decide that when you turn around the scene will be transformed into an island paradise, or if you fancy having a chat with a friend you can simply decide that they will walk out of a nearby building and greet you. But you cannot make things 'just appear' from nowhere in lucid dreams – they have to arrive in some way that makes sense, perhaps because your concepts of physical laws are back in operation. This does not, however, prevent you from enjoying more or less any physical sensation you care to imagine. Different people do different things in their lucid dreams – some fly, listen to glorious music, enjoy orgasmic sex with dream lovers or leave their bodies.

One in two people report experiencing lucidity during dreaming, but the state is a fragile one and it takes practice to maintain it.[4] There is a strong tendency for lucid dreaming to slide back into normal dreaming, or for the dreamer to wake up fully. The in-between states (when lucid dreaming is slipping one way or another) can be unpleasant. There is, for example, the 'false awakening', in which the dreamer thinks they are properly awake and fails to realize that they are still in a dream. Typically they go through the motions of getting up, dressing and perhaps even setting off for work. The dreamscape in a false awakening is often gloomy and may feel as though it is charged with a sinister atmosphere. Movements have that 'glued to the ground' feeling, because the dreamer becomes aware of the sleep paralysis that still affects their body.

Lucid dreaming occurs when some of the changes in brain activity which switch us from sleep to wakefulness happen, but others do not. The disconnection between cortical areas which produce the unreflective mind-set we have in ordinary dreaming is due to a plunge in noradrenalin and serotonin, while sleep paralysis and the generation of dream images are due to the ebb and flow of other neurotransmitters. Usually all these changes are reversed, swiftly and together, when we wake up, so normal self-consciousness returns at the same time as the dream imagery disappears and sleep paralysis lifts.

In lucid dreaming what seems to happen is that the noradrenalin and serotonin levels rise slightly and trigger activation in the prefrontal cortex. If you have primed your brain with the thought 'this is a dream' by repeating it before sleep, the neural activation related to the thought will be 'warm' and therefore more likely to occur. If it does, and if the activation is strong enough, it may 'burst through' the blocked pathways in the conceptual processing areas of the brain and bring the entire package of autobiographical memory,

Dream Caused by the Flight of a Bee around a Pomegranate One Second Before Waking Up
Salvador Dali, 1944.

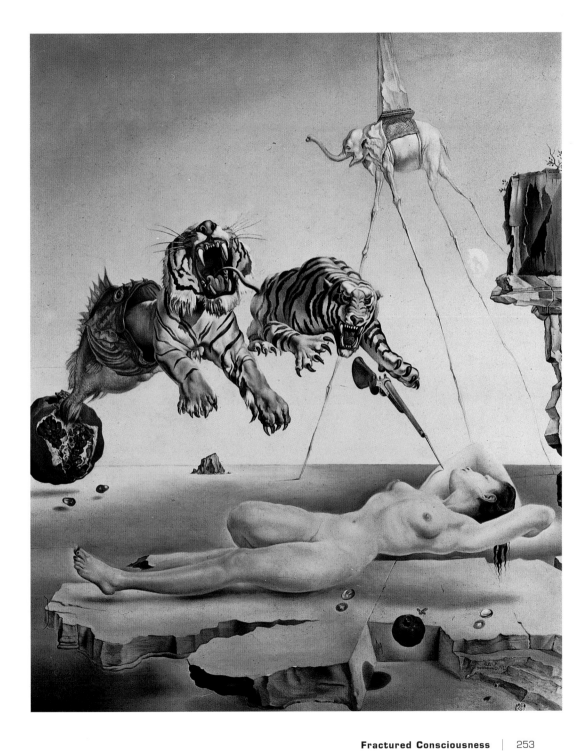

working memory, and so on back on-line. Your 'self' is reinstated. The further increase in serotonin and noradrenalin created by the activation of these concepts tends to tip the chemical balance of the brain back into the waking state, but if you can relax into the dream and avoid turning your mind to thoughts like 'is it time to get up?', you can remain poised in a half-sleeping, half-waking state. You can continue your dream while remaining entirely aware of who and where you are, and that the dream is a self-generated hallucination that you can turn into anything you want. Come morning your dream will remain as a clear memory – not quite as clear as a real event, perhaps, but much more retrievable than an ordinary dream, because it will have taken place in a brain state which allows it to be encoded into long-term memory.

As well as serving as a playground for the mind, lucid dreaming is proving to be a useful tool for examining some aspects of normal consciousness. It is possible – although it takes perseverance – to train yourself to become lucid more or less at will. Although lucid dreamers are paralysed, and therefore cannot report on their dreams as they happen, they can communicate with people in the outside world by making pre-arranged eye movements which can be seen beneath the eyelids or detected by mechanical sensors.

In a series of studies carried out by Stephen LaBerge and his colleagues at the Lucidity Institute in California, experienced lucid dreamers carried out various pre-arranged tasks while they were dreaming. In one study, the subjects first indicated when they became lucid by sweeping their eyes from side to side three times. Then they summoned up a circular object in their dream and traced its outline with their eyes. The researchers then monitored the eye movements and compared them with movements made by the same subjects when they were awake and tracing the outline of a real round object, and separately that of an imagined one. The experiment showed that in the dreaming state, the subjects' eye movements followed the contours of the object smoothly. They did this, too, when the people were awake and looking at a real object. When the object was imagined, however, the eye movements were jerky.[5]

This study rather confirms what most of us recall about dream imagery – it seems, like waking perception, to be solid and fine-grained, like a high-quality photograph. By contrast, visual imagination (except in eidetic imagery) is more vaporous or bitty. This, in turn, gives us a clue to the nature of internally generated imagery.

One of the ongoing debates in neuroscience and philosophy concerns whether imagination is closer to abstract thought or to sensation. Brain-imaging studies should be able to answer the question by revealing the area of the brain which generates it: if it is mainly sensation the brain areas that light up most when someone is imagining something would be the primary sensory cortices – those that are active when they 'really' see (or hear or touch) it. If it is a matter of abstract thought, however, the areas involved would be further forward in the brain, in the conceptual processing areas.

In fact brain-imaging work in this field is conflicting – some experiments show activation mainly in the primary cortices when a person sees something in their 'mind's eye',[6] while others show most activity in 'higher' brain areas.[7] If consciousness necessarily involves both bottom-up and top-down processing then these conflicts are not surprising – they just show that imagination, like consciousness of externally generated perceptions, is a matter of both sensory and conceptual processing. They do not help to answer the question of which is the greater factor.

LaBerge's lucid dream studies suggest that REM dreaming is very much a bottom-up process, rather like a highly attentive waking state or eidetic memory. Imagination, by contrast, is one step further towards abstraction. Our daydreams remain grounded in physical sensation, but they feel less solid than our dreams and perceptions of the outside world because they incorporate less bottom-up information.

Lucid dreaming experiments may also give an indication of how many waking perceptions we memorize. During lucid dreaming it is easy to alter the world you are in – all you need do to change a frog into a prince is to turn your back and wish it. Much more difficult, though, is to keep things the same. Only those things you concentrate on are likely to stay stable and if you turn away from something for more than a moment it is likely to be different when you look back at it. If you are reading words, for example, in a lucid dream, the ones you are actually reading at any moment will seem quite clear. But if you go back a few lines you will probably find that the ones you read a moment ago now say something else. These changes are not necessarily willed, and trying to prevent them is very difficult – 75 per cent of a group of lucid dreamers who tried the reading experiment reported that words changed however much they willed them to stay the same.[8] These involuntary changes, however, tend to be rather subtle, unlike the dramatic metamorphoses you can bring about deliberately. The words in the book, for example, will only have altered a little and a person may have a slightly different hairstyle on second viewing, but is unlikely to have changed into a chair.

If, as seems likely, dream sensation (as opposed to content) is almost the same as in waking, this rather backs up the idea that normal vision is fragmented. When you look attentively at something during normal wakefulness, turn away and then go back to it, it nearly always looks the same as it did before. But, as change blindness experiments show (see page 14), the surrounding environment could change dramatically and you would probably not notice. You simply assume it is the same. When you look away from a dreamscape it continues to exist only to the extent that it lingers in memory. When you look back the neural activation in the sensory cortices that produced the previously attended-to images is re-triggered by the top-down expectation that the objects they encode will still be there. However, unlike in real life, this activation is not refreshed by incoming information, so it is slightly degenerated and thus produces a different image. Objects that you did not consciously see first time round don't seem to have changed because you don't have a concept of them to compare with the new perception. The involuntary changes seen in lucid dreams may therefore uncover the shortcomings of our normal waking visual consciousness by reflecting the number of 'items' we are conscious of – waking or dreaming – at any one moment.

Dreaming demonstrates that the self-concepts that underpin normal consciousness – unity, agency and so on – can be flipped on and off by chemical changes in the brain. Provided the physiological changes that induce sleep are orchestrated in the normal way we lose the concepts only when we are safely asleep and paralysed, so however crazy it makes us doesn't matter – no-one else is going to be affected and the worst it can do is to give us a nightmare.

Schizophrenics are not so protected. This illness is primarily a disorder of the self in that the insanity associated with it is born out of the disruption of the sense of ownership and/or agency, and a resulting alteration in experience. In some patients, at certain stages in their illness, the self effectively disappears and they sink into catatonic inertia. At other times they lose the sense of ownership of their perceptions, emotions and thoughts, or fail to realize that they are the agent of their own actions, blaming shadowy external manipulators for inserting alien ideas into their minds. In other schizophrenic states the self is hugely amplified – conceptually extended to such a grandiose degree that it subsumes everything in its surroundings. The owner of this inflated self may believe they have God-like agency – control over all they survey. The strange beliefs held by schizophrenics are probably a creative way of explaining their altered consciousness, an attempt to make sense of what is happening to them rather than the root cause of their illness. When their perception is normalized, their beliefs tend to become normal too.

This ties in with brain-imaging studies which show that in schizophrenics, parts of the frontal cortex concerned with constructing the self are underactive during stages of the illness in which the feeling of free will is undermined. Conversely there is some evidence to suggest that it is overactive in patients with grandiose ideas about their powers of control.[9] In these cases what may be happening is that plans of action, or just vaguely imagined ideas of what one might do, which are concocted in the frontal cortex, are overwhelmingly strong and cannot be cancelled out by the intentional areas in the parietal cortex when they fail to occur. The result is that they seem to have been executed. The subject sees some effect – the sun passing across the horizon, say – and feels that they have acted to make it happen. Consciously, of course, they recognize that they have not done this physically but the conviction of agency is so strong that they contrive an elaborate explanation, usually involving thought-waves or mysterious rays.

Schizophrenics are often very intelligent, and the battiness of their ideas is testimony to the strength that the sense of agency can attain. It seems overwhelmingly certain to them that the cause lies in themselves, and to deny it seems even madder than supposing they have the power to move the earth.

Schizophrenics sometimes become catatonic, and may stay frozen in strange postures for weeks. The state is associated with a lack of activity in the frontal cortex.

Such beliefs severely affect some schizophrenics' ability to function in the outside world, for obvious reasons. But their elaborate rationalizations probably serve to make their inner world more comfortable because they remove the clash between what they feel and what they know to be true. Unable to change what they feel, they change what they know, trading external 'madness' for inner sanity.

Beyond this the neurological basis of schizophrenia is little understood. It seems to be to some extent 'hard-wired' – there are strong genetic and structural differences in schizophrenics' brains which suggest that something goes wrong in brain development early on. Yet the symptoms can often be eradicated by drugs. It seems likely that the bouts of insanity occur when the normal to-and-froing of information between various brain modules is disturbed – either blocked, or amplified – but drugs can make this brain activity more normal.

Autism, by contrast, is resistant to treatment. In its severer forms this condition produces a profound fragmentation of experience in which the sense of self – if it exists at all – is severely and permanently compromised.

Autism is coming to be seen less as a single, invariant condition, and more as a spectrum of disorders marked by an almost total inability to function at one end of the scale, to mere oddness or eccentricity at the other. Autistic people invariably have an obsessive insistence on sameness and indulge in obsessive rituals which involve placing things in some sort of order. They might endlessly arrange objects in a particular formation, or be fixated with lists and schedules. Another invariable is their lack of intuitive grasp of what is going on in others' minds. Some autistic people have islands of extraordinary talent – so-called 'savant' skills like the ability to memorize huge amounts of data, do lightening calculations, draw brilliantly, or play a musical piece on an instrument note-perfect after hearing it only once.

Severely impaired autistics are unable to speak, so it is impossible to know what their consciousness feels like. But the behaviour of such people suggests that it is fragmented to such an extent that they have only a very basic idea of self. It is possible therefore that the perceptions created by their brains remain unowned, unreflected-upon and unbound. The repetitive physical rituals (head-banging, swaying, clicking fingers, etc.) so often observed in the severely autistic may be an attempt to integrate physical motion and sensation. Thus they try to form the connection between these two things which normally gives the sense of ownership and agency (which creates consciousness-with-self), that is, experience as we know it.

Travel along the spectrum a bit, and imagine a mind that is slightly more connected in that sensory perceptions are bound, but still disconnected from higher conceptual processes. Such a brain would know its perceptions to be 'out there' and itself as the 'in-here' 'I' that experiences them. But its experience would be narrow and concrete – a set of discrete objects without meaning.

Along a bit more, and consider a person with some working connections between sensory and conceptual processing areas. Now they can link perceptions to labels, producing 'tokens' such as words, and create a skeleton conceptual self. However, without rich input from the 'higher' conceptual processing areas in the prefrontal cortex such tokens would remain deeply grounded in the body. An 'apple' would refer to the object – its image and taste – and would not come to be associated with love ('the apple of my eye'), or temptation (the apple that seduced Adam), or tidiness ('apple-pie order'). Similarly, a threat to such a person's self would be something that imperilled them physically – there would be no 'notional' self to be hurt by humiliation or insult.

The consciousness of such a person would be locked into the moment. There would be little anticipation, so no disappointment at things that don't turn out as imagined, nor fear of things to come. Memories would be laid down perfectly and completely because there would be no top-down processing to prejudice the selection of one element over another. Once stored they would remain intact because they would be isolated from others and therefore not be altered or swamped by them. Similarly objects would be seen with immense precision and clarity because they would not be occluded by an onslaught of expectations. Unable to bind their experience into a conceptual 'big picture' the contents of their consciousness would consist of trillions of tiny details like a photograph magnified so much that it decomposes into pixels.

How to make meaning in such an atomized universe? The brain would still try, because that is what brains do, even severely damaged ones. Unable to grasp big patterns, it would therefore focus obsessively on what it *could* compose – physical order. By arranging objects, or events, in some set form, the autistic person would have a concrete reference on which to base concepts: the idea of a cup of tea, for example, might be linked to a particular sequence of observed movements involving a particular kettle, a particular cup, a particular tea-caddy, manipulated in a certain order. So long as the physical form remained constant the concept would hold together, but alter one tiny part and the idea would shatter because a cup of tea is that physical activity and there is no abstract 'cup of tea' that remains when it is gone.

Hence sameness would become essential: alter the physical form and the concept is shattered.

Something of the experiential distortions suffered by people with schizophrenia and autism are shared by many people who would not be considered mentally ill. The conceptual framework that organizes our perceptions and makes them ours are pretty robust, but severe stress may cause it to break down, a phenomenen known as dissociation. The resultant

Alzheimer's disease eats away at the self as the brain dies. This series of self-portraits chart the course, over five years, of the artist's idea of himself as he became increasingly demented.

disturbances in perception are known as derealization, and disturbances in self-perception are known as depersonalization.

Dissociation involves, to a greater or lesser extent, a loss of self. It may manifest as the sense of 'losing' a part of the body, rather as in neglect, or the inability to access information about oneself or one's past life (psychogenic amnesia). In some cases the most fundamental qualities of consciousness: ownership and unity, may be compromised.

Severe depersonalization and derealization (which often go together) are mercifully rare, but almost everyone has experienced them mildly at some time or another. It is what happens when you are in an accident and feel as though you are 'watching' it rather than perilously involved; it is when you feel inappropriately detached during what you would expect to be a highly emotional experience such as watching someone you love die; and when you find yourself 'going through the motions' of behaving normally when you are desperate. Depression and severe anxiety usually involve a degree of depersonalization and/or derealization, as do acute fear and exhaustion, the aura of migraine and the prodromal stage of a seizure. One study found that nearly one in four of a large sample of people had experienced the symptoms of one or other condition within the previous year.[10]

Depersonalization is marked by a feeling of being unreal, disembodied and

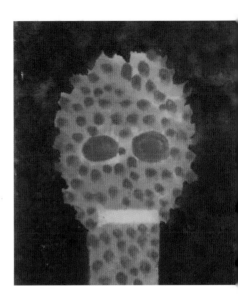

floating or like a puppet or robot. Some people report 'watching themselves' as though through another's eyes, or as being an observer of their thoughts and actions rather than the agent. One chronic sufferer, Aeleis, describes it as though she is split in two: 'When I look back I have generally at least two clear memories for any given event ... One of these was extremely detached. This "me" felt unemotional, and not connected to anything in particular. Kind of like this thing sitting in the back of my head observing everything. The other was very "raw" and experienced sensory overload on a near-constant basis. ... The thing is, neither of these two seemed to have control of my body. It was like something separate that was moved by something else and not something I could feel attached to. [At one stage] I started to experience drastic changes in my levels of connection. One minute I would be floating away from myself, and then I would be floating away from the world.'[11]

Derealization is closely related to depersonalization, but differs in that it consists of altered consciousness of the outside world rather than of oneself. A person in this state might feel that their surroundings are unreal or distanced; objects may seem tiny and far away – as though seen through the wrong end of a telescope; or the world may seem to be flat, artificial and cardboardy, or shifty and shimmering. There may be episodes of deja vu, or its converse, *jamais vu*, in which familiar scenes or people seem strange.

Depersonalization and derealization do not, in themselves, cause people to lose touch with reality. Although those who suffer from the conditions may feel as though they are going crazy their thinking and behaviour is entirely sane given the information available to them. Their state of mind is that of a normal person who is struggling to make sense of an alien sensation or environment. However, depersonalization and derealization very often occur in mental states which lack this crucial insight and are frankly psychotic.

Capgras delusion, for example, is the belief that one's nearest and dearest have been replaced by robots, or taken over by aliens, or in some other way 'switched' for the real thing. It is an inappropriate rationalization of intense derealization with regard to familiar people. Although these people look like themselves, and talk and move and behave like themselves, the patient with Capgras delusion feels these once-loved beings are not themselves in some indescribable but fundamental way. So convinced may the patient be of this that they will attack their family or friends, blaming them for 'doing away with' the real people they are impersonating. In one sad case a patient with Capgras delusion slit his father's throat to look for the wires that would prove he was a robotic simulacrum.[12]

Severe depersonalization may also be interpreted in a delusional way. When all normal sense of self is lost some people actually become convinced that they are dead. Patients with Cotard's delusion, as it is known, may say that they are invisible, and will insist that their body is lifeless or even long-dead and rotting. No amount of persuasion will disabuse them of their conviction, and conversations designed to do so are foiled – if the sufferer is intelligent – by a curious circular logic that deluded people often employ in order to maintain their belief against all the evidence. There is a joke that captures this frustrating aspect of the phenomenon:

A man is convinced he is dead. Everyone tells him it can't be true: 'Look, you're not dead: you're walking and talking and breathing; how can you be dead?' But he continues to insist he is. His family finally takes him to a doctor. The doctor spends hours with the man trying to convince him that he is not

The cortical 'who?' recognition pathway ends in the frontal area with the conscious acknowledgement that a person is familiar

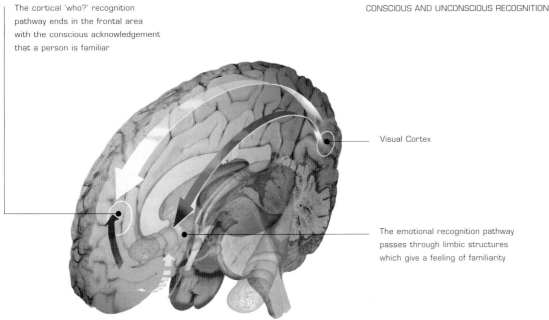

Visual Cortex

The emotional recognition pathway passes through limbic structures which give a feeling of familiarity

dead. He lets him listen to his heart beat ... not convinced. He draws attention to his breath ... still not convinced. Not to be out-done, the doctor pulls out some medical books and determines that the true proof of whether a man is dead or alive is that dead men do not bleed. After some time, the man admits that dead men do not bleed. The doctor then takes the man's hand and pokes it with a needle. The man starts bleeding. At which point he looks at his finger and says, 'Well, what do you know? Dead men DO bleed!'

Capgras delusion occurs when the emotional processing pathway fails to produce the normal jolt of recognition in response to a familiar person.

The resistance to disproof shown by patients with Cotard's delusion suggests that the condition is brought about by a combination of severe depersonalization combined with altered thinking. But it is not the *way* they think that is screwy – if you are dead and you bleed it does, indeed, prove that dead man bleed. Rather it is the beliefs informing the thought process that are wrong.

However diminished, or denied the self may be in such a state, it at least maintains one of the essential qualities – unity. Even when depersonalization causes a person to 'see' themselves as two beings, or believe they are dead, there remains a single conscious entity which does this seeing and believing. It is an 'as-if' experience of duality or demise, not the real thing.

Friends ...

'It is true that many multiples do experience dreadful disorganization and emotional difficulty in connection with their ... 'household', as we multiples refer to our selves. However, not all multiples endure this ... some households ... work in harmony. We communicate, share and help each other. In fact we have enabled each other to survive. We are happy the way we are and have no desire to become singular.'

Letter to New Scientist
(22 January 2000).

Sometimes alters do not succeed one another but pop up at the same time, sharing a conjoined consciousness. One personality might 'see' what another is seeing, for example, without regarding the seeing as 'theirs'. Donnie, for example, claimed to have watched while a college student known as John Woods killed two women. While it was happening, Donnie said he felt too scared to think. It was, he said, as if he was back in his childhood where everything was 'wild and confused ... [I] wanted to leave, but I was trapped.'[18] The feeling of entrapment was unusually literal in this case because Donnie was inside Woods' head at the time – he was one of two alters that periodically popped up there. The event Donnie saw was viewed through John's eyes, yet he described feeling like an observer. The murderous actions were those of a body he shared but at that moment was not controlling.

Sometimes co-existent alters are mutually aware of each other's consciousness. This is not the same as the 'as-if' duality experienced by Aleis – In simple depersonalization the two 'selves' are both seen from the point of view of an outsider – and this observer is the unified self. But the dual consciousness of 'conjoined' alters is experienced from the inside – there is no 'other' self to observe it. Sue described it on *Horizon* thus: 'It's hard to explain but I can see all of them here and we sit and we talk and then we, we discuss and a lot of times we argue, unfortunately, until we can come to a compromise ... because there's only one body and we have to share it.'

Although dissociation manifests itself in many different ways what all the states have in common is that consciousness is in some way fragmented or incomplete, as though its fabric has been shot through with holes or ripped apart and reconstituted in the wrong way. To what extent can these holes and rips be mapped onto the brain processes which construct the self?

It would be reasonable to assume that derealization – the feeling of something being 'not quite right' with the outside world, might be due to some glitch in early information processing, where sensory information itself is bound together. The brain areas primarily involved are toward the back of the brain – the sensory cortices, sensory association areas and the parietal cortex. Where it involves the sensation of not knowing what one is seeing, the problem is likely to be located in the lower 'what's that?' pathway that links sensory stimuli to associated memories and concepts. Where it involves distortions of location like the Alice-in-wonderland shrinking and distancing of objects, the problem is more likely to lie along the upper pathway that relates outside stimuli to the body. And the feeling that familiar objects are changed and alien – as in Capgras delusion – probably relates to a disruption in the flow of information to the limbic system.

The flattening of emotion that characterizes depersonalization is almost certainly due to abnormal activity in the pathways leading to and from the limbic system. It may be that information that has the potential to affect a person's own mind and body is simply not getting through, hence it is not evaluated and seems meaningless. Or perhaps the information is getting down to the limbic system and being duly evaluated but is not getting out again because the two-way pathways that connect this part of the brain to the rest are working in one direction only. 'Stuck' in this part of the brain, the information cannot flow up to the prefrontal cortex to create conscious emotion, nor can it form a memory or be translated into words. Depersonalization during acute trauma – a road accident, say – might be of this nature. At the time the event is experienced in a distant way, seemingly without emotion. But in fact the emotional memory is being formed in the limbic system and later, maybe much later, it will flood back. Because it was laid down in isolation, without being bound to words, such a memory may not have any describable content – it will just be felt as a replay of the emotional state that the person was in when it was laid down. Panic attacks and post-traumatic stress disorder may be a late effect of this type of depersonalization.

Dissociative Identity Disorder, too, seems to be associated with changes in limbic system activity. One intriguing brain-scanning study gives a glimpse of the self actually in the process of disappearing and giving rise to an alter.

Neurobiologist Guochuan Tsai and psychiatrist Don Condie, in Massachusetts, carried out a series of fMRI scans on a woman with DID who could switch, more or less at will, from one of her many personalities to another. The scans showed that her hippocampus was abnormally shrunken, and when her primary self gave way to an alter the activity in it ebbed, remaining low for the duration of the alter's domination. When her main self returned, the activity sparked up again. Control experiments confirmed that this activity was distinct to the switch in personalities – when she merely imagined she was another self there was no such dip.[19]

The hippocampus is the organ in the limbic system which encodes and triggers recall of personal memories – the stored autobiographical episodes that comprise our individual life narrative. The sense of continuous self depends on our ability to have these memories 'on tap'. In someone with DID therefore it figures that the hippocampus would be more active when the primary self is in charge, because – by definition – this is the self that is attached to the largest bag of memories. Each moment of primary self-consciousness is therefore likely to involve a bigger neural firing pattern 'set' than a moment which contains an alter.

Even in a normal brain though, the self-construct must be flexible. It is the slow change in the self-patterns, due to learning and maturation, that distinguishes the self we were as children from the self we are as adults. And a certain amount of plasticity is needed for the adult self-construct to allow us to adapt to changes in the environment.

To function well in unusual or novel circumstances the habitual, or primary, self-structure needs to recruit mini-networks that fulfil particular new, or rarely-required functions. Sometimes the new recruits will be entirely fresh – firing patterns brought into existence during an intense learning experience. Others will be old alliances – networks which were formed in the past and remain intact, but only rarely link up with the core self. If you are suddenly required to do something uncharacteristically aggressive – to shoot someone in order to save your own life, say – you will need to activate patterns that may not have been exercised since you had a punch-up 20 years ago in the school playground. Such mini-networks may represent a particular characteristic – sentimentality, rage, frivolity – which are not usually present in the core and therefore not usually exhibited by the person concerned.

An analogy is a company that normally ticks over on a permanent staff of full-time workers, each of whom knows everything about the entire set-up – its customs and regulations, its files and working practices. Most of the time these workers do everything the company needs to keep functioning and the set-up is adequate for day-to-day business. However, if the firm suddenly finds itself up against problems – especially a threat to itself – it may draft in extra free-lance workers from outside. Some of them will be known and trusted (kept permanently on hand by way of a sort of retaining contract) while others will be, literally, 'made' for the job in hand. Once they have fulfilled their emergency function they sever their links with the company and lie low until they are needed again.

In most people the outriders to the primary self manifest merely as fluctuations or conflicts in a single character, as when we speak of being 'in two minds'. To outsiders they may appear as moodiness or sudden changes in behaviour, as in: 'He's really nice – but if you cross him he can be vicious.' In some these flash changes are so unlike the primary personality that they inspire bewilderment (even fear) in those who observe their brief appearances. And they are the root of many a superstition: odd characteristics in children gave rise to the idea of changelings – sinister lookalikes planted by the fairies; while the notion of demonic possession is still reflected in colloquial phrases: 'I've got the devil in me tonight.'

There is, though, an essential difference between fluctuations in personality (however extreme) and DID. In the first the alters are absorbed into the primary self which 'owns' them, while in cases of DID the primary self 'switches' off and allows an alter, temporarily, to stand alone. When an alter is activated the sensations and perceptions experienced while it is 'in residence' are owned by it rather than by the non-activated primary self, so over time the alter accumulates its own autobiographical memory which is inaccessible to the primary self. So when an alter pops up it can report on events that happened when it was last active.

Co-awareness and shared perception in DID – as, for example, when Donnie watched John Woods murder his victim – are different from total switches in that the primary self and the alter(s) both may have access to each other's autobiographical memory store. Such states have yet to be studied by neuro-imaging techniques (to my knowledge) so they remain obscure. Possibly what happens is that, during co-consciousness, the hippocampus activates both sets of memories and concepts, each of which link with the pattern produced by the sensory experience of the moment, so perceptions are integrated with both selves while the thoughts, emotions and memories owned by each self remain separate. They are, in effect, micro-consciousnesses brought into existence by virtue of containing sufficient 'self' elements to provide an experience.

Dissociation (apart from that caused by overt brain injury) is frequently linked to childhood trauma – so much so that the more extreme types, like DID, are commonly thought to be evidence of parental abuse. This is a dangerous assumption though, and not necessarily correct. However, there is little doubt that a child who is repeatedly thrown into a state of terror during which they are helpless is more likely to develop the habit of dissociation.

In both adult and child, the nervous system is primed to produce certain responses to threats. These are mediated by neurotransmitters which affect the brain and the whole body. The adult response to fearful stimuli is the familiar fight or flight reaction: excitatory neurotransmitters, especially noradrenalin, flood the brain and produce a state of hyperarousal in which sensual information is amplified, attention closely focused, and the body geared up for action. This reaction clearly evolved because it has terrific survival value. In very young children, however, it would be pointless – a babe-in-arms cannot run away, let alone fight a marauding predator, and if it started thrashing about it would only increase its chances of becoming lunch. So the immature brain responds to the flood of noradrenalin in a different way – instead of producing aggressive behaviour or flight, it triggers a cry for help.

If crying fails to bring help (as it would when the source of the threat is the very people charged with caring for it) the infant brain produces a second response – it causes the child to freeze. This, too, has survival value – an immobile body is less likely to be seen, and by staying quiet the child maximizes its brain's ability to localize threatening sights and sounds.

If the threat goes away, noradrenalin levels in the brain decrease and the child returns to normal (probably via a crying stage – one reason why children (and adults) often cry *after* a frightening experience). If it continues, however, something else happens in the brain: other neurotransmitters, (including endogenous opioids) kick in and switch the child's attention from whatever is happening on the outside to its own internal world. This distances the self from pain and fear and marks the, rather merciful, start of dissociation. It is similar to the 'defeat' reaction of animals caught in a trap – the child simply 'gives up', and absents itself from the scene. Outwardly this is marked by dreaminess, vacancy, passivity – behaviour which, again, is probably the best survival policy for a terrorized creature whose options have expired.[20]

Dissociation provides a release, of a sort, from the hellish situation, and so the next time the child finds itself under threat it may pass more quickly through the first and second stage responses to the relative peace of dissociation. Each time this happens it increases the chance of it happening again, because, like all brain states, the more often the dissociative pattern is activated the more ingrained it becomes, and the more likely to fire up in any situation that resembles the one in which it was first (or subsequently) created. Hence a child that is subjected to repeated abuse 'learns' to dissociate earlier and earlier in the abusive episode. They may then start to dissociate as soon as they perceive a threat – and then in situations where the threat is merely implicit. Eventually it will happen whenever they feel anxious, which is probably quite often, because they have come to expect things to turn nasty. And so the child victim becomes the adult truant – absenting herself from the world, or experiencing it from a distance.

In DID the information which is cut off during dissociation is not just what is coming in from outside (or bits of it) but a large part of the internally generated sense of self (the neurobiology underlying this may be slightly different from those above, which would typically produce derealization rather than depersonalization.

Imagine a young child in a normal state of mind. The core self-structures in her brain are mature, so she is fully aware of the outside world. However, the cortical areas which support the autobiographical self are only just being formed. Her self is therefore a frail, flittering thing, capable of producing only sparks of self-consciousness. Furthermore, her brain is still cluttered with cells so she has the potential to 'make anything' of her experiences. She has not yet laid down the learned concepts and memories which, in an adult, ensure that experiences are interpreted in a particular way and integrated with a particular self-construct.

Now what would happen if, in this formative state, that child's brain was suddenly flooded with excitatory chemicals? Whatever was happening to her at that time would be instantly bound with the fragile self-construct that happened to be active in her brain at the time. But remember, that self-structure – that particular pattern of neural activity – is not a deeply ingrained, complex mesh as it is in adults. It is new and weak, because it has not yet fired up day after day, garnering memories and spinning ideas about itself until it is solid, stable and weighty enough to provide a ground of consolidated experience on which new events might stand apart. In fact, if a trauma occurs while this splintery self is active, the patterns produced by the event may be so overwhelming that it cannot experience it as an *object* of consciousness at all. Rather the event subsumes everything else and the child 'is' it – and her newly minted little self is bound for ever to this terrible happening and is incorporated into it. When the event is then dissociated, the self goes with it, and so long as the memory of the event remains unconscious, the little self interwoven into it remains unconscious too.

However, given the right stimulus – the perception of a situation that is very similar to the one encoded by the traumatic memory – the memory may be triggered, and with it the half-baked self within it. If the primary self is already dissociated from this new situation, the former child-self may take ownership of the perceptions currently being generated. It will experience the new trauma on behalf of the primary self, and when it is over it will return to unconsciousness, embellished with its new memory and leaving the primary self to return unscathed.

Something similar to this seems to happen in certain hypnotic states (themselves a form of dissociation). In one experiment, for example, people who were about to undergo surgery were put under hypnosis and told that they would feel no pain, even though the operation was to be done without anaesthetic. However, the hypnotist told the patients that the pain would be felt by a 'hidden observer' in their mind. After the operation the patients duly reported that they had felt nothing. But when they were hypnotized again and the hypnotist addressed the 'hidden observer', they reported excruciating pain.[21]

Much of this description of DID is, admittedly, speculation – but it fits well with what evidence there is. Alters range widely in age and disposition, but children – naughty children, sad children, mean children, guilty children – pop up again and again. They are usually frail, unformed personalities, and they tend to emerge in the circumstances that they are most familiar with. There is no reason why any number of fragmentary selves could not be tucked away in the brain of a person who has suffered continual abuse. Such a person would have to re-build their primary self each time an alter was created, so it figures that it might take many years for them to establish a strong enough personality to hold the stage during threatening events, and thus see off whatever alter popped up.

The disadvantage of repeated early dissociation is that the primary self may be stunted or splintered into a host of 'hidden observers'. And if the primary self remains frail these alters may wreak havoc with their lives. Less dramatic forms of derealization and depersonalization may also be horrible and disruptive.

However, it is worth remembering that dissociation is a natural function of the brain, and it has its uses. Although it usually only occurs in extreme circumstances it can also be induced through various types of hypnosis, including self-hypnosis, and it may be useful to develop the knack of dissociating it – to cope with intractable pain, for example, or even to cope with stressful or tedious situations. If you have to do something you find terrifying a little dissociation may help you to float serenely above it without impairing your performance. And if you are stuck with a job which threatens to drive you nuts with boredom, disappearing into a dream-world may save your sanity.

For some people, learning to dissociate is easy because their brains are naturally predisposed to it. The part of the brain which produces fight, flight and freeze responses is the amygdala, a small module in the limbic system. In some people, the part of it which produces the fight response is most sensitive to stimuli, in others it is the flight bit, and in others the part that causes freezing.[22] The amygdala is one of the first parts of the brain to mature and unlike many other brain areas it functions from the moment of birth. The way it functions is determined partly by the action of various hormones and neurotransmitters, some of which act on it while the child is in the womb. If it is subjected to high levels of stress hormones leeching across the placenta from an anxious mother, the amygdala may be sensitized to fearful stimuli from the start. Sex hormones also play a part. The 'y' chromosome of a male foetus triggers a flood of testosterone in the uterus and this affects the development of various parts of the brain. One of the things this hormone 'bath' seems to do is to alter the amygdala, priming the parts of it that produce an aggressive reaction to threatening stimuli rather than a fearful one. Hence the female amygdala, like that of an infant, is more likely to produce a crying or freezing reaction than that of a male. This is also probably why women are more likely to suffer dissociative disorders than men, who instead tend towards hyperarousal (attention deficit hyperactivity disorder in boys) and aggression.

Another physical factor that probably favours dissociation is the tendency to an abnormal balance of dopamine, noradrenalin and serotonin. Indeed, drugs which alter the balance of these neurochemicals can produce dissociation in anyone, and, conversely, may 'cure' a person of a dissociative disorder.

Drugs are generally the quickest and surest route to altered experience, and it is unfortunate that the use of radically mind-altering substances is, in many societies, severely curtailed by law. This does not prevent people using them, of course – there is massive consumption of drugs such as 3,4methylenedioxymethamphetamine (Ecstasy), cannabis, heroin and cocaine throughout the Western world. It is now fairly widely acknowledged that the Western 'War on Drugs' makes this activity unnecessarily dangerous (because it prevents proper quality control and the development of safer products) and socially disruptive. What is not often pointed out is that it prevents us from using (legally) a powerful technique for exploring our potential ability to construct subjective reality in different ways. Though there is no shortage of drug-created experience (a million brains will be having one come Saturday night in any major city), the research data it could provide is more or less lost and does not generally inform the study of consciousness except in the form of cultish art and literature.

It is almost impossible in the US and UK for a researcher to get legal permission to study the effects of psychotropic drugs for anything other than the narrowest therapeutic purposes. So, in order to gather and publish research about drug-induced altered states (without risking legal comeback) researchers are increasingly turning to societies in which altered consciousness is regarded as a valuable eye-opening exercise (or even a sacred rite) rather than something to be forcefully discouraged. Among tribes of the Upper Amazon region of South America, for example, ritual use of the hallucinogenic herbal brew Ayahuasca is absolutely central and the experiences it produces are regarded as, in some ways, more real and more important than day-to-day existence. One of the (many) radical changes the drug brings about is in consciousness of time – it typically produces the sensation of being 'outside' of time and space. In doing this it eradicates the most fundamental building blocks of normal experience.

The fact that the nature of experience can be radically altered by the ebb and flow of chemicals demonstrates that 'normal consciousness' is actually just one type of awareness – the sort known by an organism that is constructed and functioning in a particular environment. It does not necessarily follow, therefore, that this standard consciousness – singular, private, bound and continuous – provides a clearer view of reality than any other. It could be that organic processes that seem to give us knowledge of the world actually act as a screen through which we glimpse only a murky, distorted glimmer of the truth.

Certainly our 'natural' view of the world – a place made of solid, discrete objects in separate spatial and temporal dimensions – is, quite simply, wrong. The classic, mechanistic model collapsed a century ago when Einstein showed that time and space, and matter and energy, are merely different manifestations of a more fundamental reality.

Since then quantum physics has revealed an even more alien picture: a universe in which nothing is definite until it is observed; sub-atomic particles are linked in some unknown way so that one will respond instantaneously to another at any distance; and all we can ever be sure of is probability.

These discoveries force us to recognize that what we think is reality is in fact only one aspect of the universe. And, as we have seen, even that part is distorted by the neurological prisms built into our bodies and brains.

So what, given this keyhole view, can we make of the world? Should we assume that it is at root meaningless, and that the fractured inner world of the autistic is nearer to a clear view of it than normal consciousness? Or could it be that the super-meaningful, all-powerful convictions of the schizophrenic, or the weird dislocations of REM sleep, are more faithful interpretations of what – if anything – is really 'out there'?

So far in this book I have concentrated mainly on the way the human brain and body creates particular forms of consciousness, the easy problems, in other words. The next chapter returns us – via the most extraordinary form of consciousness of all – to the hard problem: the nature of consciousness itself.

A Conscious Universe?

'Mind no longer appears as an accidental intruder into the realm of matter; we are beginning to suspect that we ought rather to hail it as the creator and governor of the realm of matter.'

Sir James Jeans, *The Mysterious Universe*

The first rule of science is to look at the evidence. This poses a tough problem for scientists who study consciousness because such scrutiny is meant to be objective. Yet the evidence in question here is, by definition, subjective.

Scientists take the notion of objectivity seriously; so much so that in presenting their work publicly they invariably write in the passive tense, as though the experiments reported just happened rather than being designed and executed by human beings. Given this reluctance even to acknowledge their own existence, it is not surprising that many scientists feel uncomfortable about using their own experience as evidence. Most of them therefore spend their time trying to find out what is going on in others' minds, peering through layers of interpretation, rather like a Victorian physician examining a female patient through her clothes.

Eastern traditions such as Buddhism, by contrast, study consciousness directly. The Experiential method is highly disciplined and refined, and over many centuries its practitioners have accrued a vast amount of empirical and theoretical data. Happily, many of them are willing to share their findings with what, if their philosophy was less forgiving they might think of as Johnny-come-lately Western scientists. And the scientists, in their turn, are starting to acknowledge that they might have something to learn from ancient contemplative disciplines. Students of neuroscience are now reading the teachings of Buddha alongside the works of William James; researchers toil up Tibetan mountains to interview members of isolated religious communities about their perceptions of time and space; and bemused (or perhaps amused) monks are regularly invited to meditate with their heads in brain scanners.

This chummy collaboration cannot, however, disguise the fact that the conventional scientific view of consciousness and the Eastern idea of it are still poles apart. The materialist view presents consciousness as something that arises from (or is) certain physical states or processes within individual systems, and it is seen almost entirely in terms of its contents. Perceptions, thoughts and feelings are generally deemed to be all there is to consciousness – blips of awareness in a fundamentally unknowing material universe.

The Eastern view (to the extent that you can talk of such a thing given the variety and complexity of Eastern traditions) is quite different. Far from being the very stuff of consciousness, perceptions are regarded as a smokescreen of illusions ('suffering' in Buddhist terms) that obscures a 'ground' of pure awareness which cannot be reduced to anything more fundamental. Sometimes we may glimpse this ground in the gaps between thoughts, but most of the time we create polluting puffs of illusory perception so thick and fast that we are blind to the reality beneath. Contemplative disciplines are therefore about learning to stop generating what most Western researchers think of as consciousness, in order to know the boundless, holistic and fundamental reality that lies beneath.

It may turn out that the (rather bleak) materialist notion of consciousness is correct. But to assume that scientific materialism has, in its couple of hundred years of existence, come up with a truer description of reality than that arrived at over centuries by philosophers dedicated to the task is (to put it mildly) presumptuous. Furthermore, the notion of an essentially materialist universe is not one that finds favour with many people, even among those who in other ways live the material life to the hilt. Nine out of 10 Americans and 76 per cent of people in the UK claim to believe in a spiritual dimension which is more fundamental than the material universe.[1] Only some of them call it God, but practically all believe it involves some form of unified, irreducible Mind that transcends normal consciousness.

The idea of transcendental consciousness does not prevail through religious dogma but because a huge number of people – anything between 40 per cent and 80 per cent depending on which polls you go by – have had a personal experience in which they have felt themselves to be lifted into a higher realm of being which is truer than the concrete world. In some it occurs spontaneously, as a sudden realization or awakening. Others find it through prayer, or in meditation, and some claim to have arrived at it thanks to mind-altering drugs.

Although transcendental experiences vary enormously there are certain core qualities which distinguish them from normal consciousness. One is the feeling of stillness and freedom from thought, perception and anxiety, which nevertheless leaves awareness intact. Another is the sensation of being beyond or outside the physical boundaries of the body. A third is ecstasy. And a fourth – perhaps the most extraordinary – is a feeling of oneness: loss of the usual subject/object divide such that the experiencer becomes what they are experiencing.

I could give you countless examples of reports of these experiences, but, in the spirit of getting as close to the evidence as possible, I will recount some of my own. You have probably experienced similar episodes yourself, and as spiritual revelations go mine are rather mundane – I have yet to be 'held aloft by a Great Force', or 'struck as though by lightning', as some have. But they are, I think, fairly typical and I know (as well as one can know) that they are pretty accurate descriptions because, although they happened years ago, they still rank as some of the clearest most intense memories I possess.

The first occurred, unsurprisingly, during meditation. There were a few years when, fancying myself treading the path of enlightenment, I sat down twice a day and intoned a mantra for 20 minutes in the hope of replacing my usual cacophony of thoughts and worries with quiet inner peace. And one day it happened. Five or so minutes into my usual routine I felt what I can only describe as a sensation of falling, quite swiftly, *up*wards. My body felt light, as though some weighty cloak had been removed from it, and I was aware of entering an infinitely vast, luminous space that was, paradoxically, also a velvety blackness. The last of a train of thoughts bubbled up, out and away and, for once, no more followed. The very noting of what was happening also evaporated, and my mind – for the first time ever, as far as I know – felt utterly silent.

I know in retrospect that I spent about 15 minutes in this state, but to describe it from within is impossible because 'I' in the sense that 'I' usually experience myself, was not there. There was no sense of time passing, and, although I am tempted to use the word bliss, there was no emotion of the usual sort and certainly no visceral 'thrill'. In fact I was not aware of my body at all, nor of being in a particular location. All there was, it seemed, was awareness itself.

My second excursion into an altered state happened in a tiny room somewhere in the suburbs of Manchester. I was working as a journalist and had spent the previous two weeks hurtling around the country interviewing people in dozens of different towns. It had involved some marathon driving sessions which I was doing in a clapped-out sports car I had bought, unwisely, from a dodgy dealer a couple of days before I set off. The car broke down on me more or less every day and sometimes twice a day. One of its more obvious faults was an ill-fitting soft-top, and as it was January and freezing cold the long waits for roadside assistance were agonizing. Added to which I had organized the trip pretty haphazardly, neglecting to book accommodation ahead, so I spent a lot of time searching for a place to stay.

In Manchester I found there was not a hotel room to be had in the entire city. As I drove off, through a hailstorm, in the hope of finding accommodation in the next town, my car made a by-now familiar burping noise, lost power, and stopped.

By the time the breakdown van arrived I was exhausted and probably hypothermic. The mechanic fixed the problem but warned that it would probably happen again, quite soon. He seemed a nice man, and as he left I asked, pathetically, if by any chance he knew of a guest house that might take in a bedraggled stranger at what was by now 3 a.m. He didn't. Apologetically he made to drive off and then hesitated. 'Except ... well ... my aunt lives near here and she has a spare room.'

Half an hour later his aunt had installed me in her house. She had insisted I had a hot bath, taken my dripping clothes to dry, lit a fire in the room and generally fussed over me in a motherly way. By the time I slipped between her pink brushed-nylon sheets I was thinking benign thoughts about almost everything and everyone (except perhaps the dodgy car dealer) and was ready to fall into a deep, grateful sleep.

When I noticed the fire – one of those built-in gas burners – was still on, I thought I should probably get out of bed and switch it off. But as I looked at it something very strange happened. I realized that I was not only looking at it from the perspective of where I lay, but – weird as this may sound – I was seeing it too from within the flame itself. I *was* the fire – absorbed into its redness and warmth, both giving and receiving its heat. At the same time (it was not a sequential realization) I became aware that I was also the bed, and the walls, and the window and the sheets. My self seemed to have bled out of its boundary and infiltrated every crevice of the room. Stranger yet, I was not just in the room, but beyond it too. Although I could not, literally, see beyond its four walls, I seemed to be outside them as well as within. Indeed, I felt that I was everywhere, and everything – embracing the most distant stars and yet also inhabiting the smallest speck of dust. All sense of space, location, boundedness and division disappeared.

As all this happened I thought – or rather, *I knew* – that what I was experiencing was the real state of things; that I was part of some much greater whole and that all my experience up until now had been in some sense unreal. Despite its peculiar nature I felt no anxiety, and – odder – no curiosity. It all felt entirely natural.

I have no idea how long the feeling lasted. At some stage I lay down and slept. In the morning the fire (still burning) was back in its appointed location and so was I. But, unlike a dream, the experience remained crystal clear and as real and significant as it had been while it happened.

The third experience (actually the first of many similar ones) happened as I emerged from a (glorious) lucid dream. Although fully awake I was still in a state of sleep paralysis, so I relaxed and waited either to slip back into the dream or to wake up fully. In this state I became aware – no, utterly certain – that someone was standing just behind me. As I was paralysed I could not turn to look, but anyway it was unnecessary because I knew that this was not a physical presence so much as an *essential* presence. And I also knew it was utterly benign, the epicentre of a pure love that encompassed me and all things entirely.

At that time I had a very strong materialist belief system that absolutely ruled out the possibility of supernatural entities. However, the certainty which I felt about this presence – that it was not hallucinated but a 'real' thing – was such that it demolished, in seconds, those deepest convictions and replaced them with what I took for years to be an unshakeable belief in (for want of a better word) God.

The materialist 'explanation' of these types of experience is that they give a no more 'true' view of reality than any other state, just a rather unusual one. Indeed, given that a wholly material world is at its base insentient, all meaning is but an illusion created by our brains. The meaning-ladenness of spiritual experience therefore suggests that it is more rather than less illusory than normal – the opposite of the traditional Eastern idea.

I have absolutely no idea which of these explanations is true. The awesome 'knowing' I felt when I personally experienced altered consciousness is now long gone, and I am inclined to assume (though no longer with utter certainty) that it was just a glorious illusion rather than a glimpse of some sublime reality beyond the material.

That being so, how might my brain have constructed it?

Normal consciousness arises when the brain integrates information to an optimum extent. Its various contents are bound together enough to ensure that our sense of self is unified so we don't splinter into lots of different personalities like someone with DID, but not so integrated that the self is indistinguishable from non-self. The view this self has of the world 'outside' is of objects, each of which consists of information put together in convenient chunks. All the visual information from the same location is integrated, for example, so we don't see the colour and form of an object as two separate images but as aspects of one. If we are confronted with a nose, eyes and mouth in a particular configuration we see it as a face – not as floating body parts, as perhaps, do people with autism. And we separate these perceptions, packaging them in 'frames' – each one a conscious moment – which are close enough to connect with one another and therefore create a running narrative, but not so close that they overlap and produce a single timeless moment in which all events are merged.

The integration of normal consciousness extends, in a vaguer way, beyond the self. It gives us a sense of belonging – to our species, our tribe, and quite intensely to our families and close friends. We empathise with those who are like us; understand, to some extent, what is happening in their inner worlds, and may share their joys, sorrows and fears. At times – when we are intimately involved with another, or engaged with a group in some common purpose – we may even feel that our minds are in some way merged with others'. However, even though our self boundary may be feel soft and permeable, it normally never disappears entirely.

It is reasonable to assume that this middling state of integration has evolved as the brain's default mode, because it is the one that serves our purposes best. Information is connected enough to have meaning (a face means a person) so we are prompted to act in response to it; but it is fragmented into discrete 'bite-sized' objects (the face is individual – not all of humankind) so we can deal with it in chunks, as required. Of course, we can zoom up and down the scale of integration – breaking down the information we get into tiny particles (a speck of dust) or a huge field (the landscape outside the window). But our view does not extend beyond the ordinary world in which matter is solid and spatially divided, and time flows smoothly forward. Other dimensions and states are known only indirectly, through metaphors or mathematical models. Their existence, when we are in a normal state of mind, must be taken on trust (e.g. belief in God); or deduced ($E=mc^2$).

Generally speaking, normal consciousness feels kind of okay – it's how we are when we are 'together'. Sometimes, of course, we feel more together (and more okay) than at others; our inner world is harmonious, we see connections that give us creative ideas, the things that happen to us 'add up', we 'go with the flow' and time lingers luxuriously. And there are days when everything seems disjointed and meaningless: we are aware of ourselves as a bunch of conflicts, others' behaviour seems perverse or impenetrable, music jars, nothing connects, and we are constantly behind the clock.

Spiritual-seeming experiences such as those I've described might therefore simply be 'what it is like' to be exceptionally together. The feeling of wholeness, purity of thought, lack of anxiety and boundlessness are due to the brain super-integrating incoming information so that the usual array of disconnected experiential objects seem to blend into a single harmonious universe.

Such experiences occur only when the brain is tipped into unusual functioning by extraordinary stimuli (rituals, sudden release from anxiety, drugs) because to be in that state is risky. If we spent our lives in transcendental bliss we would not run from danger because we would have no fear; nor discover anything beneficial (because we would have no curiosity). Indeed, we would not do anything much at all to ensure our survival because we would feel too good just 'being'.

If the sense of spiritual transcendence is just this: the way it happens to feel when one's brain is functioning in an unusual way, a description of this altered functioning should be enough to explain the subjective features of it in the same way that a description of normal brain function explains the way we usually see things.

Such a description is starting to emerge from the work of a number of neuroscientists who have investigated the biological correlates of 'higher' consciousness.

One of them, Andrew Newberg, of the University of Pennsylvania, scanned the brains of eight highly-skilled meditators of the Tibetan Buddhist school. This discipline involves what is known as focused meditation: clearing the mind of clutter by concentrating on a single action or perception such as the current breath or a mantra. As meditation deepens, all thoughts fade away, giving way to a state most commonly referred to as Pure Consciousness.

Newberg's studies were, for obvious reasons, rather more difficult than most to set up. Having one's brain scanned is not conducive to contemplation because, whichever imaging method is used it involves being subjected to some sort of noisy, obtrusive, uncomfortable or invasive bit of technology.

Newberg used SPECT (Single Photon Emission Computed Tomography) which requires injecting the subject with a radioactive substance which attaches to the blood cells. For a short period thereafter the 'tagged' blood leaves a trace which can be detected by an imaging machine. Brain areas which are active use more blood than others because neuronal activity is fuelled by blood-borne oxygen. SPECT brain scans therefore detect which bits of the brain are working hardest by showing up concentrations of the radio-active marker.

The experiments were designed to be as meditation-friendly as possible. Before a session began Newberg inserted an IV line into the volunteer's arm so when the time came for the dye to be injected it could be done quickly and easily. The subject was then left to meditate in a candle-lit room scented with jasmine essence while Newberg waited outside. Between them trailed a long piece of string, and when the subject entered a state of higher consciousness he gave his end of it a tug, which was a signal to Newberg to come in and inject the radioactive tracer. Newberg then whisked the volunteer off to the scanning machine.

The resulting scans were very different from those that would be expected from the brains of people in a normal state of mind. Some of the differences simply indicated extreme calmness and intense concentration. The amygdala, for example, which generates anxiety, was unusually quiet; and hypothalamic activity altered in such a way as to damp down the sympathetic nervous system – the 'fight or flight' response – and reduce metabolism. Other differences, though, seemed to be specific to the transcendental state. They included changes that indicated prolonged orientation (fixation on a particular target); an increase in frontal lobe activity (up to 20 per cent) and a startling decrease in parietal lobe activity.[2]

Knowing what we do about the brain areas and systemic activity that are altered in meditation it is possible to construct a hypothesis – a very speculative one I stress – about how the brain creates the weird subjective features of transcendence.

Take, first, the prolonged orienting stability. Orienting is the 'what is it?' reflex that directs attention to a particular target. It is automatic, and happens when one particular stimulus (which may be sensory or internally generated) overrides competing stimuli, usually because it is especially salient. The neural activity associated with the target stimulus is then amplified by excitatory neurotransmitters which are 'pulsed' up to the cortex from an area at the base of the brain called the locus coerulius.

In normal consciousness, we change orientation every few seconds because the brain is naturally exploratory. Even if we are not literally 'looking around us', our brains are. Holding orientation on a single, not very interesting thing, like a mantra, is therefore unnatural, and it usually takes a lot of practice to achieve.

Zen

Imaging studies of experienced meditators show very clear differences in brain function when they are in a state of meditation.

These include:

- unusually prolonged orienting (the 'what is it?' reflex);

- inhibition of the sympathetic nervous system (the flight or fight response);

- greater EEG synchrony across right and left hemispheres and across the cerebral cortex generally;

- inhibition of sensory input;

- up to 20 per cent greater frontal lobe activity (especially right frontal);

- changes in the hypothalamus leading to decreased body metabolism;

- reduced parietal lobe activation.

Once orienting has directed attention to a target stimulus other brain areas click in to keep it there. The prefrontal cortex (PFC) for example, locks attention on to one thing by actively inhibiting information coming from everything else. The effect is that competing stimuli are prevented from getting access to consciousness. This is not quite the same as the sensory blockade that occurs in sleep. In that case input is blocked by the thalamus before it reaches the cortex. During focused attention, by contrast, sensory information may still enter the brain, be constructed and represented at a quite high level.

This high-level representation might allow it to be 'filed' in memory so that, unlike much 'of the moment' consciousness, the sensory information could be reported if the person is prompted. Information laid down in this state of 'absence' may even be recalled more fully and accurately than that which is attended to, because in filing it away it is not 'polluted' by top-down interpretations. A simple example of this might be a situation in which a person addresses another who is deeply involved in some task and appears at first not to have been heard. 'Did you hear what I said?', they ask – at which point the second person 'clicks to', thinks for a second and repeats the words back. Were they conscious of them the first time, or are they just accessing information that had entered their brain while they were mentally elsewhere? It is impossible for anyone to know, including the person repeating back the words.

The changes in the meditators' prefrontal cortex suggest that they were so firmly locked on to their single target of meditation that sensations could not have been conscious. However, this conflicts with the usual description of meditation as being a state in which one is acutely aware of sensations (extraneous noise, for example) but not *affected* by it. Are these reports actually true reflections of what was happening in the meditative state, or are the subjects just accessing knowledge that entered their brains while they were meditating and assuming they experienced it at the time it occurred? Again, there is no way of knowing.

Normally, attention is rarely so narrow and focused that we 'lose ourselves' in its target entirely. Even when we are absorbed by something (and fail to hear someone addressing us), the body maps which monitor our physical boundaries keep humming, so the concept of the physical self is maintained, however faintly. In meditation, however, the cranking up of prefrontal activity through prolonged orienting may be so extreme that even this concept is lost as the brain area responsible for it closes down. As a result even the unconscious recognition of one's physical boundaries might disappear.

Without the normal conceptual boundary the sense of self usually contained by it bleeds outwards, like vapour, to incorporate everything. So instead of seeing the world from 'inside' the person feels that they see it from all sides. They are everywhere and nowhere – and instead of being separated from everything else they feel they *are* it.

At first, in focused meditation there is a 'target' perception to merge with, but after a while meditators report that even this single 'blip' of content disappears.

This is not, actually, surprising because attending to a single object means that a small subset of neurons fire in a characteristic pattern for much longer than normal. As a result the neurotransmitters which seep out of their axons and keep the electrical activity going become depleted. So gradually their firing rate diminishes until it drops below that required for consciousness. This process is known as habituation.

Yet now we have an odd situation. The brain has been coerced into shutting off its usual generation of perceptions by saturating its consciousness with a single object. And now the object has disappeared. It would follow – given the vacuum-abhorrent nature of the brain – that the competing stimuli which were previously kept out by the target would now flood back into consciousness. Yet they do not.

What seems to happen in meditation, then, is that the frontal brain areas that are normally busy turning first-level representations of objects into higher-level, conscious. representations, are dissociated from the brain areas that create the low-level representations. The knowledge is still in the brain (Newberg's scans showed quite high activity in the primary sensory cortices) but consciousness does not – if you like – 'embrace' them.

The physical concept of self is, as we have seen, already inactive due to parietal shutdown. In addition, the disconnection between the front and back of the brain disrupts the feedback that produces the normal sense of ownership. And the system that produces a sensation of agency is brought to a standstill by physical and mental stillness. (You have to move – externally or internally – in order to generate thoughts and actions, and meditation techniques inhibit movement.)

Sensory stimuli therefore no longer has a self to own it. Although it is present in the brain it floats there as a micro-consciousness – available for action should it be required, but not experienced in the normal consciousness-with-self way, so the individual does not sense it to be part of their consciousness, even though it could be argued that it is, in *itself*, conscious.

No. 1.

The Ordinary State.

SEPARATE PERSONAL
SPHERES.

The above represents the
operator and subject beginning
the magnetic process.

No. 2.

The Psychological State.

PARTIAL BLENDING OF
SPHERES.

The above condition is fa-
vorable to sympathetic and
transitional phenomena.

No. 3.

The Somnambulic State.

COMPLETE BLENDING OF
SPHERES.

The above state brings out
excursional, examining, and
medical clairvoyance.

No. 4.

The Superior Condition.

MENTAL SPHERES SEPA-
RATED.

The above state leads to independent clairvoyance and in-
tuitional wisdom.

Spiritualists believed that hypnotically
induced trance allowed people to
share a common consciousness.
From Andrew Jackson Davis,
The Magic Staff (1864).

Now, normally there would be no consciousness in this state, because unowned consciousness does not have a subject to be conscious of it. Attention therefore has nothing to lock on to and 'amplify' to consciousness. In meditation, however, the attention mechanism remains on, and in the absence of other things to illuminate it, it latches on – if you like – to its own workings. In other words, 'pure' consciousness is not exactly consciousness of nothing but consciousness of consciousness – the brain listening to itself.

This conclusion is, of course, very similar to the one arrived at by meditators themselves. Except that they would say it was mind listening to mind rather than brain listening to brain.

Not all spiritual-seeming experiences involve 'pure' consciousness. The experience of feeling a presence, for example, is certainly not contentless. The presence may not be an ordinary sort of perception but it is certainly something rather than nothing.

The 'sensed presence' is a very common experience, especially during sleep paralysis. When it is benign, as mine was, it is often described as feeling like being in the presence of God. These sensations are particularly common among people with temporal lobe epilepsy, who have localized 'storms' of neural activity. Such storms may also be triggered by lack of oxygen or glucose (e.g. when the brain is exhausted or traumatized) or when a state of high anxiety suddenly gives way to one of relief. This may explain why people often 'find God' at moments of crisis.

The experience can also be induced by deliberately stimulating certain areas of the temporal lobes. Various rituals have been devised to create this, and it is also possible to do it by sending magnetic pulses through the skull. Michael Persinger, at Laurentian University in Canada, devised a helmet that does this, and nearly all who have used it report the sensation of a presence. Many also see religious visions such as the Virgin Mary or Jesus.[3]

Henry Fuselli, *The Nightmare* (1781).
The incubus – a malignant entity which
squats on sleeping women – is one
of the more fanciful, and enduring,
interpretations of the 'sensed
presence' that people experience
in certain brain states.

The 'God' experience is ecstatic, but the sensed presence may also be felt as something evil such as a sinister ghost, an incubus (a suffocating spirit) or the devil.

The mechanisms that give rise to these feelings are not clear, but it seems likely they occur as the result of several interrelated changes in brain function. One is the dislocation of the self-generating mechanisms in the left and right hemispheres. Persinger, for example, speculates that assymetrical temporal lobe hyperactivity separates the sense of self into two – one twin in each hemisphere. The dominant (usually left) hemisphere then interprets the other part of the self as an 'other' lurking around outside. The 'otherness' is then coloured by emotion – ecstasy or fear – according to which hemisphere is most active. The temporal lobe is the home of the amygdala. In the right hemisphere, amygdala stimulation is associated with a sense of fear and dread, while left hemisphere activation seems to inhibit this.[4]

There seems, then, to be a plausible mechanistic account for each of the core qualities of mystical or spiritual experience. Put very crudely: 'pure' consciousness emerges when a tension is maintained in a perceptual vacuum; 'oneness' is created by the close-down of the 'boundary-making' parts of the self; ecstasy come from turning off the right amygdala; and the sense of presence is formed by the splitting of the self system into two.

Every type of spiritual-seeming experience could be explained in this way: near-death experiences; out-of-the-body experiences; incubi and succubi; visions and ghosts. Even the feeling of universal love may just indicate lack of amygdala activity in a super-integrating brain.

Is this, then, all there is to spiritual experience? Is transcendence merely an aberration of consciousness – an unusual way of viewing the same old material universe?

Perhaps. Yet it is difficult to hold this position unwaveringly once you have had such an experience. You know in a transcendental state that at base the universe is holistic, sentient and non-material. And that knowledge carries a degree of authority which information received in normal states of consciousness lacks.

Intuited knowledge is not (by definition) reasonable – but that doesn't necessarily mean it is incorrect. We just don't know enough about intuition to weigh it against publicly demonstrable deduction. The cognitive processes that give rise to intuited knowledge cannot be examined directly because they are unconscious, so we don't know what they are or even what information they draw on (think how long it has taken us even to detect human pheromones on account of them being unconscious). So the conscious inability to see why something may be true does not necessarily mean it is not true. Even Einstein claims first to have intuited his major discoveries and only later to have worked them out. Perhaps spirituality is just awaiting its Einstein.

If the timelessness and boundlessness of transcendental experience is not an illusion but a glimpse of a true reality, unbounded by ordinary physical laws, you might expect to find evidence for it other than inner certainty. Such evidence would show, for example, that in certain states of mind it is possible to see into what we normally think of as the future or the past (precognition); to know what is happening in a distant location (clairvoyance); to alter the physical world without physical interaction (psychokinesis); or to join with one or many others' consciousness (telepathy).

Such 'impossible' things (according to scientific materialism) are known collectively as psi phenomena. There is, of course, a massive body of anecdotal evidence of 'supernatural' happening, much of which is undoubtedly sincere, fascinating, and – for many – persuasive. For scientists to take it seriously as a challenge to materialism, however, psi phenomena needs to be demonstrable in the same way that material 'facts' are demonstrable – i.e. consistently and in methodologically sound experimental conditions.

In the last 10 years there have been enough rigorously conducted psi experiments, you would think, to prove one way or another whether these phenomena exist. Yet the debate goes on ... and on ... and (believe me) on. On one side psi researchers claim that meta-analysis of their work shows that in each broad category of psi (clairvoyance, psychokinesis, telepathy and precognition) there is a small, but significant and consistent effect. On the other side sceptics claim that meta-analysis show no such thing. As soon as one side presents what seems to be the clinching study of studies the other side counters with a conflicting one. You cannot (trust me on this) draw a decisive conclusion from the evidence.

One problem is that both sides of the argument are driven by prejudice. Conventional science dictates that psi is by definition impossible, so those who hold to the standard scientific model assume that any psi researcher who gets positive results must be deluded, careless or dishonest. Given that psi results are thus meaningless, they see no reason to examine them (why waste time?). So science sails serenely on, holding its conventional model intact by refusing to allow anomalous findings to be taken into account.

This attitude is maddening to the small group of scientists who are dedicated to psi research because, in general, they are far more careful to

Entering Other Minds

Transcendental consciousness creates the sensation of being 'at one' with everything, including other minds. And psi researchers claim that thoughts and feelings can be shared directly or transferred from one mind to another.

One possible explanation is that we are indeed fundamentally 'all of one mind' – a conscious field that is the fundament of the universe. However, quite a lot of apparently telepathic or shared experience can be understood just by looking at known brain mechanisms.

Human beings are a highly social species and the ability to empathise with others and thus to experience oneself as an interactive part of society is central to our nature. Although we each have our own point of view, the way we see the world implies that it is a shared experience. When we look at a chair, for example, we know, without having to think about it, that it would look different to a person standing on the other side of it. Our personal perspective therefore includes the shadowy presence of other observers even at the most basic level. Instead of being locked into a single point of view we can 'throw' our minds into those of others.

The recognition that experience of the world is shared is one of the concepts which seems to be hard-wired into the normal human brain. Although it develops over time its various manifestations emerge at more or less the same age in everyone, whatever their background. This suggests that it is not learned but is genetically programmed.

Empathy is founded largely on mimicry. When you see someone making a facial expression you unconsciously copy it. People shown a photograph of Adolph Hitler smiling broadly will start to smile themselves in the 200 milliseconds or so before the picture becomes conscious – then they will swiftly inhibit the action.

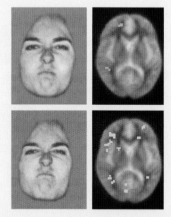

Seeing a picture of someone showing disgust (top left) automatically triggers activation in the part of the observer's brain that reacts when they feel disgusted themselves (top right). And the more intense the expression they see (bottom left), the more active their brains (bottom right).

Facial expressions are not just outward signs of what a person is feeling – they actually create the feeling they signify. Activation of the face muscles involved in smiling, for example, sends feedback signals to the brain which create feelings of pleasure. And brain scans show that the area of the brain activated by seeing a particular expression on another's face is identical to the area activated when we feel whatever is being expressed.

Another type of mimicry that is evident almost from birth is the automatic following of another person's gaze. When someone suddenly swivels their eyes to a new location it is very difficult to resist looking that way

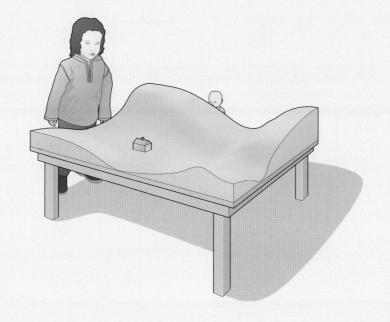

The ability to see things as though through the eyes of another develops naturally in most people around the age of four – they do not have to learn it consciously. The 'mountain range' test (left) provides one way of telling if a child has 'got' the concept of other points of view. The child observes the range from their point of view and is asked if they can see the house. They say yes. Then they are asked if a doll, placed on the other side of the range, can see it too. Children who have yet to develop 'theory of mind' say yes (even though from the doll's viewpoint the house is hidden), because they cannot imagine a view that is not their own. Older children say no.

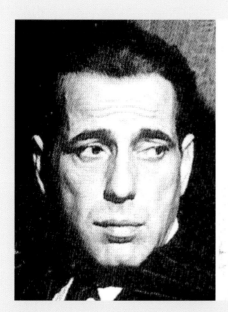
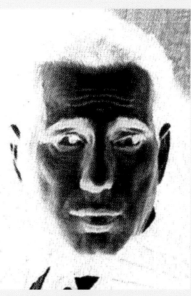

The brain seems to have a special 'module' devoted to gaze detection. If you look at a negative of a photograph of a person looking to the side the direction of their eyes seems to be reversed. This is because the brain overrides your knowledge that in a negative dark and light are reversed and insists that the dark area is the iris. This shows that 'making sense' of eye direction is a task that is processed unconsciously and thus by a different brain area to that which interprets other aspects of the image.[1]

Around the age of four, normal children develop what is known as 'Theory of Mind' (ToM). This is the intuitive ability to know that other people have a point of view that is different to their own. One of the 'markers' for the emergence of a sense of self in humans is the ability of a child to recognize itself in a mirror. The test of this is to dab a bit of rouge on a child's face, hold it up to its reflection, and see if it reaches up to its own face to wipe off the mark. The mirror test has been tried on many species. Chimpanzees are one of the few that consistently 'pass'.

yourself. So we automatically find ourselves sharing the experience of what others are seeing.

Mimicry seems to be dependent on special brain cells called 'mirror neurons'. Single-cell recordings of monkey brains show that certain cells became active when the animal sees another monkey doing a very particular action. These neurons are precisely those which would be activated if the animal was doing the action itself. Interestingly, these cells also seem to fire when the animal *imagines* the other is doing the action.[2] In other words, the monkey knows how the one it is watching is feeling because it is doing the same thing, albeit without carrying the action through to the point where it is externally visible.

In humans, brain-imaging studies have found that watching an experimenter handle an object activates two brain areas.[3] One is in the motor area that would

It is obvious to most people which chocolate bar Charlie wants, but autistic people don't automatically know, even if they are very intelligent. They have to work it out, like a puzzle. This suggests that the ability to know what is going on in other peoples' minds is determined by a brain mechanism which is quite different from other forms of intelligence.

carry out the act (a similar finding to that in monkeys) and the other is Broca's area.[4] Broca's area is the part of the brain concerned with articulating speech, so the finding suggests that, in addition to mimicking the observed action physically, we also activate the language-based concept of it. This, perhaps, is the basis of Theory of Mind (ToM) – an abstracted form of mimicry in which we create in ourselves concepts which match those in another's mind.

In our social lives ToM is essential because it gives us a basis for predicting other people's behaviour and for judging what effect our own behaviour will have on them. Of course, any intelligent person can work out how another person may be seeing something, but ToM does not involve deduction – like mimicry it is automatic, and very difficult to 'turn off'.

ToM is paradoxical in that it partly eradicates the very division between people that it allows them to recognize. The question is: how far can ToM and mimicry take us in creating shared consciousness? They clearly give us the ability to *copy* another's state of mind – but might they also allow us to create a form of communal consciousness, like that we seem to see in beehives?

Individual honey bees are capable of surprisingly high-level cognition. Some studies even suggest they are capable of abstract generalization (distinguishing a stimulus that is similar to one they have previously seen rather than identical, for example).[5] This type of conceptual task is suggestive of the ability to create a higher-order experience (HOE) and might therefore suggest that they have individual consciousness.

Hives of bees, termite colonies, shoals of fish and flocks of birds exhibit group behaviour which seems to reflect some sort of shared consciousness.

Yet when they are in a hive the insects seem to lose these markers of individuality and become subsumed into the group in a way that goes far beyond mere co-operation. It is as though the hive itself becomes conscious – a consciousness, perhaps that 'emerges' from the interaction of its parts.

The mechanisms that allow honey bees to function as a single unit are largely unknown. It is possible that their neuronal activity becomes entrained, much as neuronal activity in a human brain is bound into sychronous oscillation. In a human brain the binding is achieved by the exchange of electrical signals along axons and dendrites. In a hive the signals seem to leap from one bee to another via sensory mechanisms such as sight and smell – and perhaps some that have yet to be discovered.

'Hive' consciousness is therefore rather similar to individual human consciousness. The 'self'-structure might be seen as the hive and the neurons within it as worker bees. So long as they are integrated into the self-structure the components have a single consciousness, but if they are separated from it they create a 'mini' self-structure and perhaps achieve consciousness of their own.

If this is the case, perhaps individual human consciousness can also be lost in the 'hive' of society. Crowd behaviour is known to be quite different from the behaviour of individuals. It is, if you like, an 'emergent property' of social interaction. Could it be that crowd consciousness could similarly emerge?

[1] Pawhan Sinha, 'The Bogart illusion', *Perception*, 29, (2000), 1005–8.

[2] David Perrett, Department of Psychology, University of St Andrews, 'Cellular mechanisms for deciphering the behaviour and intentions of others', Institute of Cognitive Neurology Workshop, 28 July 2001.

[3] Giacomo Rizolatti, 'Resonance Behaviours and Mirror Neurons', *Archives of Italian Biology*, 137, 85–100.

[4] A finding also reported by Marco Iacoboni, 'Cortical Mechanisms of Human Imitation', *Science*, 286, (1999), 2526–8.

[5] Martin Giurfa, *Nature*, 410, (2001), 930–33.

adhere to scientific discipline (sound methodology etc.) than those in other fields. This is precisely because they know that if they get positive results their work will be assumed to be flawed, and they are determined that it will withstand the most critical scrutiny (should it be scrutinized at all).

However, it is very, very difficult for a scientist to be in the business of psi research if they are not certain they are on to something. The rest of the scientific community is scornful or dismissive towards their work, and so long as they remain rigidly scientific they are unlikely to have the consolation of riches or fame. So those who do it tend to be believers.

Beliefs operate at an unconscious as well as a conscious level, so once a person believes something it is impossible for them, however hard they try, to refrain from seeing evidence in the light of that belief. Careful experimental design – double-blind controlled trials and so on – may prevent belief from influencing how results are arrived at, but at some point those results have to be interpreted. There is thus nearly always a crack through which unconscious prejudice might skew things.

And yet, quite a lot of psi research has now been carried out in such a way that no-one has been able to identify any ordinary way that belief can affect the results. Even in what seems like watertight experimental conditions, those who believe tend to get positive results while those who don't, don't. The same experiment, undertaken in the same laboratory, produces different results depending – it appears – on nothing more than who is nominally carrying it out.

The 'easy' explanation for this is that one or other side is somehow defying the methodological security system. But this does not solve the mystery so long as no-one can explain how it is done. It also suggests that even the most sophisticated experimental protocols allow erroneous results to slip through time and time again. And that, in turn, suggests that *all* scientific results may be skewed – which in turn raises the awkward possibility that the evidence upon which materialists rely to discount psi is itself resting on shaky foundations. So anyone who genuinely holds to the scientific method is forced at least to consider whether there may be some other explanation for weird phenomena.

One place to start is with the slippery nature of psi research results. The fact that believers get better results than sceptics could be due, not to error, but to the nature of the phenomena itself. Not only, perhaps, is it very weak and erratic, but it may be essentially subjective, so the beliefs, attitudes and intentions of those investigating it cannot be removed from the experiment without removing the thing itself.

Quantum Minds

Quantum mechanics is weird, and so is consciousness. And the weirdness of each is in some ways similar: both, for example, seem to defy space and time, and both exist in a different dimension from material systems ordered by classical physical laws. This is enough, for some, to convince them that consciousness will eventually be explained in terms of quantum theory.

Others, however, maintain that quantum approaches are simply attempts to solve one mystery with another. Consciousness, for them, is the product of physical – though complex – dynamics which will eventually be fitted into the material framework.

Stuart Hameroff, of the University of Arizona Centre for Consciousness Studies is one of the most enthusiastic champions of the first view. His colleague and friend, mathematician Alwyn Scott, is convinced of the second. Scott believes that non-linear dynamics – the branch of mathematics which describes the recursive type of information processing which occurs in the human brain – will eventually explain how consciousness emerges from physical systems without recourse to quantum weirdness. Hameroff is unconvinced. This is the transcript of a conversation between the two:

Stuart: Tell me, Al, why are you so negative about quantum theories of the mind?

Al: Before trying to answer that, let's remember where we are in agreement. We both feel uncomfortable with the notion that the mind is nothing more than the switchings off and on of the brain's neurons, and we are both looking for something more. But we're looking in different places. I don't have anything against quantum theory – but I don't see any need for quantum theory to explain the strongly nonlinear dynamics that are observed in the brain.

Stuart: What needs to be explained are the tough questions of consciousness – in particular qualia, or conscious experience: the 'hard problem' – as well as binding and other enigmatic features. I agree that nonlinear dynamics is necessary, but why not quantum theory also if it can answer these tough questions?

Al: Sure, we need to understand the riddle of subjective experience. I completely agree with you there. But quantum theory doesn't help much because the binding of stable and globally coherent states is a phenomenon that arises more naturally in classical nonlinear systems than in the linear theory of quantum mechanics. You simply don't need quantum theory to explain global coherence.

Stuart: I agree that consciousness is a globally coherent state, but globally coherent classical states are merely couplings and correlations of separate individual activities, e.g. 'neurons fire synchronously'. Being coincidental doesn't necessarily solve the binding problem. On the other hand, there are macroscopic quantum states – superconductors, for example – which are qualitatively different. They are globally coherent in the sense of 'being one entity'.

Al: There's lots more to classical nonlinear dynamics than neurons firing synchronously. A generic feature of classical nonlinear dynamics is the emergence of stable dynamic entities at each level of description to provide a basis for the nonlinear interactions at the next higher level. You don't need to assume that quantum theory is required for such behaviour: tornadoes emerge from the nonlinear dynamics of air and sunshine, just as cities and cultural configurations emerge from the very nonlinear interactions among human beings. Each of these is indeed 'one entity'. You can't have half a tornado.

Stuart: But tornadoes and cities are not conscious ...

Al: The special thing about consciousness – it seems to me – is that it emerges from all the levels of the brain's dynamics; not just one (the neurons for example) but all of them.

Stuart: Including quantum coherence at the level of intra-neural microtubules?

Al: I don't have any philosophical problems with quantum coherence playing a role in conscious phenomena, but at the level of biochemistry, these effects are very small. Even if they apply at the level of protein dynamics – which I agree is possible – it doesn't mean they are necessary to explain consciousness. [Pause.] Taking another tack, let me try to express my position this way. Brains are composed of neurons, synapses and glial cells in the same sense that living organisms are composed of chemical atoms, and the functional organization is equally intricate. Just as one would not attempt to describe the life of an organism in terms of the motions of its constituent atoms, one cannot describe the mind in terms of the switchings of its constituent neurons. But the intricacy of this picture doesn't require quantum effects. Life and mind emerge from the immensely complicated nonlinear and hierarchical structures of body and brain. That's where the mystery lies.

Stuart: How would you explain the intelligent, adaptive behaviour of a single-cell organism like a paramecium, which leads a rich existence without a neural network or synapses?

Al: That's a good point. Maybe these little guys could be using their cytoskeletons to compute.

Stuart: One might need something like quantum theory to describe a fundamental life process of the bacterium. How do we know? What is life?

Al: One cannot think of the brain merely in terms of individual neurons. Neurons organize themselves into assemblies of neurons, each of which exhibits global coherence, binding and threshold phenomena, as does an individual neuron. Thus assemblies of neurons can organize themselves into assemblies of assemblies, which in turn organize themselves into assemblies of assemblies of assemblies – and so on – up to the functional dynamic entities that provide the basis for the immensely complicated behaviours that underlie human consciousness.

Stuart: Granted. But what is it that these behaviours are underlying? What is consciousness?

Al: Stuart, if I knew, I would certainly share it with you, but these statements about the functional organization of the brain – which are supported by many experimental studies – are far removed from the considerations of quantum mechanics. There is no need to cast about for sources of mystery here; fully organized thoughts are immensely (in a precise technical sense) complicated entities, and the experiments of present-day electrophysiology tell us little about how they might interact.

Stuart: And they tell us nothing about the nature of conscious experience – the 'hard problem'. There is a need to cast about for something.

Al: Yes, and I'm suggesting that the immensely intricate nonlinear structure of the brain's dynamics is a much richer source of mystery than quantum theory will ever be. In my opinion, physicists who turn to quantum theory for explanations of such intricate phenomena are looking in the wrong direction. Quantum theory tells us how atoms interact, but little about protein dynamics and nothing about the electrophysiology of the brain.

Stuart: I disagree. Regulation of protein conformational dynamics is not understood, and some evidence supports quantum effects. For example, quantum coherence apparently does occur in certain proteins, and quantum spin correlations are preserved in cytoplasm ...

Al: Well, yes, protein dynamics are very complicated. That's also my point. But – to repeat – it's not clear that you really need quantum theory to describe this intricacy. I spent about 10 years studying quantum theories of polaronic effects in protein and at the end of the decade it was difficult to point to anything of experimental significance that could not be just as well described classically.

Stuart: That's not to say that quantum effects in proteins may not be experimentally shown subsequently. It's an extremely tricky business – quantum effects are, in general, unobservable.

Al: If physicists are truly interested in contributing to our understanding of phenomena related to consciousness, they should acquaint themselves with the relevant neurological facts, which are far more intricate than can be expressed in a quantum formulation.

Stuart: I think a theory of consciousness must integrate philosophy, physics and neurobiology, so I basically agree. However the 'relevant neurological facts' may turn out to include quantum effects.

Al: It's my view that physics and mathematics will play minor roles in this integration. [Pause.] And I have the impression that some physicists cling to the quantum approach because they are subconsciously aware that their knowledge is of limited value for understanding really interesting questions – like the natures of life and mind. Physics is a science of the past.

Stuart: Not being a physicist, I don't take this personally, but I do think it's unfair and incorrect. Face it – neither the hard problem of experience nor the nature of the universe is understood. Physics may offer solutions for both, particularly if experience is a fundamental property of the universe.

Al: I don't feel comfortable with blithely assuming the existence of some new force field (or whatever) without experimental evidence for it. I would have no problem with a quantum theory of neural behaviour if there were some experimental evidence to support it, but there is none that I know of. So I prefer to concentrate my very limited powers of analysis on the vast and unexplored realms of hierarchical nonlinear dynamics.

Stuart: Your work on hierarchical emergence is extremely important. And it is true that there is currently no hard evidence for quantum coherence and wave function collapse in microtubules. However, I might add there is currently no experimental evidence for consciousness. It is unobservable (except in ourselves).

Al: Isn't the fact that we are having this conversation clear experimental evidence for consciousness?

Stuart: Not necessarily. I could be a zombie.

Al: Ah! Don't get started on zombies; the whole idea is kooky! Look. At the end of the day, I suppose, it comes down to intuition. My whole professional life – 35 years – has been devoted to the study of classical nonlinear dynamics. [Pause.] My little finger tells me that quantum effects aren't important. [Pause.] Of course, that's not an argument, is it?

Stuart: Perhaps not, but I have great respect for intuition. It's a non-computable process. It's just that my intuition is that quantum effects are necessary to explain enigmatic features of consciousness.

Al: Anyway you can't claim that your conclusion is inescapable because so many see it differently.

Stuart: Well it's inescapable to me.

Al: [Sigh.]

Charles Tart, a former professor of psychology at the University of California and now a full-time psi researcher offers a thought experiment in the alien-brain-implant tradition to illustrate the problem of trying to 'prove' psi by traditional objective methods:

'Imagine that some very technically advanced (but error-prone) aliens came along one night and implanted a physically undetectable transceiver (which works on some unknown frequency) in the brains of all humans while we slept. We remember nothing about this surgery. Unfortunately they made one of their errors, and instead of connecting the transceiver controls to the conscious areas of the brain, they hooked up the controls to the subconscious area. And, as a government economy measure in this project, they bought the transceivers from the lowest bidder, so the units tend to be unreliable and usually (but not always) have a lot of noise mixed in with both their sent and received signals.

'Now imagine you're a psychologist carrying out experiments, unaware, as are all people, of this alien project. You do an experiment where you precisely (by the old reality standards) control what sensory information your subjects are exposed to, so you can control the independent variables you stimulate them with. Except now sometimes a subject's implanted transceiver operates, for reasons that may be unknown to the subject, or that are only roughly related to conscious factors that stimulate unconscious factors, and the subject picks up additional information about the experiment. For example she may find out that she is in the control group and the experimenter does not expect her behaviour to differ from random behaviour. Or that the experimenter has an enormous emotional investment in her behaviour changing in a certain way as his next promotion depends on getting data that supports the theoretical position he is already publicly committed to. Or that the experimenter would really like to go to bed with her but is controlling himself and acting very professionally. Or that the experimenter finds her ugly ...

'Sometimes, for subconscious reasons, the experimenter's transceiver operates to send information to the subject's transceiver, which may or may not be in receiving mode. He may send information about how confident he is in his hypotheses and understanding, or about his repressed feelings of uncertainty and conflict, or ...'

Under our new, flaky-transceiver-implanted conditions, asks Tart, how could we possibly develop an 'objective' science of (para)psychology?

The answer, obviously, is with great, great difficulty. However, this does not necessarily mean that psi is doomed to remain shrouded in the dark mists of superstition beyond the enlightened kingdom of science. It may never be incorporated into the traditional stronghold of scientific materialism (indeed it cannot be, by definition), but science itself is expanding its boundaries, and those at the leading edge are developing theories that could incorporate anomalous events in a new, expanded model of the natural world.

The established scientific paradigm – the one accepted by even the most dyed-in-the-wool conservatives – includes phenomena which, if they could be scaled up and witnessed directly, would seem to be magic. They include particles which are in two or more places at the same time; particles which effect one another across (apparently) limitless distances with no detectable means of communication; and events that are decided by the act of being observed.

Quantum physics has been with us now for more than a century and the quantum phenomena I have described are no longer just mathematical predictions but have been demonstrated repeatedly and even put to use in technology such as lasers and superconductors.

Nevertheless, it is still generally thought that quantum phenomena have very little to do with our day-to-day lives. The human-scale world in which we operate is still assumed to be entirely ordered by the laws of classical physics; replete with matter, space and linear time – a closed system of physical cause and effect. At smaller scales – atomic particles, nanoseconds and so on – and at the cosmic end of things, it may be very different. But the weird stuff – mysteriously entangled particles; dead-and-alive cats; wormholes and superstrings – can be left to theoreticians because none of it actually affects us.

Now consciousness undoubtedly does have some presence in the human world. Whether or not we think it is part of the physical universe, we very physical beings know about it, so the only way the current scientific model can account for it is either by claiming it is material (identity) or that it emerges from the material. Either way, matter is primary.

If, however, one supposes that the weird stuff goes all the way up – from atoms to galaxies – matter may not be fundamental at all. The material world 'sandwiched' between quantum weirdness and the equally strange universe of black holes, vacuum energy and infinite space may just be a curious emergent property of some more basic 'stuff' such as energy and information or – even more fundamental than that – sentience. Individual consciousness could then be seen as a droplet of condensation in this ocean of knowing. Its normal contents, being things material, would obscure its real nature. Transcendental experiences and psi phenomena, by contrast, would manifest their real nature. Precognition, for example, would be a reflection of the mind's essential freedom from time. Clairvoyance would occur when it is allowed to roam outside the boundaries set by our physical senses. Telepathy would be a demonstration of its essential oneness.

The appeal of quantum mind/brain theories is that they solve the 'hard problem' automatically. If the universe is consciousness then there is no need to explain how it can emerge or interact with it. Instead, however, it raises an equally hard problem: how can matter arise from mind?

So far the matter-from-mind solution has proved as elusive as the mind-from-matter one. If there is any consensus on it, it is this: a single 'bit', or quantum, can be described as an item of information which may be either 'yes' or 'no'. Which it is is not decided until it interacts in some way with the environment. It may be that the environmental interaction must be the observation by a sentient observer – but this is not known because (rather as with the fridge light problem) the only things we can observe are those that have been observed by a sentient being. So we can never know what they might have been like if we hadn't observed them. Might they have remained undecided? Mere 'potential'?

A large number of quanta may all be in this undecided state, and when they are like this they are entangled. This means that if one is observed the others appear to alter (magically – for no-one knows how) to complement it.

A system like this (before it is observed) is known as coherent quantum superposition. The event that occurs on observation is called quantum decoherence or collapse. A collapsed state is a definite 'answer' to the question of observation. And one theory is that that 'answer' is the material universe – collapsed into concrete existence by the question posed by the observer. In other words, we create a part of the material universe every time we invoke the question of attention.

The trouble with quantum theories about consciousness is that the weight of evidence suggests that quantum effects simply don't happen at the human scale. They can only be observed at microscopic level and in the sort of extraordinary conditions that can be achieved in laboratories. As soon as there is any interference from the macroscopic environment quantum states collapse, so the warm, wet, macro-environment of the human brain is not the sort of place where they could occur except, perhaps, for nanoseconds. Certainly not continuously, as would need to be the case if they were responsible for creating our ongoing awareness.

Now there is a school of thought that holds that mind is not so intimately connected with brain that this necessarily matters. Charles Tart, for example, cites a story of a patient who witnessed her own heart surgery (from outside her body) while her brain was completely inactive.[5] And a survey of 63 cardiac patients undergoing surgery at Southampton Hospital found that at least 6 per cent of them appeared, by their own reports, to have been conscious while clinically dead.[6]

Most quantum mind theorists, however, take the more reasonable view (in my opinion) that personal consciousness (if not consciousness *per se*) is intimately connected with the workings of a live brain.

Quantum mind theories tend to be rather vague, but the British mathematician Sir Roger Penrose, with Stuart Hameroff, has developed one that pins down the processes precisely. They have tried to get around the 'environmentally unsuitable' problem by locating quantum processes in microtubules – tiny filaments of protein in neuronal cell walls. Microtubules are very complex and it is possible that, just as individual neurons are information-processors within the greater information-processing system of the brain, micotubules may be information-processors within the neuron.

The interior structure of microtubules is largely shielded from the outside environment, and Penrose and Hameroff suggest that delicate quantum states may therefore be able to survive in them for periods of up to half a second. During that time the subunits would be in the yes/no state of superposition, and able to interact with other subunits (including those in different neurons) through non-local entanglement. This interaction would be a form of quantum computation. At a certain point the quantum system would collapse through a physical process dubbed decoherence, due to the action of gravity. It would then be reduced to a state which conforms to the laws of classical physics. Each collapse, according to this theory, would be a 'blip' of consciousness – the 'answer' to the computation.

This theory, known as 'Orchestrated Objective Reduction' (Orch OR) is probably the best worked-out quantum theory of consciousness yet, but it still has huge holes. Quantum gravity, for example, has yet to be shown to exist. And it remains debatable (most physicists would say unlikely) that even the relatively sheltered environment of a microtubule could sustain a coherent quantum superposition for the length of time needed to carry out the computation at the heart of the theory. Even Stuart Hameroff admits it is but 'a speck on the horizon'.

Nevertheless, the development of Orch OR demonstrates that it is at least plausible that consciousness may be incorporated into the scientific paradigm without recourse to hard materialism. Descartes' *res cogitans,* the indivisible, infinite stuff of mind, may turn out to be, not just part of the natural world, but the very basis of it.

It has become fashionable in recent years to speak of science reaching a dead end. In a sense that may, indeed, be true. Objective science may not be able to probe beyond the limits of the physical world because there may not be an objective world beyond – only a field of possibilities which become facts by the very act of observation. To proceed past the concrete limits of materialism, then, scientists may have to abandon objectivity and place themselves within the scheme of things, recognizing themselves as creators as well as observers of the natural universe. From this subjective perspective, the hard problem of consciousness may simply dissolve.

' ... understand how great is the darkness in which we grope, and never forget the natural-science assumptions with which we started are provisional and revisable things.'

William James, The Principles of Psychology *(1890).*

References

Chapter 1

1 T. Nørretranders, *The User Illusion: Cutting Consciousness Down to Size* (New York, Viking, 1998); Gerald Edelman and Giulio Tononi, *A Universe of Consciousness* (New York, Basic Books, 2000)

2 *'Mack I and Rock I', Inattentional Blindness* (Cambridge, MA, MIT Press, 1998)

3 J. Grimes, 'On the failure to detect changes in scenes across saccades', in K. Akins (ed.), *Perception* (New York, Oxford University Press, 1996), 89–110

4 D. J. Simons and C. F. Chabris, 'Gorillas in our midst – sustained inattentional blindness for dynamic events', *Perception*, 28 (1999).
(http://www.wjh.harvard.edu/~viscog/lab/demos.html)

5 J. Kevin O'Regan, Ronald A. Rensink, James J. Clark, 'Change Blindness as a result of "mudsplashes"', *Nature*, 398 (March 1999), 34

6 Rita Carter, *Mapping the Mind* (London, Weidenfeld & Nicolson,1998), 200

7 J. Kevin O'Regan, 'Change Blindness and the Visual World as outside memory', Towards a Science of Consciousness Conference, Tucson, 2000

8 George Riddoch, 'Dissociation of visual perception due to occipital injuries, with especial reference to appreciation of movement', *Brain*, 40 (1917), 15–57

9 C. A. Heywood and R. W. Kentridge, 'Affective blindsight?', *Trends in Cognitive Science,* 4 (2000), 125–6

10 L. Muckli et al, 'Blindsight in Normal Observers?', *Neuroimage,* 5:4 pt 2 (1997), S144 Academic Press.

11 T. Radil, 'Anosmic and Hyposmic Olfaction – a blindsight-like phenomenon', Towards a Science of Consciousness Conference, Tucson, 2000, abstract no 169

12 P. Stoerig and A. Cowey, 'Blindsight in man and monkey', *Brain*, 120 (1997), 552–9

13 J. Grimes, 'On the failure to detect changes in scenes across saccades', in K. Akins (ed.), *Perception* (New York, Oxford University Press, 1996), 89–110; reporting on G. W. McConkie and David Zola, 'Is visual information integrated across successive fixations in reading', *Perception and Psychophysics*, 25 (1979), 221–4

14 M. V. C. Baldo, Department of Physiology and Biophysics, Insitute of Biomedical Sciences, University of Sao Paulo, Brazil, 'Temporal Modulation of the Attentional Blink by Target Complexity', Towards a Science of Consciousness Conference, Tucson, 2000.

15 For a discussion of this see Walter J. Freeman, 'Perception of Time and Causation through the Kinethesia of intentional action', *Cognitive Processing,* 1, (2000),18–34

Chapter 2

1 Christof Kotch, in discussion,Towards a Science of Consciousness Conference, Tucson, 2000

2 Max Velmans, *Understanding Consciousness* (London, Routledge, 2000)

3 Jonathan Barnes, in Richard L. Gregory (ed.), *The Oxford Companion to the Mind* (Oxford, Oxford University Press, 1987)

4 For a discussion of this see Nigel Thomas, California State University, Almagination, Eliminativism, and the Pre-History of Consciousness;
http://www.u.arizona.edu/~chalmers/online.html

5 Sir Geoffrey Warnock, in Richard L. Gregory (ed.), *The Oxford Companion to the Mind* (Oxford, Oxford University Press, 1987)

6 George Rey, 'Reasons for doubting the existence of even epiphenomal consciousness', *Behavioural and Brain Sciences*, 14:4, (1991). 692. Quotes in Max Velmans, *'Understanding Consciousness'* (London, Routledge, 2000), 32

7 Daniel Dennett, 'Instead of Qualia' in A. Revonsuo and M. Kampinnen (eds.), *Consciousness and Philosophy and Cognitive Neuroscience* (Hillsdale, NJ, Lawrence Erlbaum Associates, 1994)

8 Paul Churchland, *Matter and Consciousness* (Cambridge, MA, MIT Press, 1984)

9 Daniel Dennett, *Consciousness Explained* (Harmondsworth, Penguin, 1991), 310

10 Adapted from David Chalmers, 'Absent Qualia, Fading Qualia, Dancing Qualia' in Thomas Metzinger (ed.), *Conscious Experience* (Imprint Academic, 1995)

11 John Searle, 'Consciousness, Free Action and the Brain', *Journal of Consciousness Studies*, 7:10, (2000), 17

12 David Chalmers, *The Conscious Mind* (Oxford, Oxford University Press, 1996), 160

13 Ibid, 298

14 Daniel Dennett, 'Facing Backwards on the Problem of Consciousness', *Journal of Consciousness Studies*, 3:1 (1996), 4–6

Chapter 3

1 Gallup poll reported in *Publishers Weekly* (September 4, 1994); in Carl Sagan, *The Demon-Haunted World* (New York, Ballantine Books, 1996), 65

2 Benjamin Libet, 'Unconsciousness: Cerebral Initiative and the role of conscious will in voluntary action', *Behavioural and Brain Sciences*, 8 (1985), 529–66

3 Hans Kornhuber and Luder Deeke, 'Hirnpotentialänderungen bei Willkürbewegungen und passiven Bewegungen des Menschen: Bereitschaftspotential und reafferente Potentiale', Pflügers Archiv für die Physiologie des Menschen und Tiere', 284 (1965), 1–17

4 Benjamin Libet, 'Do we Have Freewill?', *Journal of Consciousness Studies*, 6 (August/September 1999), 47

5 Patrick Haggard et al, 'On the Perceived Time of Voluntary Actions', *British Journal of Psychology*, 90 (1999), 291–303; Patrick Haggard et al 'On the relation between brainpotentials and awareness of movements', *Experimental Brain Research*, 126 (1999), 128–33

6 John Searle, in discussion, Towards a Science of Consciousness Conference, Tucson, 2000

7 Mark Ridley, *Mendel's Demon – gene justice and the complexity of life* (London, Weidenfeld & Nicolson, 2000)

8 For more on this see Paul Cisek, 'Behaviour as Interaction', *Journal of Consciousness Studies* (November/December 1999), 133

9 For a fuller discussion of this see Todd Moody, 'Conversations with Zombies', *Journal of Consciousness Studies*, 1:2 (1994), 196–200

Chapter 4

1 Charles Jonscher, *Wired Life. Who are we in the digital age?* (London, Bantam Books, 1999)

2 B. W. Connors et al, 'Intrinsic firing patterns of diverse neocortical neurons', *Trends in Neuroscience*, 13 (1990), 99–104

3 D. Schwender et al, 'Anaesthetic control of 40-Hz brain activity and implicit memory', *Consciousness and Cognition*, 3:2, (1994), 129–47

4 A list of such studies is contained in Bernard Baars, 'The conscious access hypothesis: origins and recent advances', *Trends in Cognitive Sciences*, 6:1 (2002)

Chapter 5

1 R. Held and A. Hein, 'Adaptation of disarranged hand-eye coordination contingent upon re-afferent stimulation', *Perceptual Motor Skills*, 8 (1958), 87–90. From Francisco J. Varela, Evan Thompson and Eleanor Rosch, *Embodied Mind* (Cambridge, MA, MIT Press, 1991), 175

2 Hans Richter and Ove Franzen, *'Neuroanatomical correlates of voluntary modulation of accomodation in the human visual system'*; First International Symposium on

Accomodation/ Vergence Mechanisms in the Visual System, Stockholm, September 1996

3 U. Castiello, Y. Paulignan and M. Jeannerod, 'Temporal Dissociation of motor responses and subjective awareness', *Brain*, 114 (1991), 2639–55

4 Ferdinand Binkofski and Richard Block, 'Accelerated Time Experience after Left Frontal Cortex Lesion', *'Neurocase'*, 2:6 (1996), 485–93

5 John McCrone, 'When a second lasts forever', *New Scientist* (1 November 1997)

6 G. Csibra et al, 'Gamma Oscillations and Object Processing in the Infant Brain', *Science*, 290 (2000), 1582–5

7 Antonio R. Damasio, *The Feeling of What Happens* (London, William Heinemann, 1999)

8 M. H. Johnson et al, 'Newborns' preferential tracking of face-like stimuli and its subsequent decline', *Cognition*, 40 (1991), 1–19

9 Richard Cytowik, 'Synaestheisa, phenomenology and neurophysiology', *Psyche*, 2:10 (1995)

10 Mircea Steriade, Laval University, Quebec, Canada, 'Cortical Resonance, states of vigilance and mentation', *Neuroscience*, 101:2 (2000), 243–76

11 For a review of brain states associated with memory formation see Michael E. Hasselmo, 'Neuromodulation: acetylcholine and memory consolidation', *Trends in Cognitive Sciences*, 3:9 (September 1999), 351–9

Chapter 6

1 Michael Frayn, *The Tin Men* (London, Collins, 1965)

2 See Mark Johnson, 'Embodied Reason', in Gail Weiss, Fern Honi, Gail Haber (eds.), *Perspectives on Embodiment* (New York and London, Routledge, 1999)

3 T. J. Grabowski, Antonio R. Damasio and Hannah Damasio, 'Premotor and prefrontal correlates of category-related lexical retrieval', *Neuroimage*, 7 (1998), 232–43

4 P. Erhard et al, 'Functional mapping of motor activation in and near Broca's area', *Neuroimage*, 3 (1996), S367. See also E. Bonda et al, 'Frontal cortex involvement in organised sequences of hand movements: Evidence from a Positron Emission tomography study', *Society for Neurosciences Abstracts*, 20 (1994), 353

5 M. Krams et al, 'The preparation, execution and suppression of copied movements in the human brain', *Experimental Brain Research*, 120 (1998), 386–98

6 Rita Carter, *Mapping the Mind* (London, Weidenfeld & Nicolson, 1998), 116–19

7 For a detailed description of the conscious and unconscious visual processing pathways see A. D. Milner and M. A. Goodale, *The Visual Brain In Action* (Oxford, Oxford University Press, 1995)

8 James Jerome (J.J.) Gibson, *The Perception of the Visual World* (Boston, Houghton Mifflin, 1950)

9 Oliver Sacks, *Seeing Voices* (London, Picador, 1991)

10 Jan Iverson and Susan Goldin-Meadow, 'Why People Gesture when they Speak', *Nature*, 396, (1998), 228

11 David McNeill, *Hand and Mind: What Gestures Reveal About Thought* (University of Chicago Press, 1992)

12 Joseph Le Doux, *The Emotional Brain* (New York, Simon and Schuster, 1996), 303

13 Ibid, 203

14 Valerie Gray Hardcastle, 'It's OK to be Complicated: The Case for Emotion', *Journal of Consciousness Studies*, 6, (November 1999), 241

15 Endel Tulving and Daniel Schacter, 'Priming and Human Memory Systems', *Science*, 247 (1990), 301–6

16 Andrew Scholey, report to British Psychological Society, March 2000, reported in *New Scientist* (29 April 2000)

Chapter 7

1 Keenan et al, 'Self Recognition', *Trends in Cognitive Sciences*, 4:9 (2000), 341

2 Ronald Melzack et al, 'Phantom Limbs in People with Congenital limb deficiency or amputation in early childhood', *Brain*, 120 (1997), 1603–20; V. S. Ramachandran, *Phantoms in the Brain* (London, Fourth Estate, 1998)

3 A. Iriki et al, 'Coding of modified body scheme during tool use by macaque postcentral neurones', *NeuroReport*, 7, (1996), 2325–30, in V. Gallese, 'The Inner Sense of Action', *Journal of Consciousness Studies,* 7:10, (2000), 35

4 Diana, Princess of Wales, resignation speech 1996

5 C. Lutz, *'The domain of emotion words on Ifaluk'*, in R. Harré, *The Social Construction of Emotions* (Oxford, Basil Blackwell, 1986); quoted in J. McCrone, 'A Bifold Model of Freewill', *Journal of Consciousness Studies*, 6 (August/September 1999), 249

6 Daniel Wegner and Thalia Wheatley, 'Apparent Mental Causation: Sources of the experience of Will' *American Psychologist,* Vol 54, (1999), No. 7

Chapter 8

1 Allan J. Hobson, *Consciousness* (New York, Scientific American Library, 1999), 170

2 For a detailed description of the neural activation during sleep and dreaming see Allan J. Hobson, *Consciousness* (New York, Scientific American Library, 1999)

3 David Kahn, '"I Just Know It's John!" Character Recognition in Dreaming Consciousness', Towards a Science of Consciousness Conference, Tucson, 2000, abstract no. 254

4 Susan Blackmore, 'A theory of lucid dreams and OBEs', in J. Gakenbach and Stephen LaBerge (eds.), *Conscious Mind, Sleeping Brain* (New York, Plenum 1998), 373–87

5 Reported by Stephen LaBerge at Towards a Science of Consciousness Conference, Tucson, 2000

6 E.g. Stephen Kosslyn et al, *Journal of Cognitive Neuroscience*, 5:3, (1993), 263–87

7 M. Cocude et al, *Psychological Research*, 62 (1999), 93–106; and Jan Kassubek et al, 'Cortical activation during visual mental imagery investigated by fMRI', *Neuroimage Poster No 65* (Academic Press, 2000)

8 Reported by Stephen LaBerge at Towards a Science of Consciousness Conference, Tucson, 2000

9 David Weinberger et al, 'Physiological dysfunction of dorsolateral prefrontal cortex in schizophrenia', *Archives of General Psychiatry*, 43 (1986), 114–24

10 Y. Aderbigbe et al, 'Prevalence of depersonalisation and derealisation experienced in rural population', *Social Psychiatry and Psychiatric Epidemiology*; quoted in Marlene Steinberg and Maxine Schnall, *The Stranger in the Mirror* (New York, Cliff Street Books, 2000)

11 Depersonalization and Derealization discussion board website at <http://www.users.globalnet.co.uk/~nogin/maurice/stories.aeleis,html>

12 G. Blount, 'Dangerousness of Patients with Capgras syndrome', *Nebraska Medical Journal*, 781 (1986), 207; and Rita Carter, *Mapping the Mind* (London, Weidenfeld & Nicolson, 1998), 123

13 James, *Principles of Psychology* (New York, Holt, 1890), 359–63

14 John Kihlstrom and D. Schacter, 'Functional Disorders of Autobiographical Memory', in Baddeley et al (eds.), *A Handbook of Memory Disorders* (Chichester, John Wiley, 1966)

15 F. Putnam et al, 'The Clinical Phenomenology of Multiple Personality Disorder', *Journal of Clinical Psychiatry*, 47, (1996), 285–93

16 William H. Smith PhD, 'Overview of Multiple Personality Disorder', *The Menninger Letter*, 1:4, (1993), 5

17 *Mistaken Identity*, BBC2 (November 11, 1999)

18 Judith Armstrong, 'The case of Mr Woods', (unpublished paper, quoted by Jennifer Radden in 'Pathologically Divided Minds', in Shaun Gallagher and Joanathan Shear (eds.), *Models of Self* (Imprint Academic, 1999)

19 Tsai et al, 'Functional magnetic resonance imaging of personality switches in a woman with Dissociative Identity Disorder', *Harvard Review of Psychiatry*, 7 (1999), 119

20 For an overview of the mechanisms underlying childhood trauma-induced dissociation,

see Bruce Perry et al, 'Childhood Trauma, the Neurobiology of Adaptation and Use-Dependent Development of the Brain: How States become Traits', *Infant Mental Health Journal*, 16:4 (1995), 271–91

21 E. Hilgard, *Divided Consciousness 2nd edition* (Chichester, John Wiley, 1986); D. Holender and J. Kihlstrom, 'The Cognitive Unconscious', *Science*, 237, (1987) 1445–52

22 Joseph LeDoux, *The Emotional Brain* (New York, Simon and Schuster, 1996)

Chapter 9

1 Gallup: *'US Key Indicators'* (January 2000); 2) Gallup UK for BBC *Soul of Britain* (June 2001)

2 Andrew Newberg, *'Why God Won't Go Away'* (Ballantine Books, 2000)

3 'Religion and the Brain', *Newsweek* (May 7 2001)

4 M. A. Persinger, 'Vectoral Cerebral hemisphericity as differential sources for the sensed presence, mystical experiences and religious conversions', *Perceptual and Motor Skills*, 76, (1993) 915–30

5 Charles Tart, satellite presentation at Scientific and Medical Network Beyond the Brain Conference, Cambridge, August 1999

6 Dr Sam Parnia, 'Near Death Experiences in Cardiac Arrest and the Mystery of Consciousness', *Network* (August 2000)

Further Reading

Philosophy of Consciousness

Conscious Experience, Thomas Metzinger (ed.) (Thorveton UK, Imprint Academic, 1995). Essays cover a wide range of philosophical issues – a heavyweight tome for the dedicated reader.

The Conscious Mind, David J. Chalmers (New York and London, Oxford University Press, 1996). Chalmers lays out his theory of consciousness (a 'modern' form of dualism) with terrific care and scholarship. Tough passages are obligingly signalled in advance, allowing the reader to skip difficult technicalities.

Consciousness Explained, Daniel C. Dennett (Harmondsworth, Penguin, 1991). Dennett's seminal work on the illusory nature of consciousness. (It is often referred to as 'Consciousness Explained Away'). Witty, wonderfully readable and – at least while you're reading it – hugely convincing.

Introducing Consciousness, David Papineau and Selina Howard (Cambridge UK, Icon Books, 2000). Pocket-sized, snappy introduction to the main theories, complete with comic-book style illustrations featuring Germaine Greer lookalike.

Models of the Self, Shaun Gallagher, Jonathan Shear (eds.) (Thorveton UK, Imprint Academic 1999). A wonderful collection of essays about the nature of self.

The Rediscovery of Mind, John R. Searle (London, MIT Press, 1998). Searle's attack on computational theories of mind that leave out consciousness. Describes his theory of consciousness as a natural feature of the mind, irreducible to mere brain mechanics.

Stairway to the Mind, Alwyn Scott (New York, Copernicus, 1995). Mathematician Alwyn Scott goes step-by-step from atoms to consciousness – showing how the 'other stuff' of mind might emerge from a material system.

Theories of Consciousness, William Seager (London and New York, Routledge, 1999). A strictly monist account of representational theories of consciousness. Text-book style will probably appeal more to the student than the general reader.

Understanding Consciousness, Max Velmans (London, Routledge, 2000). Velmans' 'reflexive monism' aims to bridge the materialist/dualist gap by placing human consciousness in the world rather than in the brain. Wide-ranging and scholarly.

The Undiscovered Mind, John Horgan (London, Weidenfeld & Nicolson, 1999). Science journalist John Horgan argues that consciousness cannot be 'explained' by science.

Embodiment and Emotion

The Embodied Mind, Francisco J. Varela, Evan Thompson and Eleanor Rosch (Cambridge, MA, MIT Press, 1991). Consciousness as a function of the body and its interactions with the environment. Not a light read, but probably the most complete and careful exposition of the notion of embodied consciousness.

The Emotional Brain, Joseph LeDoux (Simon and Schuster, New York, 1996). Mainly concentrates on the amygdala – the brain organ that generates negative emotions.

The Enigma of Reason, the Seat of the Soul, Paul M. Churchland (Cambridge, MA, MIT Press, 1999). A hard-line materialist sets out the case for identity.

The Feeling of What Happens, Antonio R. Damasio (London, William Heinemann, 1999). The biological basis of consciousness, or how what's 'out there' comes to be 'in here'.

How to Build a Mind, Igor Aleksander (London, Weidenfeld & Nicolson, 2000). Can a silicon brain in a metal body have a mind? AI researcher Aleksander thinks so…

Psychology and Neuroscience

A Universe of Consciousness – How matter becomes imagination, Gerald M. Edelman and Guilio Tononi (New York, Basic Books, 2000). Edelman describes how consciousness is bound by synchrony and 're-entrance' – the back and forth 'conversation' between brain modules.

A User's Guide to the Brain, John Ratey (London, Little, Brown, 2000). Down-to-earth handbook about brain functions – better than anything you get with a computer.

Consciousness, J. Allan Hobson (New York, Scientific American Library, 1999). Concentrates on sleeping and dreaming – and what it tells us about the nature of consciousness.

Eye and Brain, Richard L. Gregory (Oxford, Oxford University Press, 4th Edition, 1995). The construction of visual consciousness, beautifully observed by one of the world's leading authorities.

Going Inside, John McCrone (London, Faber and Faber, 1999). Solid and detailed, yet highly readable description of the brain mechanisms underlying experience.

Hare Brain Tortoise Mind, Guy Claxton (London, Fourth Estate, 1997). Engaging account of the conscious/unconscious divide and how it affects our lives.

Hidden Minds, Frank Tallis (London, Profile Books, 2002). A history of the unconscious, charting the discovery, neglect and rediscovery of the backrooms of the brain.

Images and Understanding, Horace Barlow, Colin Blakemore and Miranda Weston-Smith (eds.) (New York, Cambridge University Press, 1990). Aspects of visual consciousness in a series of illustrated essays.

Inevitable Illusions, Massimo Piattelli-Palmarin (New York, Wiley, 1994). Intriguing analysis of the 'built-in' concepts that mould consciousness.

The Mind's Past, Michael S. Gazzaniga (University of California, Berkeley, 1998). The mind as memory.

Phantoms in the Brain, V. S. Ramachandran and Sandra Blakeslea (London, Fourth Estate, 1998). Largely informed by Ramachandran's work with amputees, *Phantoms in the Brain* gives fascinating accounts of how consciousness is moulded by the body. Also covers the now-familiar areas of alien hands, blindsight and neglect.

Understanding Other Minds, Simon Baron-Cohen, Helen Tager-Flusberg and Donald J Cohen (eds.) (Oxford, Oxford University Press, 2000). Theory of Mind, empathy, mimicry …

Wet Mind, Stephen M. Kosslyn and Olivier Koenig (New York, Free Press, 1992). The brain as a neural network.

Altered States/Experiential/Holistic/ Quantum Approaches and Weird Stuff

Bright Splinters of Mind, Beate Hermelin (London, Jessica Kingsley Publishers, 2001). The strange world of autistic savants.

The Conscious Universe, Dean Radin (New York, HarperEdge, 1997). Panpsychism, supported here by the author's experiments with anomalous (psi) phenomena. More persuasive than most of its type.

Exploring the World of Lucid Dreaming, Stephen LaBerge and Howard Rheingold (New York, Ballantine Books, 1990). Psychologist LaBerge is now the leading researcher in this field. This book is a 'how-to' manual as well as a description of lucid dreaming.

Lucid Dreams, Celia Green (Oxford Institute of Psychophysical Research, 1968). Celia Green is the pioneer of lucid dreaming, and her descriptions of her's and others' experiences at a time when the phenomena was largely unrecognized (and often flatly denied by sleep researchers) make fascinating reading if you can find a copy.

The Near-Death Experience, Lee W. Bailey and Jenny Yates (eds.) (New York and London, Routledge, 1996). A sober look at a strange type of experience.

The Noonday Demon, Andrew Soloman (New York, Scribner, 2001). An exceptionally cogent analysis of depression.

Simple Zen, C. Alexander Simpkins and Annellen Simpkins (Dublin, Newleaf, 1999). DIY meditation.

Spiritual Intelligence, Donah Zohar and Ian Marshall (London, Bloomsbury, 2000). Panpsychism revisited via quantum physics.

The Stranger in the Mirror, Marlene Steinberg and Maxine Schnall (New York, HarperCollins, 2000). The 'hidden epidemic', according to the authors, of dissociation. Largely based on case studies.

Journals, associations and websites

Journal of Consciousness Studies - an extraordinarily eclectic, and often ground-breaking multi-disciplinary platform for consciousness studies. Published monthly by Imprint Academic. For details see http://www.academicpress.com. There is also a lively, informative and well-hosted JCS online discussion group which is worth listening in to if you want to keep up with the latest (and very wide-ranging) thinking on the subject.

Trends in Cognitive Sciences – neuroscience and psychology relating to cognition and consciousness. Published monthly by Elsevier. For details see http://www.trends.com

Psyche is an online journal devoted to the mind – http://psyche.cs.monash.edu.au/ The Association for the Scientific Study of Consciousness holds regular conferences with the emphasis on neuroscience. http://www.assc.caltech.edu

David Chalmer's home page includes a comprehensive list of online papers about every aspect of consciousness, as well as links to other sites and news of conferences and seminars: http://www.u.arizona.edu/~chalmers/

There is also a bibliography of papers on consciousness at: http://www.home.earthlink.net/~dravita/

Other websites worth visiting are
The Global Consciousness Project at http://noosphere.princeton.edu/
And http://www.psiresearch.org

Index

Acknowledgements

My thanks to David Papineau and Chris Frith for their constructive comments – respectively philosophical and scientific – on the early draft of this book; to Malcolm Godwin for his artistry (and ravioli) and Nic Cheetham, my editor, for his patience.

Picture Credits

Moonrunner Design Ltd **p2, 10, 20, 23, 29, 37, 38, 41, 48, 58, 67, 78, 102, 107, 108, 110, 114, 120, 131, 132, 135, 142, 148, 156, 160, 164, 173, 176, 187, 191, 196, 197, 208, 210, 212, 215, 223, 235, 246, 263, 276, 285**; Patrick Mulrey **p25, 84, 118, 122, 136, 138, 141, 144, 146, 159, 161, 162, 163, 167, 172, 183, 203, 204, 205, 216, 225, 293, 295**; Patrick Mulrey/based on 'The Ames Demonstrations in Perception', William Ittelson **p221**; National Gallery, London and Experiment results, Derby University Enterprises Ltd **p13**; Simons D. J., & Chabris C. F., Gorillas in our midst: sustained inattentional blindness for dynamic events' *Perception* 28 (1999) issue 9, Pion, London (http://www.wjh.harvard.edu/~viscog/lab/demos.html) **p14**; Change Blindness 'Flicker Paradigm', Ronald A Rensink and Corel **p15**; R Gregory, *Eye and Brain*, (London, Weidenfeld & Nicolson, 1966), **p44**; Fischer, E., Haines, R. F., & Price, T. A., Cognitive issues in head-up displays, (NASA TP-1711) Moffett Field, CA: NASA-Ames Research Center (1980) **p17**; SCALA **p94**; Science Photo Library Ltd **p123, 138, 179, 210, 213**; Cataract 3, 1967, Bridget Riley, Emulsion PVA on linen, 223.5 cm x 222 cm, **p127**; *Notre Dame* by Stephen Wiltshire **p137**; Sally P. Springer and George Deutsch *Left Brain, Right Brain* (Worth Publishers, 1981, 1985,1989, 1993, 1998) **p147**; W. Penfield and P. Perot, BRAIN, Vol. 86, No 4, (1963) pp 595-696, Used by permission of Oxford University Press **p154**; *The Persistence of Memory*, 1931 (oil on canvas) by Salvador Dali (1904-89) Museum of Modern Art, New York, USA/Bridgeman Art Library/DACS **p158**; Experiments on dogs, at the Digestion Physiology Department in the Pavlov Institute, for 'L'URSS en construction', June 1934 (b/w photo) by French School (20th century) Bibliotheque des Arts Decoratifs, Paris, France/Archives Charmet/Bridgeman Art Library **p170** (We have been unable to trace the copyright holder of this image and would be grateful to receive any information as to their identity.); MGM Courtesy of The Kobal Collection **p179, 214**; Sistine Chapel Ceiling: *Creation of Adam*, 1510 (fresco) (post-restoration) by Michelangelo Buonarroti (1475-1564) Vatican Museums and Galleries, Vatican City, Italy/Bridgeman Art Library/DACS **p192**; *Chirologia, or the Naturall (sic) Language of the Hand* John Bulwer (1664) **p195**; Lorna Selfe: *Nadia: A Case of Extraordinary Drawing Ability in an Autistic Child*, (1977) **p206**; Unfinished Stereoscopic Painting by Salvador Dali (1904-1989) Alt Emporda, Catalonia, Spain/Index/Bridgeman Art Library/DACS **p211**; *Self Portrait*, 2002 by Gloria Hamlyn; *Self Portrait*, 2002 by Liam **p217**; NASA Jet Propulsion Laboratory **p224**; Fortean Picture Library **p226**; *The Innocent Eye Test*, 1981. Courtesy of Mark Tansey/Gagosian Gallery **p239**; *Dream Caused by the Flight of a Bee around a Pomegranate One Second before Waking Up*, 1944 by Salvador Dali (1904-89) Thyssen-Bornemisza Collection, Madrid, Spain/Bridgeman Art Library/DACS **p253**; Bill Utermohlens/ Galerie B.O.B. Lancet 2001: 357:2129-2133, fig 3 **p260-1**; *The Nightmare*, 1781 (oil on canvas) by Henry Fuseli (Fussli, Johann Heinrich) (1741-1825) The Detroit Institute of Arts, USA/Bridgeman Art Library Founders Society purchase with Mr and Mrs Bert L. Smokler and Mr and Mrs Lawrence A. Fleischman funds/DACS **p289**; Michael Badger **p296**; Pahwan S, 'Last but not least: here's looking at you kid', *Perception* v29 issue 8, Pion, London, **p293**; Cognitive Evolution Group, University of Louisiana at Lafayette **p294**;